A **YORKSHIRE POST** publication


in association with

THE YORKSHIRE COUNTY CRICKET CLUB


Produced by  G R E A T  N O R T H E R N

British Cataloguing in Publication Data
A catalogue for this book is available from the British Library

# Contents

THE YORKSHIRE COUNTY CRICKET CLUB

# THE YORKSHIRE COUNTY CRICKET CLUB

From the President, Robin Smith

If there is a sporting venue in the world with a greater claim to fame than Headingley, I am not aware of it. The scene of cricket drama throughout the last century, and the home of Yorkshire cricket, Headingley has a unique place in English sporting history and pride of place in the affections of all Yorkshire cricket lovers.

After 109 years since Yorkshire played its first game at Headingley, the Club has acquired a new long leasehold interest in the ground, and, with the support of Sport England and Leeds City Council, has been able to commence a comprehensive redevelopment scheme costing £10 million, the first phase of which is chronicled in this book. When complete, Headingley will have the facilities to stage Test, International and County cricket to the very best modern standards. The Yorkshire members and wider public deserve no less.

This book has been published by the Yorkshire Post, in collaboration with the Club, to mark the redevelopment, and I have great pleasure in giving it a very warm welcome.

There can be no more appropriate publisher of a book about Headingley than the Yorkshire Post, which, as Yorkshire's newspaper of record, has chronicled cricket at the ground throughout its history. Nor can there be a more suitable author than Robert Mills, whose incisive match reports and perceptive comment in the Yorkshire Post have graced Yorkshire cricket, and both delighted and challenged readers, for the last eleven years.

By recording triumph and defeat, hope and despair, athletic and tactical prowess, and that special brand of pride and determination which identifies Yorkshire people, this book is a reflection of Yorkshire life itself. The Yorkshire County Cricket Club is proud to be associated with it.

## ENGLAND AND WALES CRICKET BOARD

From the Chairman, Lord MacLaurin

I am delighted to have this opportunity to wish all involved with Yorkshire County Cricket Club great success in the redevelopment of Headingley.

This historic ground, over many years has been the scene of some magnificent cricket matches, both at International and at County level.  Those of us that have followed cricket closely will have our own special memories of famous matches.  In more recent years, I will never forget the amazing Monday, some three years ago, when England beat South Africa.  The match only lasted an hour or so that morning, and England were cheered to victory by a tumultuous and knowledgeable Yorkshire crowd.

All in cricket will rejoice in the redevelopment of this wonderful and historic ground.  I wish you all well.

# Introduction

CHARACTER, not beauty, is the word generally applied to Headingley Cricket Ground. It seems to epitomise what most outsiders think of Yorkshiremen - dour, prone to bouts of mournfulness and generally a bit odd.

Its development over the years has not really been development at all, but rather a patchwork, patched-up mess which has left the place looking as if it has been put together by a hyper-active seven-year-old with a few Lego bricks left over.

Even the buildings which have gone up and the refurbishments made have not met with universal approval. The 'improved' old pavilion, for example, is said to have all the character of an airport lounge; the Main Stand, though for years the symbol of Headingley's grandeur and of its international standing in two games, has for a long time looked careworn and delapidated; the new pavilion, though serving a purpose in bringing the club's offices from town to the ground, was criticised when it also housed the players' dressing-rooms and is still derided as an architectural eyesore.

The North Enclosure trees have gone, which is a pity, and the Western Terrace went through a period when it was a no-go area for decent human beings unless they were willing to dress up as a carrot.

In terms of specatator viewing, Headingley has always been an odd place. Test match punters have been far better off booking a room in one of the adjoining guest houses, where they could gain a panoramic view of the cricket from a balcony at no extra charge, than actually paying for a front-row seat in the ground, where their view would be constantly interrupted by people promenading around a cycle track which has served no useful purpose for donkey's years.

In terms of creature comforts, the ground has been bottom of most people's list of Test and even of county venues for years, both for members and for the general public. In this respect it has improved greatly in the last couple of years, but there was a time when you half expected to see Headingley's pork pies on The Antiques Road Show. Serving good, basic food at good, basic prices in pleasant surroundings where paying customers can get a view of the cricket is still a trick that has to be mastered.

Even so, the ground does have a character of its own. It is part of the growth of Leeds as a city and from the higher vantage points the view over a mass of chimneyed houses is imposing. The Main Stand is uniquely grim and austere and the slope of the field down from the North end has if anything been made more visible by the erection of the new West Stand.

The reason why Headingley reached the need for urgent and drastic improvement was twofold.

First, the relationship between Yorkshire as tenants and Leeds Cricket, Football & Athletic Company, the owners, was initially and for a long time too cosy. Although Lord Hawke is rightly regarded as the man who shaped much of what we and the world now regard as the ethos of Yorkshire cricket, he was uniquely well placed to safeguard its financial future but did not take that chance.

Secondly, the relationship between Yorkshire and their landlords in the last quarter of the 20th century became so fractious and tetchy that the ground stagnated when it needed to move forward to keep pace with a more demanding sports-watching public. Sitting at home and watching the Tests on TV was an option open to all and when paying to go to Headingley was the alternative TV began to look like a very attractive option.

Not enough was done by past committees at a time when Yorkshire cricket was a huge public attraction and could have afforded to invest in the ground's future. The present committee has been left to take the financial risk or be in danger of losing Test match status to, say, the Riverside ground at Chester-le-Street.

As President and committee chairman, Sir Lawrence Byford saw the problem with crystal clarity and thought he also had the solution, which was a move lock, stock and batting pads to Durkar, near Wakefield.

Those intentions were already clear when Paul Caddick took charge at Leeds CF & AC and on his first day made it equally clear that as far as he was concerned his figures did not add up without Yorkshire and Test match cricket and that he would do everything in his power to keep the club at Leeds.

Whatever they may think about him, no one connected with Yorkshire can accuse Caddick of being anything other than straightforward, to the point of ruthlessness when he issued writs in the amount of millions of pounds against several individuals connected with the club. It was a deafening warning shot.

The gradual subsidence of the Wakefield funding package and Caddick's determination to hold Yorkshire to the terms of a lease which they had signed brought us to the stage where the club and the ground owners went back into talks with a clearer understanding of where they stood and where each wanted to be in the future. Caddick's negotiators were in the happy position of knowing that Wakefield was no longer a viable alternative.

We are now about to see the fruits of the compromise. Initially it will be confined to the new West Stand, which will accommodate 7,500 from the Main Stand to the Wintershed and gives spectators more leg room and better sight lines. If

you envisage the 2001 structure being extended round though the North Enclosure and beyond the office block (which Yorkshire plan to demolish) you get a clearer idea of how Headingley is being shaped into an homogeneous ground at long last.

The cycle track is to go and has already disappeared in front of the West Stand. In future access to seats round the ground will be behind the stands. The cricket field is extended by 20 feet to reach up to the foot of the West Stand, which will bring into play two more pitches on the square.

The Training Ground near the railway line is being resurfaced to provide match-day car parking. It will also house grass nets so that players can practise outdoors during the course of a match.

Plans to rebuild the Main Stand to include hospitality boxes have been shelved and these executive boxes will be in the new East Stand on the Bowling Green, which has for years been the site for a temporary structure at Test matches.

Again, the cycle track will be eliminated and 2,000 seats for members installed leading up to a first-floor Long Room with bar and catering facilities. Underneath the terracing will be indoor nets, classrooms for school parties, changing rooms and gym and physiotherapy facilities. This building will be the home of the Academy.

Yorkshire will convert the nets in the East Stand into a hospitality area during Test matches and will take all the income apart from the catering element. The income from the executive boxes atop this stand will be shared with Leeds CF & AC.

The frontage to the ground in St Michael's Lane will be dramatically altered, the Sharman Gates must be re-sited and the indoor school across the road from the ground is to undergo a major refit, not just a refurbishment.

The funding package amounts to nearly £9,900,000, made up from: Sport England (lottery) grant £2.9m; Leeds City Council grant £1.5m; Yorkshire CCC contribution £1m; Yorkshire CCC bank borrowing £3.8m; Sports Grounds Initiative grant £250,000; Leeds CF & AC contribution (for a half share of the executive boxes) £400,000.

A new 999-year lease gives Yorkshire control of cricket activities and the chance to buy various income streams now enjoyed by the owners, including catering, advertising, hospitality and parking.

# Chapter One

# Yorkshire to 1914

IT IS one of the eternal truths of nature that if you put two Yorkshiremen in a room together the result is likely to be an argument.

As a tribe we have squabbled over just about everything, from whether to bow down to the Romans to whether Arthur Scargill talked more sense than Margaret Thatcher.

Nowhere has been this trend towards sometimes unreasoned disputation been more evident than in our cricket, largely because ever since a club recognisable as a county organisation came into being there have been rows about where it should play.

This was the scenario in the late 1880s. Until then Sheffield had been the powerhouse and the central focus of the Yorkshire club, whose progress was intrinsically linked to that of Sheffield United Football Club at Bramall Lane.

The foresight, influence in high places and sheer persistence of the visionary Michael John Ellison had, in 1854, led to a meeting at the city's Adelphi Hotel where he announced that through his working connections with the Duke of Norfolk's estates in Sheffield he had managed to acquire the lease to nine acres of land on Bramall Lane.

The following year the venue staged its first match and in August 'Yorkshire' also played there. A heavy defeat by Sussex could not spoil Ellison's satisfaction at having fashioned a top-class ground to rival that already in existence at Nottingham.

But diminishing support for matches between local teams was insufficient to make the venture profitable and Ellison soon saw the need to establish a proper county club, more easily identifiable as such than the somewhat makeshift teams gathered together under the name of Yorkshire until that time.

So it was that on January 8, 1863, a presumably smoke-filled room at the Adelphi Hotel was again the birthplace of the formalised Yorkshire County Cricket Club. For the next 30 years or so Ellison, in the dual role of president and treasurer, and Joseph Beckett Wolstinholm, who was the club's secretary, ran Yorkshire cricket from Bramall Lane, which also prospered as a football venue.

These two men were the first of a line of fine leaders and administrators with which Yorkshire has been blessed. Whether it is because they know when they are on to a good thing (surely not) or because of loyalty, the secretaries in particular tend to be long-servers.

Including the present incumbent, David Ryder, Yorkshire have had only five secretaries since their inception in 1863. Wolstinholm, a fierce defender of Sheffield's position, held the office from 1864 to 1902, Sir Frederick Toone from 1903 to 1930, John Nash (Mr Nash to you) for 40 years from 1931 and then Joe Lister from 1972 to 1991. Yorkshire have succeeded in establishing a clear line of succession and have benefited from it.

For a time, Sheffield's pre-eminence as the home and natural base of Yorkshire cricket was unchallenged but by the late 1880s this was causing resentment among the movers and shakers in West Yorkshire, particularly in Leeds, which had also burgeoned in the urbanisation that accompanied the industrial revolution.

Some battles are more significant than others. It is somehow fitting that Yorkshire should, for the first time, have staged a Second XI fixture in the year 2000 at Stamford Bridge, where nearly 1,000 years ago one such helped change the course of this country's history.

For almost its entire history the Yorkshire club has argued internally about where it should play, partly because it is always a good excuse for a row and also because of the size of the county. There have been periods of peaceful accommodation and compromise but by 1890 there was trouble brewing between the great city rivals, Sheffield and Leeds.

Sheffield's near-monopoly of the county's cricket rankled with many of the monied and influential Leeds citizenry. There had been a handful of games at Hunslet and at Holbeck but Leeds could not mount a sustained challenge to Sheffield because of the absence of a ground to match Bramall Lane.

Without any reference to the National Lottery (this was a time when such things, along with world wars and batting bonus points, had not been imagined) a group of sports-loving businessmen founded the Leeds Football, Cricket and Athletic Company Ltd. This has subsequently been known for short as Leeds CF & AC and occasionally, in times of strife between the company and Yorkshire, as "those money-grabbers at the rugby club."

The first chairman of the company was the future Lord Hawke. His deputy was a member of the Tetley brewing family and the board included the father of FS Jackson, soon to become a towering figure in the county's history and a glorious personification of what has come to be known as the Golden Age of cricket, the period up to the outbreak of the First World War.

The land on which the Headingley ground now stands then belonged to the Cardigan estate and the company purchased one lot for the sum of £25,000. It was opened on May 27, 1890, with a match between Leeds CC and Scarborough; in September of that year the inaugural first-class fixture took place between the North and the Australians and in in the following year Yorkshire made their debut on the ground in a match against Derbyshire, who were not a first-class county at that time but still managed to win by 45 runs.

In August of that year the first county championship match at Headingley, whose origins may lie in the Saxon 'Forest clearing belonging to

Hedde', was between Yorkshire and Kent. It rained and it was a draw, Yorkshire making 148 and 78-5 and the visitors 126.

Nearly all the grounds Yorkshire used in this era had all-year usage as homes for semi-professional cricket clubs in the summer months and football clubs in the winter. In the Sheffield area football meant the Association variety but in the West Riding it was the rugby code at Batley, Bradford, Halifax, Holbeck, Huddersfield and Hunslet. After the great schism it was Northern Union, the forerunner of rugby league.

At Headingley the 22-acre site allowed for more than two sports. There was room for an athletics and cycling track around the cricket field, for bowling greens and tennis courts, and although from the start it was primarily a rugby venue in winter it dabbled with football in the 1890s in the form of exhibition games and Amateur Cup finals.

The first buildings, which went up in 1889, were the pavilion in the south-east corner and a double-fronted grandstand separating the cricket from the rugby field, both built and designed by Smith and Tweedale. The other great feature was the banked terracing on the west side of the ground and in all £30,300 was spent on the site, in excess of £750,000 in modern terms.

The emergence of Headingley as a first-class venue in all senses of the term marked a shift of power from Sheffield which was mirrored in changes in committee representation, gradually lessening Sheffield's stranglehold on club policy.

It was no coincidence that the changes were wrought at a time of deeply unsatisfactory playing performances, which fuelled discontent.

The club had produced some fine players in the years leading up to 1890, including fast bowlers George Freeman and Tom Emmett and Allen Hill, slow left-armers Edmund Peate and Bobby Peel, the earliest links in a chain of spin wizards, and batsmen Ephraim Lockwood, George Ulyett and John Thewlis, who was the most distinguished product of the amazing Lascelles Hall production-line of Yorkshire cricketers.

But the results from the team were mostly disappointing, sometimes downright poor, and the all-round effort frustratingly erratic. The usual Yorkshire theory was followed – when in doubt, blame the committee. So it was that the club was overhauled and Sheffield's stranglehold was further loosened. That city's influence, once seen as benign, came to be regarded by some (mostly in the West Riding) as suffocating and sterile.

The move to Headingley alone proved to be no panacea. In 1891 Yorkshire finished second bottom of the championship table with a record of five wins, 11 defeats and a draw. They had won the title three times in four seasons from 1867 (once jointly with Nottinghamshire, who were then the pre-eminent county side) and it must be added that the barren period, which lasted until 1893, was in an era when 'least losses' was a key factor in deciding the title. Yorkshire tended to play more games than most of the other counties and so gave themselves more chance of losing.

But that was an excuse not accepted by the club's supporters of the day. The poor season of 1891 brought much debate in the Press and Wisden had the temerity to suggest that the lack of representation of areas other than Sheffield might be undesirable.

During the period from 1889 to 1892 the make-up of the committee was altered to afford a wider spread of representation and so, under the guidance of Martin Bladen Hawke, was the selection policy. Yorkshire has undergone a similar committee upheaval in recent times, of course, but to prove that some things never change there is a committee meeting minute from December, 1891, which says that "the President (Ellison) asked that members of the Committee would not be interviewed by newspaper reporters."

It is easy to imagine what had transpired in the previous few months.

Lord Hawke is the greatest figure in Yorkshire's history, one who generates such awe that we mention only in passing the fact that he is one of 40-odd players to have worn the white rose who were born outside the county.

He came into the world in 1860 in a Lincolnshire rectory but his family, made famous by the naval exploits of Rear-Admiral Edward Hawke in the mid-18th century, soon moved to Wighill, near Tadcaster.

This was no ordinary family. His grandmother had danced at the balls in Brussels on the eve of the Battle of Waterloo and the following day rode out on a horse to a vantage point from where she could see how things were going for the English.

Martin Bladen, the seventh Baron, was as extraordinary as any of his ancestors.

He went to Eton and to Magdalene College, Cambridge, where after appearing a couple of times for Yorkshire in 1881 he won a blue the following year and later became the Cambridge captain.

Military duties a Captain of the 3rd Battalion of the Princess of Wales's Own Yorkshire Regiment at times interrupted his cricket career.

It seems that Yorkshire were inclined to give him the county captaincy as early as 1882, when he was 22, but he preferred to look and learn under the leadership of Tom Emmett for another year and the official appointment did not come until 1883.

His appearances in his first three seasons as captain were sporadic but he used them to assess the strengths and weaknesses of the team and, more important, to gauge the character of the individual players. In 1886 he was firmly established and in full charge and the first true flowering of the White Rose (he was responsible for the introduction of the players' white rose badge) was about to begin, though it would be another seven years before it reached fruition in the winning of the championship.

Yorkshire had until then relied on professionals, so their upsurge cannot be seen as a romantic triumph of working-class methods. The professionals had failed the club, not through lack of skill, which many of them had in abundance, but because they were somehow not quite a team. They needed a dose of autocracy to bring the best out of the large number of gifted cricketers being produced in the Broad Acres and Hawke provided it.

The 1892 season was, however, another disappointment with as many defeats as victories (six), nine draws and a final placing of sixth. Headingley, where there were some teething troubles with the pitches (no change there, then) inspired the opposition more than it did Yorkshire and an encouraging start to the 1892 campaign came to an abrupt halt at Leeds when they lost to Surrey, the reigning champions and the side which largely through the bowling of George Lohmann had become the major force in the land.

Bobby Peel, later one of the players discarded by in Hawke's character-driven shake-up, took 7-43 as Surrey, after a wash-out on the first day, were dismissed for 151. But Yorkshire made only 87 on a worsening track with Lohmann claiming 6-37 and Surrey's 81-7 left Yorkshire with just over two hours of batting.

They refused to give up hope of winning even after being reduced to 21-4 with Ted Wainwright, a good all-rounder from Tinsley, Sheffield, (998 career wickets for the county) hitting out to make 44 in 50 minutes. But Lohmann was in full cry and his second-innings return of 8-70 gave Surrey victory by 17 runs with three minutes left for play.

Later in that season Yorkshire lost again at Headingley, this time to Middlesex by nine wickets. They were bowled out for 100 and although limiting the visitors to a lead of 22 runs the batting on the third and last day was a sorry sight and they were all out for 46, Stanley Jackson making half of the total.

But Hawke's revolution had started. Though an amateur, he did much to advance the cause of the professional cricketer and although he left no one in any doubt that he was in charge he took the advice of the senior professionals into account.

He did away with the old system of £1 for 50 runs or six wickets and instead awarded talent marks for outstanding effort and performance taking into account the conditions, the state of the game and the strength of the opposition. Until this time Yorkshire's fielding had at times been described as execrable but under Hawke it improved hugely with several players gaining national recognition in specialist positions.

At the end of a season the whole team would be invited to Wighill Park, there to be given their merit money. In the case of George Herbert Hirst this once amounted to £52, worth well over £1,000 at today's values.

Hawke was captain from 1883 until 1910 and also held the presidency of the club from 1898 when he succeeded Ellison, another indication of Sheffield's gradually waning influence.

Like most men who emerge as leaders in Yorkshire cricket, he was occasionally accused of blinkered autocracy but there is no doubt that he was responsible for shaping Yorkshire into a dominant, sometimes domineering, playing force as well as directing the club towards financial prosperity.

There was plenty of scope for improvement in the latter area. In 1891, just two before the championship triumph, subscriptions produced only £90 and even two years later there were only 175 names on the members' list.

He introduced the Yorkshire cap at a time when Lancashire's players were already wearing a red rose on navy blue. But he improved on nature and designed a white rose of his own, with 11 petals to denote the First XI, to be worn only by capped players, and the Hawke colours of Cambridge blue and Oxford blue-and-gold were adopted by the county.

He is usually described as only a moderate batsman, though there were times when he perhaps under-rated his own abilities and Pelham Warner wrote that though Hawke was an edgy starter he drove and pulled strongly and with style and more than once dug the side out of a hole.

At this time it was enough for an amateur to be merely competent as a player, but vital that he should have the leadership qualities and strength of character to impose discipline and establish a unity of purpose within the team.

This Hawke achieved in glorious measure, the amateur-professional dichotomy in cricket only mirroring that in other walks of life in this era, such as in the army and the navy and in the factories and on the farms where the owners provided leadership and left it to bailiffs and foremen to provide or buy in the skill and hard graft.

Until Hawke took a grip some Yorkshire professionals had been inclined to socialise themselves into a stupor, though lager was no one's tipple and a lager-lout mentality was a thing of the future. Even when drunk, men rarely behaved badly. Unusually for a man based near Tadcaster, he outlawed excessive drinking and acted, firmly though regretfully, against anyone who transgressed his code of decent behaviour and dress, as Peel was to discover.

In 1893 Yorkshire beat the Australians at Bramall Lane by 64 runs. If you think pitches these days are poor, there were some rough ones about then and the comment after the tour match was that "seldom has a worse wicket been played upon by first-class teams."

They moved up to Headingley to play Sussex who, after a good start, collapsed to 125 all out with Peel, then in his pomp, taking 7-55. Yorkshire fared even worse in stumbling to 61-9 but Hirst and David Hunter lifted them to 111 and this partnership proved to be the platform for a four-wicket win.

But Headingley could bring the worst out of Yorkshire in the early years and was the scene of their first defeat of that season, a humbling innings reverse against Lancashire on another bowlers' pitch. Yorkshire lost nine wickets for 27 runs to be all out for 107 and Lancashire took command through Archie MacLaren, another majestic figure of the Golden Age, who made 54 in nearly three hours out of a total of 169. Peel took five wickets but was outshone by Lancashire's rotund all-rounder Johnny Briggs, who demolished them with 8-19 in a total of 53 all out.

Heavy rain again put the bowlers on top when Yorkshire lost to the Australians at Leeds later that season and Briggs was again the architect of victory as Lancashire completed a championship double at Old Trafford in front of massive crowds.

But despite this setback Yorkshire were still narrowly ahead of their Roses rivals in the table and the title was won at Bramall Lane with an easy win over Kent in the penultimate game. They won 12 out of 16 championship fixtures even though Hawke played in only six of them, George Ulyett leading the side in his absence, apparently without much official recognition for his endeavours.

It was a tough time for batsmen. J T Brown topped the list with 712 runs followed by 'Long' John Tunnicliffe on 653. Only two other players averaged more than 20 but between them Peel and Wainwright took 155 wickets.

From its inauguration Headingley was popular with the Leeds public, even though one disgruntled resident, James Bedford of Cardigan Road, wrote to the Yorkshire Post in 1890 complaining about the disgusting smell emanating from the ash-pit refuse being used to raise the level of the ground.

"At this time last year typhoid fever raged about here, several deaths taking place; it therefore appears most iniquitous to plant fever-breeding matter in such a position."

Perhaps those seeking fresh air as they attended the sporting events got more than they bargained for but they certainly turned up in great numbers. Some 5,000 watched the first cricket match between Leeds and Scarborough and Leeds FC, formed out of the old Leeds St John's club, also proved a big attraction.

It was not long before the ground became one of the major sporting venues in the country. In the 1893 Yorkshire Cup final Pontefract beat Wakefield Trinity and in the same year 30,000, the largest gathering for a rugby union match, saw Scotland defeat England by two drop-goals to nil.

In 1895 the ground staged the FA Amateur Cup final in which Middlesbrough beat Old Carthusians 2-1 and in 1902 the Americans beat England in something called pushball, which must rate as the most unusual spectacle witnessed at Headingley until the famous incident when water started oozing over Dickie Bird's shoes during a Test match.

The 1893 championship triumph brought in more members and by this time Yorkshire were also paying some league clubs 15 shillings a week for agreeing to include promising young professionals such as Tommy Foster and Frank Mitchell in their teams.

Mitchell, who also played international rugby for England, was educated at St Peter's School in York and then went to Cambridge University. In this era

Yorkshire's Oxbridge connections were productive and strong. He served in the Boer War and later lived in South Africa and remarkably led their sides to England in 1904 and 1912.

In 1894 F S (Stanley) Jackson became the first batsman to make a century at Headingley, scoring 145 as well as taking 5-37 in the first innings of a victory over Nottinghamshire. They won on the ground again that year, against W G Grace's Gloucestershire, despite being 19-9 in the second innings before Hirst and Hunter added 42 for the last wicket, leaving Wainwright to claim 7-34, take his tally for the season to 97 at the stunning average of 10.17 and secure a 26-run win. It was, however, Surrey's title and although Yorkshire were badly hit by the weather at crucial times, notably in their final fixture, they could hardly complain since they had lost twice to their arch-rivals.

Yorkshire won the title again in 1896, a Roses victory at Leeds proving crucial in the final reckoning. Peel, who during the previous season had taken 15 Somerset wickets for 50 runs at the ground, was in his prime and it was his bowling which set up a comfortable 123-run win. In that year he scored more than 1,100 runs, often making vital middle-order contributions after early wickets had fallen, and taking 97 wickets at an average of less than 20.

Yorkshire showed during this campaign that they were the equal of any side on dry batting wickets and had such formidable bowling resources that they were better than the rest on wet ones. There are of course many old-stagers who played in a later era of uncovered pitches who dearly wish that the same variations in conditions could be allowed to prevail in the modern game.

It was also the year of the record total of 887 against Warwickshire at Edgbaston, in which Peel hit 210 and there were centuries for Wainwright, Jackson and Hawke. In those days first-innings declarations were not permitted and it was a sign of the increasingly ruthless nature of Yorkshire's approach to the game that they refused to throw their wickets away cheaply even in the later stages of the innings.

Peel and Hawke put on 292 for the eighth wicket, but the latter's determination to drive heavy drinkers out of the game led to Peel's abrupt dismissal in 1897 and to the rise of another towering figure for England and Yorkshire, Wilfred Rhodes, who eventually replaced him, though for a time it was a toss-up between Rhodes and Albert Cordingley of Eccleshill.

There was already Brown and Tunnicliffe and later there would be Holmes and Sutcliffe, but as the century drew to a close it was the omnipotent combination of Hirst 'n Rhodes which turned Yorkshire into a relentless cricketing machine. There is no doubt that one of the most significant entries in Yorkshire's minutes' book was on August 5, 1889, that "G Herbert Hirst of Kirkheaton be engaged for the Lancs match" though at the time his duties were probably confined to those of 12th man.

Another title followed in 1898 and at the start of the new century the only question was who would finish second as Yorkshire gained a hat-trick of championships from 1900 and then another three in 1905,1908 and 1912.

Under Lord Hawke's guidance the archetypal Yorkshire professional developed and pride in craftsmanship and reputation was passed down from one generation to the next.

Many a cricketer gleaned precious information and learned priceless 'tips' about how to play it from listening to the members of Hawke's pre-war team, though it has been said that this era was also the source of some of the less endearing Yorkshire traits, of excessive caution, affected bluntness, exaggerated solemnity and smugness. Yorkshiremen, smug? Surely not.

The more likely truth is that Yorkshire folk were inclined towards smugness long before this but that their cricket gave them something on which they could practise it to perfection.

Along with Garfield Sobers, Hirst and Rhodes stand as the greatest all-rounders to have played the game, the former bowling his left-arm swervers to devastating effect and gathering many of his runs from the pull shot. Shortish but sturdily-built, in 1906 he achieved the unique double of 2,000 runs and 200 wickets in the season, a feat that must make modern practitioners exhausted just thinking about it. In all first-class cricket he took 2,739 wickets and scored 36,323 runs, including Yorkshire's highest score of 341 against Leicestershire.

Rhodes, another jewel in cricket's golden crown, was also from Kirkheaton and like Hirst was a right-handed batsman and left-arm bowler. He mastered both skills to such a degree, not merely through his natural gifts but through dedicated practice and attention to the minutest detail, that he became the supreme professional cricketer, the only one to do the double 16 times and the only bowler to take 4,000 first-class wickets.

At the top of the batting order there was the long and short of it, the squat and stylish J T Brown, from Driffield, who died at the age of 35 in 1904, and 'Long' John Tunnicliffe, from Lowtown, Pudsey, who tempered his youthful aggression to become the ideal dour foil for Brown. He also excelled as a slip fielder and took 665 catches.

David Denton, from Wakefield, was a stylish and daring batsman whose career tally of nearly 38,000 was bettered in his era by only W G Grace, J T Tyldesley and Tom Hayward.

Ted Wainwright, a craggy and somewhat cantankerous all-rounder from Sheffield, performed sterling deeds as a purveyor of big off-breaks and a batsman of sound method and grit. Wainwright later coached at Shrewsbury School and Neville Cardus wrote: "There was something sinister about him. Every night he got drunk as a matter of course, quietly and masterfully."

Schofield Haigh, coached by Louis Hall at Armitage Bridge, was professional at Aberdeen and Perth and took 7-12 for Scotland against Yorkshire before becoming the third member of the triumphant triumvirate of all-rounders. If some of Yorkshire's players were more respected than loved, that did not apply to Haigh, who was universally liked. "There is no nicer professional cricketer," said Pelham Warner.

He was content to stand in the shadow of Hirst, his hero, and Rhodes, but for 18 years was "the sunshine of the Yorkshire Eleven," according to Old Ebor.

For all their brilliance, Hirst, Rhodes and Haigh would not have achieved as much without the prowess of wicketkeeper David Hunter, the best never to play for England. If it was not quite working for the bowlers, Hunter would talk the batsmen out with polite, soft-spoken 'sledging' from behind the stumps.

Many others contributed to Yorkshire's glory – T L Taylor, who was designated as Hawke's successor but never took up the captaincy, left-handed batsman Irving Washington, from Wombwell, Major Booth, Alonzo Drake, the first to take all 10 wickets, Roy Kilner, Rockley Wilson, wicketkeeper Arthur Dolphin and Edgar Oldroyd.

In the title hat-trick period from 1900 Yorkshire lost only two county matches, both to Somerset, and one of them (in 1901) ranks as one of the most remarkable games in the competition's history.

At first everything went as predicted. Somerset took a gamble by batting first on a wet pitch at

*This is how Headingley looked in 1897.*

Headingley and were skittled for 87 by Rhodes. Haigh smote 96 in Yorkshire's total of 325, adding 118 in 55 minutes with Rhodes, every hit cheered by a partisan crowd of 10,000.

There was a dinner party that night for the amateurs and as liqueurs were drunk the genial host, Mr Hepworth, said that he would give £100 to county funds if Somerset won. He was taken up on the bet by Sammy Woods, who also put £10 on Lionel Palairet to score a century. Both bets were won but neither was paid.

Palairet was Somerset's one true Golden Age batsman, a true stylist. Born in Lancashire, he went to Repton School with C B Fry, played football for the Corinthians and was five times England's champion archer.

He and fellow-opener Len Braund had been out for ducks in the first innings but set off at a furious rate when they batted again, though a slip catch was denied by the umpires, one which Tunnicliffe went to his death-bed swearing was fairly taken.

Braund was a superb all-rounder, perhaps the best in England in the Golden Age apart from Yorkshire's. Both openers made hundreds and in

155 overs of violent batting Somerset made 630, a record total on the ground.

Somerset, sensing a two-day defeat, had asked for an extra carriage to be tacked on to the afternoon train but in the event did not have to catch the 5.30 from Leeds. Indeed, they won the match, only Tunnicliffe offering much resistance as Yorkshire folded to 113 all out on the third and final morning.

It was one of county cricket's most extraordinary results, Yorkshire's 48-match unbeaten run surrendered after they had built a colossal first-innings lead. Despite some doubts about at least one umpiring decision, Yorkshire were sporting in defeat, the crowd hailed Somerset's players with such enthusiasm that they could hardly get to their charabanc and back home in Taunton they were heroes.

Poetry was written to commemorate the win, which was greeted with glee throughout the land by players and spectators who had become convinced that Hawke's men were invincible.

Later that season 31,000 watched the first day of the Roses match at Leeds with play curtailed because of the size of the crowd and snow interrupted the game against Sussex the following year, which included one of the greatest feats in the annals of Headingley.

The Australians had brought their most powerful side since tours began and were unbeaten. They were bowled out for 131 in their first innings, with Hirst and Jackson taking four wickets apiece, but Yorkshire could muster only 107.

The Australians were then dismissed for 23, Hirst and Jackson again the destroyers, and this is the lowest team total on the ground. The last six wickets fell for three runs and Yorkshire gained a glorious five-wicket victory.

The 1904 Roses match at Headingley over the August Bank Holiday was Hirst's benefit and Yorkshiremen showed what they thought of him. Crowds of 31,826, 31,579 and 15,387 were recorded for the three days of a draw which helped Lancashire to take the title with Yorkshire second. Hirst's purse was £3,703.

Yorkshire were runners-up to a fine Kent side in 1913, fourth in the last season before the First World War, but in general had a side of such talent, know-how and experience that they seemed capable of dominating the scene for years to come.

Instead, something else dominated lives from for four years from 1914, the season when Alonzo Drake took 158 wickets, Major Booth 155 and both scored more than 800 runs. Booth was killed in the Somme battles of 1916, in the same action as Roy Kilner, another of the Leeds Pals, was injured. Drake was turned down for military service on health grounds and died months after the end of the conflict. Behind the grief was the question how much more they would have achieved.

# Chapter Two

# England to 1914

YORKSHIRE'S gifts to the country had been manifold before Headingley staged its first Test match in 1899 against Australia.

Five of their players – George Ulyett, Tom Armitage, Allen Hill, Tom Emmett and Andrew Greenwood – had been on James Lillywhite's tour of 1877, which marked the beginning of Anglo-Australian conflict.

Australia won the first game but in the second, again at Melbourne, the five Yorkshiremen contributed 219 of England's total of 261 to lay the platform for a four-wicket win and a 1-1 series draw. Ulyett made a half-century in each innings and Hill, who had learned his cricket while working as a handloom weaver in what turned into a cricket factory at Lascelles Hall, made a vital contribution with the ball.

The players on that trip were lucky to get home. When they went to New Zealand and tried to cross a gorge in two coaches they were overtaken by a sudden flood and waded to safety, up to their waists in the torrent. Hill said that he expected to go under at any moment.

Emmett was a lovely man from Halifax, after W G Grace the most famous player of his day. He is also well remembered for his sense of humour and his stock of one-liners. "There's an epidemic here today and it ain't catching," he said after a bad day for Yorkshire in the field. He once even forgot that he was captain of the side and having bowled unchanged from the start until lunch moaned:

"Why doesn't the old fool take me off?"

Billy Bates, another product of Lascelles Hall highly regarded by Grace, had produced a stunning all-round performance at Melbourne in 1882-3, becoming the first England bowler to do the hat-trick, finishing with 14 wickets in the match and scoring a half-century.

J T Brown showed that he could manage without Tunnicliffe at the other end when he smote a 28-minute 50 at Melbourne in 1894-5; Ulyett scored England's first Test century in Australia in 1881-2 and Bobby Peel took 102 wickets in 20 Tests, all against Australia, at an average of 16.81. He would not have understood the term 'strike-rate' but his was a wicket every 50 balls, much better than that of Wilfred Rhodes.

Headingley's credentials were fixed by the turn of the century, the ground's cause no doubt helped by Lord Hawke's influence in high places and by the fact that it had in county cricket drawn a number of 20,000-plus crowds by 1899.

At its inception some had criticised the siting of the ground at Headingley as being too far from the city centre, but the rapid development of the suburbs and the bus and tram systems introduced to cater for it – perhaps, dare one day it, somewhat more efficient than in some subsequent times – dispelled those anxieties. The even more rapid rise in car-ownership has brought fresh problems, far harder to tackle.

They were three-day Tests in those days (what's changed?) and rain before the start of the inaugural Leeds Test on June 29 caused widespread concern about the state of the pitch. They worry about it these days without bad weather.

Joe Darling, the Australian captain who was born on the same day as Yorkshire's F S Jackson, elected to bat first on the assumption that conditions would only worsen. The tourists recovered somewhat from an appalling start to reach 172 and at the close England had replied with 119-4, the tiny Willie Quaife of Warwickshire, probably the smallest man to play for England against Australia, taking nearly two hours over 20 runs.

The newspaper report says that "exceedingly pleasant weather prevailed during the greater part of the afternoon, although there were times when some heavy clouds threatened rain, but a slight breeze carried them away and the first stage of the encounter was concluded in brilliant sunshine.

"The match proved a huge attraction and before lunch time there were nearly 20,000 people on the ground and this number was largely increased as posted in Queen Victoria Street, drawing a crowd of city gents and bringing the horse-drawn carriages to a halt until the next news arrived.

The most significant event took place not on the field but hours after the end of the first day when the delightful Lancashire all-rounder Johnny Briggs, who with Peel had bowled England to an amazing 10-run win in Sydney five years earlier, suffered a violent fit while watching a performance at the Empire Theatre. It is thought to have been triggered by a blow over the heart from a drive by Tom Hayward.

He had to retire from the match and although he did return to first-class cricket the following year he suffered another breakdown and died in an asylum in Cheadle, where he was given to imagining bowling up and down the corridor and then announcing his figures to the nurses.

Hayward, the Surrey run-machine who was the inspiration for Jack Hobbs, put on 93 with wicketkeeper Dick Lilley to give England a handy lead and Australia were in danger of defeat as they lost their first four wickets before the first-innings arrears had been wiped out.

The crowd was at fever pitch as Jack Hearne, who delivered right-arm nippy medium pace with a glorious side-on action to take more than 3,000 wickets for Middlesex and England, did the hat trick with the wickets of Clem Hill, Syd Gregory and Monty Noble.

Australia recovered to 224, thanks in the main to Frank Laver, who in the previous Test at Lord's had claimed three prized scalps by disposing of Hayward, Johnny Tyldesley and Gilbert Jessop, and the Victorian all-rounder Hugh Trumble, who made 56. England needed 177 to win and the scene as set for a fascinating last day. It rained and the match was drawn with the home side on 19-0.

The rise of Headingley as a cricket venue had by no means meant the total demise of Bramall Lane and when the Australians next toured in 1902 it was Sheffield which staged the Test match, its only one, which resulted in a big win by the tourists.

But Sheffield suffered another blow with the retirement of Joseph Wolstinholm, who had served as Yorkshire's secretary from 1864. A brusque, single-minded man, he was not universally liked, but was a fine administrator, so good indeed that although from 1882 he had been paid £25 a year the club had to offer his successor £350.

The following year, perhaps because Wolstinholm was no longer there to argue against it, Yorkshire

*A view of the austerely imposing pavilion in the late 19th century.*

the afternoon advanced. To keep the crowd in order there were over 100 police present and though they had no great disorder to deal with several thousand people forced their way right up to the boundary after lunch, obstructing the view of those who occupied the proper seats and for the rest of the day the cricket went on to a ceaseless accompaniment of shouting and cries of 'sit down.' Except for this nuisance the first stage of the match passed off quite satisfactorily."

There was huge interest in the game in the city centre, where bulletins of the latest score were

*No bowler in Headingley's Test history has surpassed Colin Blythe's match figures of 15-99 in England's victory over South Africa in 1907.*

felt emboldened to move the club offices from Sheffield to Leeds, though there was not enough room at Headingley and so Yorkshire cricket, which now could be considered a proper county organisation, was run from leased offices at Old Bank Chambers, Park Row.

Wolstinholm's successor was Frederick Charles Toone, a highly-paid import from Leicestershire, where he had spent five successful years. He was in office for 27 years, during which time the membership of the club doubled to 6,000. He also revised many of the rules, organised players' benefits and edited the Yearbook, which has changed little and remains revered throughout the county circuit to this day with journalist Derek Hodgson as editor and Roy Wilkinson in charge of statistics. The manager of three MCC tours to Australia, Toone was knighted for his services to the game.

Pelham Warner thought him "the perfect manager" and his skills were recognised by the Government when he was appointed to a 'Crowds Committee' to examine the safety of spectators at sporting events in the wake of Wembley's first FA Cup final in 1923.

After its inauguration as a Test venue in 1899, Headingley had to wait six years for its second match and although it again ended in stalemate between England and Australia it was worth the waiting.

It was Golden Age cricket in microcosm. Yorkshire's great gift to this era, F S Jackson (later the Rt Hon Sir Francis Stanley Jackson), achieved the distinction of scoring the first Test hundred on the ground in what was his golden year.

He strode to the crease at 57-3, lost Hayward seven runs later but was given good support by his county team-mate Hirst and batted for 268 minutes for his unbeaten 144, hitting 18 fours. He offered just one chance, when on 130. England reached 301. Arnold Warren took Victory Trumper's wicket twice in the match and claimed 5-57 as Australia were bowled out for 195 but this was the Derbyshire fast bowler's sole Test appearance.

The tourists bowled largely negatively for containment when England batted again but Johnny Tyldesley responded by stepping to the leg side and hitting through the off to make 100 in England's 295-5 declared.

Jackson could do no wrong in this series. He won the toss in every game, topped both the batting and bowling averages and led his country to a 2-0 success, but at Headingley there was criticism that he prolonged their second innings for too long.

Even so, England came close to victory. Kent's slow left-arm bowler Colin 'Charlie' Blythe took three early wickets but crucially dropped a return chance offered by Noble, who went on to make 62 as Australia closed on 224-7 and escaped with a draw.

The 1905 series marked the crowning of Jackson's career as he averaged more than 70 with the bat and took his wickets at 15.46. Tall and well built, he was a graceful right-hander with sublime timing and a medium-pace bowler with a model action and subtle changes of pace. He personified the late Victorian and Edwardian approach to the game and to life. Cricket was never going to be the be-all and end-all of his existence. He was a sportsman, a businessman, a soldier and a politician.

An extract from the Vanity Fair periodical of 1902 describes him as "a nice young fellow of two-and-thirty, who may not be obnoxious even to Rudyard Kipling since he was patriotic enough to give up cricket to serve his country in South Africa, whence he is returned safe and sound and captain of the 3rd Royal Lancasters as well as of the Yorkshire Eleven." This is incorrect. He was never made captain of Yorkshire even though he did lead the side on numerous occasions.

Born in Chapel Allerton in 1870, he was the son of Lord Allerton, a member of the cabinet in Lord Salisbury's second government. Jackson went from prep school in Hemel Hempstead to Harrow, where he was fagmaster of Winston Churchill. His father promised him a shilling – not pocket money in those days – for every run made and a sovereign for each wicket taken against Eton. Seizing the moment, he scored 80 and took 11 wickets. He was a blue in all his summers at Cambridge.

He was their captain for two years and in 1893 led them to a decisive win in the University match as well as playing for Yorkshire and for England with outstanding success while still an undergraduate. He scored 91 and 103 in his first two Tests against Australia at Lord's and The Oval, an early sign of his ability to rise to the biggest of occasions.

After serving in the Boer War he returned to be the best batsman in the 1902 series against Australia, defying a high-class attack for more than four hours to make 128 in a famous match at Old Trafford which the tourists eventually won by three runs.

He played as an amateur for Yorkshire for 17 seasons, hitting 21 centuries for them and five more in his 20 Tests, all against Australia, but because of business and military duties and his years at Cambridge he was rarely able to play a full season for the county. When he did play, it was big news. In 1900, when home on leave from the Boer War, he was invited to play at the Scarborough Festival and newspaper placards cried out the message: "F S Jackson Will Definitely Play." He scored 134.

He was MP for the Howdenshire constituency from 1915 to 1926, Financial Secretary to the War Office and became chairman of the Conservative Party. Vanity Fair said that he had "a jaunty step, a lordly manner and exceeding confidence in himself" but was "full of childish simplicity" with no pomposity.

His popularity was, however, not universal. His dazzling career took him to the governorship of Bengal from 1927 to 1932 and there he narrowly escaped an assassin's sword-thrust with what he shrugged off as "the quickest duck I ever made." He was good at most games and, like many of today's cricketers, was particularly keen on golf.

When due to make his maiden speech in Parliament, the Speaker handed him a note saying; "I've dropped you in the batting order, it's a sticky wicket at the moment."

As president of the MCC in 1921 it was he who suggested the simple phrase 'The Great Cricketer' to be inscribed on the Grace Gates at Lord's. He later became chairman of England's selectors, succeeded Lord Hawke as Yorkshire's president in 1939 and died in 1947 in Knightsbridge having failed to recover from being knocked down by a taxi.

Jackson was a contemporary of and Yorkshire's near-equivalent to the great Charles Burgess Fry, the archetypal figure of the Golden Age, who could never quite spare the time to tour Australia but played at home against them from 1899 to 1912.

Fry, who said that he delighted in Jackson's captaincy, is as a cricketer most famous for his phenomenal batting exploits with Ranjitsinhji for Sussex. He also played football for England, earned a Cup Final medal with Southampton, played rugby for the Barbarians, held the world long-jump record for years and was an Oxford blue at football, cricket and athletics.

He was also a brilliant scholar and (doesn't it make you sick?) was regarded as one of the most handsome men of his time. "Fry could, alike in form and feature, have stepped out of the frieze of the Parthenon." someone once wrote. C B went one better than F S abroad in that Fry was actually offered the throne of Albania but turned it down: they got King Zog instead.

Headingley's next match provided England with their first win, over South Africa in 1907, when, for the first time, the South Africans' games here were granted Test match status. Their tour of 1901 had been criticised in some quarters as being in poor taste since it coincided with the worst year of the Boer War and Wisden dismissed it as being of little meaning to the cricket public since the South Africans were not in the same class as Australia.

But in 1907 the picture was different. Pelham Warner's team had lost 4-1 on the matting wickets over there and South Africa boasted a quartet of googly bowlers, one of whom had learned about the delivery from its inventor, B J T Bosanquet.

They and the South Africans were hugely successful on the 1907 tour, even though it did not bring them a Test victory. At Leeds they bowled out England for 76 in their first innings. The tourists made 110, England fared a little better with Fry making 54 out of a total of 162 and South Africa were then skittled for 75 to lose by 53 runs.

This was Colin Blythe's match, the Kent slow left-armer taking 15 wickets for 99 runs in the match. In all he took exactly 100 Test wickets in only 19 appearances for his country. In this series he took 26 in the three Tests and in the same year, in a county match at Northampton he claimed 17 wickets in a day (10-30 and 7-18).

The success of the South African googly men had a significant effect on English batting from then on until the war, for it became less dashing and generally more studious and defensive as batsmen fought shy of the flourishes which had characterised their approach hitherto.

Blythe was artistic, highly-strung and prone to epileptic fits. He admitted to finding Test match cricket emotionally taxing, though his brilliant performances gave little hint of it. He was killed in action at Passchendaele in Belgium in 1917 and a monument to him stands in Canterbury.

In 1909 the Australians were back and this time they won all five tosses. The series stood at 1-1 when they arrived in Leeds for the third Test, Hirst and Blythe having taken all 20 wickets in an easy England win at Edgbaston before the Australians hit back with a nine-wicket success at Lord's.

This match brought into conflict three of the outstanding cricketers of this or any other age – Charlie Macartney of Australia and Sydney Barnes and Gilbert Jessop of England. The fact that Jessop hurt his back in the field on the first day and was unable to bat in the match probably had a decisive effect on the result – a win for Australia by 126 runs. This time Macartney outbowled Barnes, taking 11-85.

Barnes is one of the most intriguing characters of the Golden Age in that although regarded as one of the best bowlers in history, not that fast but able to combine swing and cut with spin, he did not play much county cricket. His career, interrupted by the war, lasted from 1894 to 1930 but he appeared in only 133 first-class games, preferring league cricket where he was destructive even into his sixties.

He had only modest success with Warwickshire and fell out with Lancashire, which proves that he must have been a fairly decent chap. He looked gaunt and daunting and was relentless, bowling long spells even when his fingers were bleeding from his grip between the first and third finger. Neville Cardus wrote that "a chill wind of antagonism blew from him even on the sunniest day" and Pelham Warner refused to take him on one Australian tour because of his moods. Barnes played when he liked and said what he liked.

When he played he was utterly devastating and has the best strike-rate in Test cricket of any of them – 189 wickets from 27 matches. Yes, seven wickets a game.

Gilbert Laird Jessop, of Cheltenham Grammar School, Cambridge University and Gloucestershire, was the Golden Age's big hitter, scoring his runs at an incredible 80 an hour over his career. Of his 53 first-class centuries 12 were scored in under a hour even though, until 1910, the ball had to go out of the ground to count as six.

A thoroughly modest man, he was no mere slogger, though a total of 18 Test appearances suggests that the England selectors sometimes thought so. One bowler was so cross that he sent down six consecutive deliveries at or over Jessop's head.

But the Leeds Test of 1909 was Macartney's match, the slow left-armer using the arm ball to good effect. Australia made 188, England replied with 182 and resolute batting by Warwick Armstrong and Macartney, who made 18 out of the 80 runs added by the last three wickets, left England needing 214 to win. It looked a tall order, especially without Jessop, but they reached 60-2 before Macartney and fast bowler Albert Cotter got to work. England collapsed to 87 all out.

In 1912 both Australia and South Africa toured and the Headingley Test match was against the latter, resulting in a 174-run victory for England.

The international career of George Herbert Hirst had ended three years earlier and it is remarkable that his achievements were comparatively modest in his 24 matches for England. Mind you, when everything is compared to his annus mirabilis of

1906 (2,385 runs and 208 wickets) it is bound to look modest.

In that season he reached the double of 1,000 runs and 100 wickets after 16 matches and against Somerset at Bath made 111 and 117 not out and took 6-70 and 5-45. Yorkshire were uniquely blessed in having as contemporaries two such prolific all-rounders as George Herbert (it was never just 'George') and Wilfred Rhodes, who appeared together more than 400 times for the county.

Hirst was at his most effective after he trimmed his run-up and reduced his pace, for this enabled him to exert mastery over length and swing as a left-arm bowler. He hit 60 first-class centuries, though none of them for England, and his 341 against Leicestershire at Leicester, including 54 boundaries, remains the highest individual score made for Yorkshire.

Perhaps at Test level he lacked the pace to trouble the finest Australian batsmen on better pitches, but he still had his moments. At Edgbaston in 1902 he and Rhodes bowled them out for 36. Rhodes got seven of the wickets but it was said that Hirst was the more dangerous bowler. In the next game, for Yorkshire against the tourists, he and F S Jackson dismissed them for 23 at Leeds with Hirst capturing 5-9. At The Oval in that same season his 58 not out rescued England from a desperate position and with Rhodes he made the 15 runs needed for the last wicket to snatch a famous victory, though the runs were not gained in singles, as legend has it.

Edgbaston was also a successful ground for Hirst in 1909 when he took nine wickets in England's win. The greatest county cricketer of his time, he departed the Test scene as well loved as when he entered it, at Sydney in 1897, for he was a genial man on and off the field.

Another of the game's finest players who also did not shine against Australia as brightly as he might have done was Kent's Frank Woolley, who made 57 out of England first-innings total of 242 against South Africa in the Headingley Test of 1912.

Barnes took six wickets as the tourists were bowled out for 147 and in England's second innings Lancashire's amateur batsman Reggie Spooner made 82 and Jack Hobbs 55 in a total of 238.

Spooner was one of the most elegant batsmen of the era, said to "handle a bat as a lady would handle her fan," his speciality being the off-drive. He was one of the first batsmen to find an answer to the googly as perfected by the South Africans at that time.

The tourists managed only 159 in their second innings with Barnes taking another four wickets to finish with 10-115 in the match. South Africa were 85-7 at one stage and their late resistance was gallant but forlorn.

In the years before the First World War the pitches at Leeds generally favoured the bowlers. In the five Test matches 182 wicket were taken for just over 3,500 runs at an average of 19.35 per wicket. It is hard to believe it now but in the years after the war Headingley became one of the best batting surfaces in the country.

The ground was not deserted during the war years. members of the Leeds Pals battalion were pictured enjoying a break from duties in 1915, seated on the boundary edge with big mugs of tea, during a specially arranged game between a Pals' side and a Yorkshire X1. They experimented with eight-ball overs and 29-inch stumps and Yorkshire won by 81 runs.

The club offices, still in the city centre and not at Headingley, became the headquarters of the West Riding Volunteers, comprising 20 battalions of infantry and two ambulance corps. The public, despite the lack of proper cricket, rallied to the cause and even in the war years Yorkshire collected £5,500 in subscriptions.

Allowances were also maintained for the professionals so that when off duty they could play in charity matches. War charities benefited to the tune of some £20,000 from these events and in addition Yorkshire did their bit to keep up the soldiers' morale by despatching 500 bundles of cricket equipment to camps in this country and abroad.

When hostilities ceased the championship resumed in 1919, but it was a different world in the wake of the blood-soaked Western Front. The Golden Age had gone. It was not blown to pieces by war; it was already fading gently away in the years before it.

The unrest of the suffragette movement and other dissatisfied groups broke through the glamour of Edwardian England. Most people came to agree that the gap between the very rich and the very poor, highlighted by Lloyd George in his 1909 Budget, was too large. Cricket at this time was a huge spectator sport, claiming a part of the life of the ordinary man that is not so these days, so it was inevitable that the game would be influenced towards change by the nation's attitudes.

Both county and Test match cricket had burgeoned for two decades and more, the amateurs playing a great role at a critical stage of the game's evolution.

They provided the unique charm of Edwardian cricket, but from now on they would be neither numerous nor secure enough to play it with such panache or make such a significant contribution.

The most telling evidence of the passing of an age came in 1915 with the deaths of W G Grace and the Australian Victor Trumper. We would never see their like again. Many cricketers did not return from the war; those who did were changed men and took part in a game whose ambience and atmosphere changed with them.

# Chapter Three

# Yorkshire 1919-1930

THE period from 1919 to 1930 takes us to the end of the greatest career in Yorkshire's history, that of Wilfred Rhodes, and to the arrival on these shores of the world's finest batsman, Donald Bradman, who exploits have become part of Headingley folklore.

When hostilities on the battlefields of France and Belgium gave way to sporting encounters on the cricket fields of England in 1919 the world had changed and those involved in the running of cricket must have wondered how the game would fit into the order of things.

After the expansion of county cricket in the early years of the 20th century some of the smaller clubs had drifted into dire financial difficulties and in 1913 there was a proposal from those mean-spirited men on the other side of the Pennines that some of the weaker brethren be ditched. The idea was rejected and the idea that the larger counties should not be allowed to bully the smaller ones continues to this day.

There were other concerns, notably the claim that bowling and field placings had become too defensive, that batsmen lacked a sense of adventure and that the fixture list was too crowded. We have heard it all many times since then and the players in the last years of the Golden Age would fall over laughing at the notion that the modern professional is overworked.

In an effort to thin out the fixture list and perhaps because of a fear that the war years might have

blunted the public's appetite for the game, 1919 brought an experiment with a programme of two-day championship fixtures, the hours of play being 11.30 to 7.30. Despite a dry summer which kept down the number of draws, the move was a failure, though Yorkshire did not mind too much as they won the title.

At this time placings were decided on the percentage of wins to games played, a somewhat convoluted system which in 1919 meant that Yorkshire did not learn of the triumph until nine o'clock at night on the last day of the season, when they had arrived at Victoria Station en route from Hove.

The Yorkshire Post's cricket correspondent, writing as 'Old Ebor', hated the method but it was he who was able to tell the players of their success having telephoned the newspaper to discover that Kent, Yorkshire's main rivals for the title, had been held to a draw by Middlesex.

The anomalies this system could throw up can be gauged from the fact that had Kent won that game they would have taken the title even though they had played only 14 games to Yorkshire's 26.

The 1919 campaign brought 10 debutants, among them Abe Waddington, the future captain Geoffrey Wilson, Emmott Robinson and Herbert Sutcliffe who, with Percy Holmes, was to forge the most celebrated opening partnership in the county's history.

It did not happen straightaway, however. The new

19

captain, D C F (David) Burton, who had first played for Yorkshire while at Cambridge in 1907 and had the good sense to take plenty of advice from Hirst and Rhodes, began the season with Holmes and Rhodes as his opening partnership with Sutcliffe at No 7. It was Hirst who persuaded him to move Sutcliffe up the order.

Waddington, a left-arm firebrand from Bradford, did not come into the side until July but ended the season with 100 wickets at 18.74, hitting the county scene like a meteor. His bowling nearly always upset even the best of batsmen and friend and foe alike were sometimes upset by the sharpness of his tongue.

After his debut Yorkshire won six of their next seven games and in one, an innings win over Gloucestershire at Headingley, Waddington took 12-126 while Sutcliffe and David Denton put on 237 for the second wicket and Roy Kilner and Hirst an unbroken 196 for the fifth.

Rockley Wilson could play only in the school holidays but crucially dismissed Jack Hearne and B J T Bosanquet in successive overs against Middlesex at Leeds, which was also the venue for the first appearance of Holmes and Sutcliffe as an opening pair, against Kent at the end of June. Holmes was out for a duck but by the end of the summer they had recorded five century stands.

In 1920, when the championship reverted to three-day play, Yorkshire slipped to fourth, mainly because Rhodes and Waddington, who shared 296 wickets, were left to carry the attack without much support in the second half of the season. That statistic alone is stark proof of how standards have changed – Rhodes 156 wickets, Waddington 140 and Emmott Robinson a mere 53, and still no title.

Headingley was now emerging as a fine batting track and Yorkshire suffered against Hampshire in 1920 when the visitors, making hay while the sun shone, rattled up 456-2 on the first day only for Yorkshire, batting after heavy rain, to be caught on a "sticky dog" and they lost by an innings.

But there was a 10-wicket win over Nottinghamshire on the ground, where Rhodes made 167 not out, helped by 55 from Sir Archibald White, who had led Yorkshire to the title in his first year as captain in 1912 and who returned in this game in the absence of the injured Burton. George Gunn held out for four hours in making 69 but Kilner ripped through Nottinghamshire's tail with 3-10 and Yorkshire were left to make 50 to win.

The 1921 season was notable for Yorkshire's record total at Leeds, 560-6 declared against

Leicestershire. Rhodes was in magnificent form making 267 not out on his way to 1,329 runs for the season to go with his 128 wickets. Yorkshire won the match by an innings with Harrogate's Maurice Leyland (his birth certificate actually gives his first name as Morris) making 52 not out and putting on 140 for the seventh wicket with Rhodes, who was 23 years his senior. Norman Kilner also hit a century.

Yorkshire then lost to Surrey at Headingley by 179 runs as Jack Hobbs, playing in his only championship game of the season, carried his bat for 172 in an exemplary demonstration of his powers.

This was the end for Hirst, who retired at the end of the season when past his 50th birthday, but one of his last services as a player to the county he served with such distinction, good humour and innate cricketing intelligence was some advice to a young fast bowler from Thirsk called George Macaulay, who had appeared briefly in the previous season.

Hirst urged him to cut down his pace and the result was a wholehearted and skilled bowler who, like Waddington before him, exploded on to the scene in 1921 with 100 wickets. He took 10 against Surrey but Yorkshire's batting failed against Percy Fender, who took 6-66 as they were dismissed for 153 in their second innings.

Macaulay came to personify the side's ruthless and relentless streak in the coming years and was probably vastly under-rated. He had a sharp tongue and was famous for his wisecracks. When Bill Bowes said that his heart was always in his mouth when Macaulay was batting he replied that there was plenty of room for it.

Yorkshire could claim bad luck with the weather in several games that season, notably in the Headingley Roses match, when it intervened with Lancashire on the ropes needing 192 to avoid an innings defeat. But they were badly beaten by the champions Middlesex at Lord's, where Sutcliffe was injured during the game and wicketkeeper Arthur Dolphin fell off a chair in the dressing-room after it.

Burton stood down as captain after three years of sound achievement, including the unexpected title triumph of 1919. He was replaced by Geoffrey Wilson, from Leeds, a Harrovian who won a blue for Cambridge in 1919. He was not a great batsman, but he was a stunningly successful captain, leading Yorkshire to three consecutive titles from 1922.

These were the years of plenty. There were plenty of wins, but also plenty of controversy and during

Wilson's time in charge relations between Yorkshire and Middlesex became so strained that at one stage Middlesex threatened not to continue fixtures.

It was a period of ruthless Yorkshire dominance, but also of dourness and a certain mean-spiritedness which transmitted itself to a following which came to regard victory as a divine right and defeat (though there were not many of them) as an offence against nature.

The gap between the good sides and the poor ones was huge and although Yorkshire were arguably further ahead of the rest than at any stage in their history they became deeply unpopular. They were at the same time cricket's first superstars but also social outcasts in the eyes of many.

Wilson was certainly not of that ilk, but may not have been strong enough to curb the excesses of some of the hard-bitten professionals in his charge. "I feel that any match...should be played in the most friendly spirit. The result should be second in importance," he once said.

This sentiment, one suspects, would have gained short shrift in the professionals' dressing-room and Wilson himself admitted that criticism of the team on their southern tour for slow, ultra-cautious batting was to some extent justified.

Yorkshire started the 1922 season with six wins and eventually won the championship from Nottinghamshire, the placings now decided on the basis of five points for a win and two for first innings lead.

The game against Kent at Leeds was Dolphin's benefit match, Waddington taking 8-39 in a 10-wicket win gained despite resistance from Frank Woolley, who made 77 for the visitors.

There was an innings win over Glamorgan in which Rhodes and Edgar Oldroyd made centuries. Oldroyd had by this time established himself at No 3 in the batting order in succession to David Denton despite a brief flurry from Cecil Tyson, who hit a century on his debut but fell out with the club over money, claiming that he could earn more playing league cricket at weekends and going down the pit during the week.

This match also brought the debut at the age of 19 of Arthur Mitchell, who just after the Second World War was to become the first full-time professional coach employed by the club.

Wilson went down with appendicitis which prevented him from witnessing the title triumph, based on the batting of Sutcliffe, Oldroyd, Holmes and Kilner and some devastating all-round displays

by Rhodes, who took 100 wickets at 12.32 and averaged 40 with the bat at the age of 44.

The 1923 campaign ranks statistically as Yorkshire's finest – they won 25 games out of 32 played and lost only once, to Nottinghamshire at Headingley in early June. They did not just win matches, they annihilated the opposition more often than not.

The Nottinghamshire game was a thriller, Yorkshire going down by three runs when they really should have won as they needed only 36 runs to win with five second-innings wickets standing. The visitors waged a war of attrition on the first day, making 197-8, and were soon bowled out for 200 when play resumed.

Yorkshire struggled to 134 all out but hit back though the slow left-arm combination of Rhodes and Kilner, who between them claimed nine wickets for 53 runs as Nottinghamshire were dismissed for 95 in the second innings. Yorkshire were left to make 162 to win and were 133-4 at one stage before collapsing to leave Macaulay stranded on 17 not out.

The game with Surrey at Headingley was another compelling contest, with Yorkshire reduced to 35-4 before Leyland hit a half-century to spark a recovery continued by captain Wilson, Macaulay and Waddington, which lifted the side to a total of 278.

Surrey replied with 224 but Yorkshire's batting failed in the second innings and the visitors were left to make 184 to win. It seemed distinctly reachable, but by this time no task was beyond Yorkshire's attack and they set about this one with a will. Macaulay bowled Hobbs but Surrey still managed to reach 127-2, at which point they looked certain winners, before Robinson took three quick wickets to disturb their equilibrium. Kilner then ripped through the tail to finish with 6-22 and clinch a stunning 25-run victory.

Yorkshire also cruised to victory over Sussex at Leeds, Rhodes hitting 88 and taking 8-60, and an intriguing game against Hampshire was ruined by rain after Yorkshire had left the visitors to make 126 in 85 minutes.

The season revealed Yorkshire as a cricketing machine. Rhodes took 100-plus wickets in a summer for the 14th time, equalling Hirst's achievement, Kilner and Macaulay also topped 100 and Robinson was not far behind with 96. Kilner was in his pomp as an all-rounder of distinction, and the individual talent at Wilson's disposal was substantiated by a standard of fielding which had probably not been seen hitherto in the county game.

*Arthur 'Ticker' Mitchell shows the prowess which brought him many a catch off the bowling of Hedley Verity.*

Yorkshire's cricket team was now the talk of the shires. They were feared, respected and grudgingly admired in the rest of the country, simply idolised by their own folk, who turned out in ever increasing numbers.

Along with Lancashire, Surrey were still the big attraction and 25,000 turned out at Headingley in 1924 for the first day of a game ruined by rain after Oldroyd had scored a century.

The Headingley Roses match of that summer ranks among the finest of its kind, setting new benchmarks of dourness and fiercely competitive cricket. The weather that Whitsun holiday was uncertain and Lancashire, choosing to bat first, took 90 overs to make 113 with Macaulay taking 6-40 in 33 overs and the dependable Kilner 2-28 in 27 overs.

Yorkshire also struggled at the crease against the bowling of Dick Tyldesley, Oldroyd top-scoring with 37 out of a total of 130 which limited the home side to a lead of 17 runs. Kilner and Macaulay were at it again in Lancashire's second innings, taking eight wickets between them as the Red Rose men were shot out for 74, an innings which occupied 56 overs. Kilner returned the remarkable figures of 4-13 in 23 overs, 16 of which were maidens.

So Yorkshire were left with the formality of making 58 to win, or so it seemed to the 30,000 spectators who caught the tram home at the end of a dramatic second day. There was a good gathering to witness the execution on the morning of Tuesday, June 10, and as they walked out to open the innings with 25 century-plus partnerships already behind them Holmes and Sutcliffe were unperturbed by the yapping of a small dog at their heels.

The spectators laughed at this, but soon had their smiles wiped off their faces to be replaced by worried frowns. Sutcliffe was out for three, Holmes and Leyland for ducks; Yorkshire were 3-3.

Oldroyd was missed at the same score, but he and Rhodes could not profit much from the escape, adding only 10 before both fell with the score at 13. Half the side was back in the pavilion, the cream of the batting. Could Yorkshire find someone to break the stranglehold being exerted by Lancashire's slow bowlers, Tyldesley and Parkin?

Rhodes had tried to attack without success and when Kilner came in the left-hander tried something similar, mustering enough confidence to hit Tyldesley for a boundary. But with the total on 16 Robinson, trying to play the anchor role, had been run out, a shocking waste, and at 23 Cyril Turner was bowled by Tyldesley.

Macaulay was not a man for half measures but it did not work this time and he fell to reduce Yorkshire to a palsied 32-8. One run later Waddington and Dolphin perished, Tyldesley finishing with 6-18. According to Neville Cardus, the conductor on the tram taking him back to City Square was so shocked by the news that all he could do was repeat "Who'd a thowt it?" over and over again.

Even so, Yorkshire claimed their third consecutive title and had a combination of talents which could be challenged by Surrey and Middlesex but not matched by them.

Their progress to the summit of the county game had, however, not been without controversy and ill-feeling towards the side reached a climax in 1924 in the game against Middlesex at Bramall Lane.

It had in many ways been a sad and bitter season, albeit another successful one, with Yorkshire's seemingly unquenchable thirst for victories tarnished by outbreaks of bad behaviour on the field. At Lord's Yorkshire had been drubbed by an innings, so they were out for revenge in the return game at Sheffield.

This was such an ill-tempered match that Middlesex publicly declared that they did not wish to arrange fixtures with Yorkshire for the following season. The behaviour of the spectators on the first day became so objectionable that the umpires, H Butt and W Reeves, wrote a protest letter to Lord's criticising Waddington, who they said had incited barracking by his reaction to some of their decisions.

Yorkshire asked the MCC to investigate the whole affair but even this could not dissuade Middlesex from their threat to remove Yorkshire from their fixture list. The MCC's report supported the umpires and suggested that the club should warn Waddington to control his temper. He wrote a letter of apology to the MCC but it took a good deal of correspondence between Leeds and Lord's to repair the damage in relations between the two counties. There was no break in fixtures.

There were also reports of bitterness between Yorkshire and Surrey, a foretaste of things to come, and this atmosphere may have been one of the factors behind Wilson's decision to step down as captain after three title-winning years. He never revealed his reasons but seems to have been the sort of man who would have accepted some of the responsibility for the unpleasantness and perhaps even felt that his departure might help mend relations with Middlesex.

Lord Hawke was by this time a hugely-influential figure within the MCC and this must have helped. It is possible that while he defended his Yorkshire players in public he privately pushed for a change of captain.

No matter, the public loved Wilson for what he had achieved as a leader capable of handling and getting the best out of some temperamental professionals. His successor was the army major Arthur William Lupton, from Bradford, who was 46 when he took over.

His twofold task was to maintain Yorkshire's supremacy while at the same time restoring discipline among the players and dignity within the club. Inevitably, because of their outstanding success, defeats came hard to the players. If they could be excused for being rather bad losers, some opponents could not forgive them for being graceless winners.

At the end of Wilson's term of office Yorkshire boasted the finest team in the land but they were not about to win any popularity contests and Lord Hawke and the committee perhaps acknowledged the need to make the players keep their aggression in the right channels.

The modern cricket follower cannot possibly imagine what the game was like in 1925. There were no Test matches. Every team was at full strength. It was a state of affairs which met with the approval of Lord Hawke, who said that English cricket should never become obsessed with Tests. One wonders if even his might have been a voice in the wilderness these days.

*Herbert Sutcliffe strides out to bat at Scarborough in 1938.*

24

Yorkshire were undefeated and won 21 of their 32 championship matches to retain the title for a fourth consecutive season. Holmes scored six centuries and both he and Sutcliffe topped 2,000 runs while Macaulay took 200 wickets. Yorkshire were unstoppable.

Middlesex set aside their grumbles and turned up at Headingley for a game that was Roy Kilner's benefit. The crowd was so large that Holmes could not get to the ground in time, so Yorkshire had to open with Sutcliffe and Leyland. It made no difference; they put on 218 for the first wicket with Sutcliffe going on to make 235 while Leyland scored 110 out of a total of 528-6. Middlesex made 184 but held out for the draw, closing on 149-4.

At one stage Yorkshire won 12 games in a row, six of them by an innings and another three by 10 wickets. Derbyshire were swept aside by an innings at Leeds in two days and such was the public's appetite for winning cricket that a record 326,000 paid through the gate in the season.

Neville Cardus was by now offering the view that Yorkshire should be awarded the title as a matter of course to let the rest of the counties get on with their own game but the period of supremacy ended in 1926 and it could hardly have been worse: Lancashire took the title.

Yorkshire were runners-up, Macaulay again demonstrating his awesome powers at Leeds against Northamptonshire with 6-26 in 25 overs, but rain intervened and the game ended in a draw.

By their own astonishingly high standards Yorkshire then went into decline, though they were still not out of the top four for the next four seasons before embarking on another period of dominance in the 1930s with Hedley Verity and Bill Bowes at the helm.

In 1927 Worcestershire were beaten by an innings at Headingley with Macaulay taking 7-17 in 20.2 overs in their first innings. He then hit 67 and added 163 for the eighth wicket with Waddington, who scored the only century of his career. Yorkshire reached 291 despite some fine bowling by Fred Root for Worcestershire and Macaulay and Emmott Robinson took five wickets each as the visitors were bowled out for 81 in their second innings.

Warwickshire enjoyed rather more than their allotted 15 minutes of fame when they won at Hull to inflict on Yorkshire their first defeat since 1924 but Headingley continued to be a fortress. Rhodes and Kilner claimed nine wickets between them as Surrey were dismissed for 172 and Sutcliffe then made 176 out of a Yorkshire total of 333. Kilner took another five wickets in Surrey's second innings

and Yorkshire romped to victory by 10 wickets.

They had a seven-wicket success against Essex but found things much harder in the Roses match, Lancashire having unearthed a fiery fast bowler in Ted McDonald. On a dodgy pitch it took all Sutcliffe's skill to fashion 95 out of the total of 157, one of the opener's finest innings for the county, but Ernest Tyldesley then hit a majestic 165 in Lancashire's total of 360-8.

Yorkshire were in danger of defeat as they slumped to 75-4 but saved the game thanks to 135 from Sutcliffe and valiant contributions from Rhodes, Robinson and Macaulay, whose 61 not out demonstrated his prowess as a late-order batsman.

Yorkshire were still good, but clearly not quite good enough and at the end of the 1927 season were even talking about a professional captain. Sutcliffe was officially invited to take charge but diplomatically declined, sensing that there was strong feeling against a professional captain within the committee and outside and that if the club really wanted to go down the professional route, Rhodes was the preferred choice of many.

Sutcliffe's sacrifice prevented a damaging rift in the club, which at the start of the 1928 season was under the guidance of Captain William Worsley of Hovingham Hall, whose family links with Yorkshire cricket went back a long way and who was himself a decent attacking batsman of good club standard.

The club and the whole county was shaken by the death at the age of 37 of Roy Kilner, who died of an attack of typhoid fever contracted during a coaching trip to India. Kilner's left-handed batting, executed in a style of his own, brought him 15 centuries and he took more than 850 wickets with his slow-medium left-arm at an average of just over 17.

On numerous occasions he batted the side out of trouble and in tandem with Rhodes, especially on a drying pitch, he was well nigh unplayable. Regard for Kilner spread far beyond his home village of Wombwell for he was not only a fine player but also a lovable man, admired and liked by friend and foe alike. It is no coincidence that many boys born in Yorkshire in the 1920s were called Roy.

Arthur Dolphin had hung up his gloves and Waddington, still temperamental but now a fading force, had refused terms. So Yorkshire were left to rely for their bowling strength on Macaulay and the two veterans, Rhodes and Robinson.

At Headingley, Leicestershire were demolished by an innings with Rhodes taking 6-55 in 40 overs. Oldroyd then hit a century, Robinson made 73 and

Left: After Tunnicliffe and Brown Yorkshire were blessed with another prolific opening pair in Percy Holmes (pictured here) and Herbert Sutcliffe, who against Essex at Leyton in 1932 compiled a world record stand of 555, even though Holmes was troubled by lumbago for much of his innings of 224 not out.

Right: Bill Bowes, who noted the strengths and weaknesses of opposing batsmen in a book, puts his research into practice.

Yorkshire built a lead of 149. In the second innings Rhodes and Robinson nagged away and another son of Wombwell, Cyril Turner, claimed 3-3 to seal a victory gained without the services of Sutcliffe, Macaulay and Leyland, all away at the Test Trial.

Yorkshire also beat the West Indian tourists at Leeds in 1928 with Sutcliffe and Cleckheaton's Wilf Barber making 98 each in a total of 284. The tourists, troubled by the bowling of Rhodes and Leyland, reached 208, largely through contrasting innings from Learie Constantine, who smashed 69 in 28 minutes, and 'Freddie' Martin, who took three-and-a-half hours to compile 60. Holmes then hit an unbeaten 84 as Yorkshire declared on 172-1 and Macaulay destroyed the tourists with 6-30 as they crumbled to 58 all out.

Against Middlesex, in Holmes's benefit game, Patsy Hendren made 169 and F T Mann 122, adding more than 200 for the fourth wicket and lifting their side to a formidable total of 488. Macaulay remained dangerous and persistent even amid this run feast, finishing with 6-130.

Yorkshire collapsed to 143-7 before Robinson, with an unbeaten 70, and Arthur Wood, the stocky Bradfordian who had succeeded Dolphin behind the stumps, managed a recovery but even so Yorkshire were forced to follow on 185 runs adrift. They had no trouble in saving the game, reaching 290-1 at stumps thanks to centuries by the old firm, Sutcliffe and Holmes, whose partnership was 290 in three hours.

The history books tell us that Yorkshire's slide to fourth place in the championship table was probably because they were a bowler short, though Rhodes at the age of 50 took 112 wickets, the 44-year-old Emmott Robinson 111 and Macaulay 117, a figure described as "disappointing by his own standards". Sutcliffe and Holmes again both topped 2,000 runs for the season. To the modern eye it seems bizarre that a side containing three bowlers with 340 victims between them should be accused of lacking penetration.

In 1929 something significant happened, albeit in a relatively insignificant early-season game at Oxford University. Bill Bowes made his debut. Born in Elland but an adopted son of Leeds, he then went on to the Lord's groundstaff but played 11 games for Yorkshire that year, the beginning of a career which flourished in the 1930s and helped take Yorkshire back to the top.

There was a draw with Sussex at Headingley in 1929 in which Rhodes, still the peerless all-rounder, made 43 not out and 55 not out, after which he boasted a batting average of 267. Yorkshire were set to make an improbable 342 to win and slumped to 12-5 before Rhodes and Robinson came to the rescue.

The game against Surrey was a rain-ruined draw but Hampshire were trounced by an innings at Leeds with Robinson making 64 and taking 10 wickets in the match. It was clear, however, that the Golden Age had passed and there was constant criticism of dull cricket and negative play.

Under William Worsley the side was winning nothing but gradually taking shape after the loss of key bowlers. Bowes was to emerge as a key piece in the jigsaw and 1930 brought another one when Hedley Verity came into the side. If Bowes's first year had been encouraging, Verity's was awesome. He topped the national bowling averages with 64 wickets at 12.44 each. This was the end of the road for Rhodes, in his 53rd year, and the pair of them sometimes bowled in tandem since Verity's pace was nearer medium than slow and so provided enough of a contrast with the old master.

After two years in charge, William Worsley handed over the captaincy to Sheffield's Alan Barber, who had led Oxford the previous year and was only 25 when he took over. He also played football for Barnet and the Corinthians. Seasoned amateur captains were one thing; a young one with little first-class experience was a gamble, but it paid off as Barber in his one season provided exemplary and inspired leadership.

Yorkshire finished third under a system of eight points for a win and five for first-innings lead. Lancashire were unbeaten and were champions, even though Gloucestershire won five more matches than the Red Rose men. Yorkshire lost at home to Kent, where Frank Woolley mastered them, but Verity's arrival as the replacement for Rhodes, bleak news for Featherstone's left-arm spinner Arthur Booth, left everyone connected with the club with a feeling of optimism. It was not misplaced.

# Chapter Four

# England 1919-1930

NEARLY 48,000 people watched the first Test match between England and the Australians in 1899 at Headingley, even though there was no play on the second of the three days and the turnstiles clicked over 55,000 times during the 1905 match between the countries.

South Africa were understandably less of a draw and after a three-day attendance of 26,000 for the 1907 Test match against them the turn-out dipped to an estimated 16,500 in the last match before the war. The pattern remained the same when Headingley played host to the same two opponents between the wars with an estimated 41,000 paying to see the 1921 match against Australia, won at a canter by the tourists.

The period immediately after the First World War was one of emphatic Australian supremacy. Led by the huge Victorian Warwick Armstrong, they flattened England by the unique margin of 5-0 in 1920-21 and so it was with a deep sense of foreboding that English spectators welcomed Armstrong's men the following summer, the teams having sailed to these shores together.

The scorecard for the Headingley Test, the third in the series with England already 2-0 down and in considerable disarray over team selection, shows one startling and significant entry. Jack Hobbs is down at No 11 in the batting order and marked as 'absent ill' in both innings.

This was the only match in the series in which Hobbs was fit enough to turn up but an attack of acute appendicitis prevented him from batting and England slumped to defeat by 219 runs. Although they ended Australia's run of eight consecutive wins by drawing the last two Tests they were destroyed by the fast-bowling combination of Jack Gregory and Ted McDonald.

At Leeds England made seven changes – they used 30 players in all in the series – and changed captain, the Hon Lionel Tennyson, of Hampshire, taking over from Essex's Johnny Douglas, whose initials J W H T became the subject of a famous cricketing joke because of his often dour, defensive batting. He became known as 'Johnny Won't Hit Today' Douglas.

For the second Test at Lord's England had even invited C B Fry back to play but the 49-year-old declined, saying he was too old.

Tennyson, an Old Etonian, was a quintessential aristocratic figure. His wicketkeeper at Hampshire, Walter Livsey, was also his butler. But he could play a bit and showed that he was not just in it for a spot of fun in an innings of tremendous courage at Headingley in this game after splitting a hand trying to stop a fierce shot by Charlie Macartney. He batted virtually one-handed against the thunderbolts sent down by Gregory and McDonald.

Macartney made 115 in Australia's imposing first-innings total of 407, which spanned less than five hours, and Tennyson, despite his handicap, blazed away to hit a bold and brave 63 in just over an hour as England replied with 259 after they had lost half their side for 67. The deposed captain Douglas made 75 and the pair put on 88 in an heroic effort which saved the follow-on. Strangely, Macartney's century was Australia's only one during the series and it followed his monumental 345 against Nottinghamshire.

There was only one Yorkshire-born player taking part in this Test and he played for Australia, wicketkeeper Hanson 'Sammy' Carter, who had been born in Halifax in 1878. As he was an undertaker by trade who sometimes turned up to matches in a hearse it seemed darkly appropriate that Carter should help dig England's grave in this game with 47 in Australia's second innings total of 273-7 declared.

The top-scorer with 92 was Tommy Andrews, a stonemason whose family owned funeral parlours. One can only guess at some of the jolly mid-pitch conversations that took place between the two.

England were left to survive for four-and-a-half hours, far too long for them with no Hobbs and with morale already shattered by the exploits of Gregory and McDonald, who took 10 wickets between them in the match.

*The crowd scene at the 1921 Ashes Test, which Australia won by 219 runs.*

Gregory did it with sheer pace, often simply scaring batsmen into submission. Tall, strong and raw-boned, the spectacular all-rounder from New South Wales achieved the double in 1921 with 1,135 runs and 116 wickets and was later to blast the fastest Test century, 119 in 70 minutes against South Africa in Johannesburg. He married a winner of the Miss Australia contest.

McDonald, a natural athlete, bowled more within himself with lateral movement and reserved his fastest pace for the top batsmen. The absence of Hobbs in this series robbed him of the greatest prize. He later signed as a professional for Nelson

and qualified for Lancashire, causing Yorkshire much grief in Roses matches in the latter half of the decade and spearheading Lancashire to four championship titles in five season from 1926. In eight seasons with the Old Trafford club he took 1,040 wickets.

He died in Lancashire in 1937 in unusual circumstances. Having crashed his car he wandered dazed into the road in an effort to stop the traffic to help him and was run over.

England did manage to maintain their dominance over South Africa, winning by nine wickets at Headingley in 1924. Hobbs did bat on this occasion, making 31, but his opening partner Herbert Sutcliffe delighted the home crowd by moving past 50, only to disappoint them by falling 17 short of a century.

Patsy Hendren, of Middlesex, made one of his seven Test match hundreds in this match, eventually falling for 132, and some useful contributions lower down the order lifted England, who had won the toss, to 396.

South Africa were bowled out for 132, their destroyer being the Sussex fast-medium bowler Maurice Tate, who took 6-42 in the first innings and another three wickets in the second. A big, burly man with heavy shoulders, he was all graceful co-ordination as a bowler after changing style from slow-medium off-breaks. Even so, his run-up remained remarkably short at eight yards.

This was Tate's golden period. From 1922 to 1925 he captured nearly 850 wickets in first-class cricket as well as opening the innings for his county. He was at his best in this 1924 series against the South Africans, claiming 27 wickets at 15.70 and in the first Test at Edgbaston he bowled unchanged with his England and county captain, Arthur Gilligan, to rout the visitors for 30 in 75 minutes.

South Africa fared much better in their second innings, only the last two batsmen failing to reach double figures, but their 323 left England to make only 60 to win and they did so for the loss of Hobbs.

It was back to the more serious business of trying to regain the Ashes in 1926, Sutcliffe and Roy Kilner having played big parts in a rare England victory at Melbourne in the fourth Test of 1924-5, which turned out to be a mere blip on the graph of Australian supremacy as the home side went on to win the series comfortably.

In that season's Birmingham Test Sutcliffe had shared in the first of his 15 three-figure stands with

Hobbs, at the first attempt, and the Yorkshire opener was now at the zenith of his powers. In the second Test at Melbourne in 1924-5 he and Hobbs batted throughout a full day of a Test. It was the first time this had been achieved and they remain the only English pair to have done it.

Sutcliffe became the first England batsman to hit a century in each innings of an Ashes Test in the same game and in the series he scored 734 runs, all this in a losing side.

By 1926 Australia had lost McDonald, who had settled on the wrong side of the Pennines, and Gregory was a fading force, troubled by a knee injury. The lack of a fast attack to compare with that enjoyed by Warwick Armstrong's side was to prove crucial.

At Leeds, Sutcliffe and Kilner were again in the England side and so was another Yorkshireman, George Macaulay. The captaincy was in the aggressive and sometimes none-too-diplomatic hands of Arthur Carr of Nottinghamshire, who asked Australia to bat on winning the toss.

It looked as if this bold decision would pay handsome rewards when Tate took a wicket with the first ball of the match, Sutcliffe pouching a smart catch in the slip cordon, but Carr's grasp proved less reliable later in the over when the captain dropped Charlie Macartney. There were massive crowds for this game – nearly 76,000 over the three days – and those who had not managed to get to Headingley in time for the first over had missed the pivotal moment of the match.

Macartney took explosive advantage of his escape, hammering the ball to all parts to score a century before lunch, reaching 100 out of 131 runs on the board in just 103 minutes. When he was caught by Hendren at mid-on to give Macaulay his only wicket of the innings he had made 151 in less than three hours of spectacular batting.

On his first tour of England, Bill Woodfull, nicknamed 'the worm-killer' because of his solid defence and limitless patience, was more circumspect in fashioning 141 and Arthur Richardson scored his only Test century at the age of 37 before being run out by Macaulay. These three big innings lifted Australia to 494 all out and left England wondering what might have been had Carr taken the early chance offered by Macartney.

Hobbs made 49 but England's reply was in a sorry state when they lost their eighth wicket at 182 before Macaulay restored some dignity by making 76 out of a ninth-wicket stand of 108 with Leicestershire's George Geary. England were all out

for 294 and still had to follow on, but saved the match as Hobbs and Sutcliffe gave the Leeds crowd a classic demonstration of their prowess with a partnership of 156, the platform for an escape to 254-3 at the close.

The fourth match of the series was also drawn but England, with a new captain in Percy Chapman, reclaimed the Ashes with a 289-run victory at The Oval, where Sutcliffe made 76 and 161 – he and Hobbs put on 172 in the second innings – and Wilfred Rhodes marked his recall to the Test team in his 49th year by turning the ball out of a worn patch at the Vauxhall end to take 4-44.

Unlike Fry, Rhodes did not think he was too old and proved it.

It was the last home Test appearance for Rhodes, whose international career came to an end four years later when he played four times in the West Indies.

Since making his England debut against Australia in 1899 he had played 58 times, scoring two centuries and achieving a healthy 30.19 average with the bat and turning his left arm over 8,231 times to take 127 wickets at just under 27 runs apiece.

His best bowling display was 8-68 and 15 wickets in the match in a victory in Melbourne in 1904 and on the same ground eight years later he made 179 in another win for England. No bowler has equalled his mind-boggling haul of 4,187 wickets, only 13 batsmen have exceeded his aggregate of 39,802 runs and only six outfielders have held more than his 764 catches.

His wonderful 32-year career cannot be measured in statistics alone, astonishing though they are. Rhodes was the supreme natural psychologist, though he probably would not have recognised the term. He taught himself to explore and expose with ruthless precision the weaknesses and fears of opposing batsmen, subtle variations in flight blending with his phenomenal accuracy to turn him into the most formidable bowling machine of his or any other time.

No only that. Rhodes batted at 10 or 11 for his first nine Test matches but within a few years had worked on his batting with such diligence and intelligence that he rose to open England's innings with Hobbs, putting on a record 323 with 'The Master' in the Melbourne Test of 1912. A more complex character than George Hirst, he probably had to work harder at his game. Rhodes was the sublime product of a strong work ethic and innate cricketing intelligence.

One of the finest tributes paid to him comes from the inimitable cricket writer John Woodcock. "Even after he had lost his sight, as he did in old age, he could have bowled a length, he had got into such a way of it."

It might never have been so had Bobby Peel not been so fond of a drink. With Peel in his pomp there was no place in the Yorkshire side for Rhodes, who left to be professional with Galashiels in Scotland. Warwickshire then moved in for him but before they could arrange a trial (a trial for Wilfred, what a thought), Peel had been dismissed.

Back came Rhodes, though even then it was a toss-up for a time as to whether he or Albert Cordingley would be the permanent replacement in the slow left-arm department.

Rhodes admitted that he and Hirst were never friends. Initially this may have been because of professional rivalry which developed into jealousy – "it was always George who had to have the wind right for his swerver," he said – but deep down the two men were too different in temperament to be close friends.

George Herbert smiled a lot and liked a joke about the game; for Wilfred, cricket was not fun, it was a job of work, and he was as sparing with words as he was with loose deliveries. He didn't have much time for either.

Pelham Warner recalled in great detail a conversation which took place between Rhodes and the MCC committee prior to his dramatic recall for the final Ashes Test of 1926, when the player was 48.

Warner said: "We think, Wilfred, that you should play. You are still the best left-handed bowler in England and in a match that has to be played to a finish it is likely that we shall have rain at sometime or the other. You can still spin 'em you know."

Percy Perrin chipped in with: "And your length is as good as ever," to which Wilfred said: "Well, I can keep 'em there or thereabouts." Arthur Gilligan said: "And you make runs for Yorkshire." Rhodes: "I can get a few." Jack Hobbs: "And your fielding is all right." Rhodes: "The further I run the slower I get."

Slow bowling of a different type was on offer for the 26,000 who attended the next Leeds Test match, against South Africa in 1929. They witnessed the leg-spin bowling of Alfred Percy Freeman, always known as Tich, who despite his small stature at 5ft 2in was one of the giants of English bowling at the time.

He probably sent down more deliveries that were begging to be hit for six than an other bowler in history but not many actually were and his record in domestic cricket for Kent is astonishing.

Freeman had taken 304 wickets in the previous English summer, a record in first-class cricket, with an action described as being "like a spring snapping." Only Rhodes in the history of the game has taken more first-class wickets and even Rhodes could not match his 3,151 in the county championship.

Freeman's career was one of success mixed with failure, however, for he never held any terrors for Australian batsmen, who probably used their feet more effectively than any others. But he was too good for the West Indies in their first tour in 1928 and the following season mesmerised South Africa with 22 wickets in the series.

He took 7-115 as South Africa, choosing to bat first, were dismissed for 236, Tate and Harold Larwood being the other wicket-takers. Opener Bob Catterall made 74 for the tourists and further down the order Cyril Vincent hit a belligerent 60.

Neville Quinn, who was highly rated by Don Bradman, bowled his left-arm medium pace to good effect to claim six England wickets, including those of Sutcliffe for 37, Hammond for 65, Hendren for a duck and Leyland for 45 but Woolley's 83 steered them to a total of 328 and a healthy first-innings lead.

Freeman, Woolley and Jack White, the Somerset slow left-armer who held the reins between the reigns of Yorkshire's Rhodes and Verity, took three wickets each as the tourists were bowled out for 275 in the second innings, though England were held up by an heroic last-wicket stand of 103 in just 63 minutes between 'Tuppy' Owen-Smith (later to qualify as a doctor at St Mary's, London), who made a magnificent 129 before being caught by Sutcliffe off Woolley's bowling, and last-man Sandy Bell, who was left unbeaten on 26.

England, set to make 184 for victory, stuttered at first as Sutcliffe and Hammond fell cheaply with only 13 runs on the board but Woolley restored order with 95 not out and he and Tate steered their side home by five wickets.

For England, this represented the calm before the storm. The following summer of 1930 brought Donald George Bradman to these shores for the first time.

The English public knew what was coming, but Yorkshire's could hardly have anticipated the love affair that was about to develop between the genius from Bowral and Headingley.

Bradman had scored two centuries in the 1928-9 series in Australia but could not prevent England from gaining a comfortable win; he made 131 in the second innings of Australia's defeat in the first Test of 1930 at Trent Bridge and 254 in their seven-wicket success at Lord's in which the tourists amassed 729-6 declared, taking the gloss off Duleepsinhji's achievement of scoring a century for England on his Test debut, a feat previously accomplished by his uncle, Ranji.

The excitement was intense as the two teams arrived in Leeds locked at 1-1, England's chances of prevailing in the series depending on their ability to hold the phenomenon in check.

Although a sufferer from seasickness, Bradman had enjoyed the first-class facilities on the voyage from Australia to Naples, on which his sharp competitive instinct was seen in the way he even noted his victories in the most trivial of deck games.

The Australians then proceeded by train and ferry, a journey which allowed them to take in the sights of Rome and Paris and enjoy some of the night-life. They had a trip to the ancient ruins of Pompeii. The photograph of the tourists, in their trilby hats and raincoats, carries the caption: "Have they gone for the Ashes?"

The tour had already been a tour de force for Bradman, who in bizarre circumstances – the Hampshire captain Lord Tennyson agreed to play on in sheeting rain on May 31 at Southampton – had become only the fifth batsman in history to make 1,000 runs before the end of that month, after Grace, Hayward, Hammond and Charlie Hallows of Lancashire. The soaked players bolted off the field as soon as Bradman had despatched a long-hop for the runs he needed to reach the landmark.

He then took a break, going to the tennis at Wimbledon and doing the sight-seeing round in London before making a leisurely drive to Leeds for the third Test, which started on July 11. It had been labelled 'Bradman v England' and so it proved. Bradman won hands down, though rain prevented a finish.

There was not a space to be had in the ground as 33,000 turned up for the first of the four days, which drew an estimated attendance of more than 77,000. The weather was miserable, with a strong, cold wind and the threat of rain, but it did not seem to matter.

Australia won the toss, Woodfull elected to bat and Tate made an early breakthrough. So Bradman made his way to the crease, his collar turned up to give him some protection from the wind and the rest of the day was carnage for the England bowlers.

Bradman followed Trumper and Macartney in scoring a century before lunch in an Ashes Test. He was 105 not out at the interval and the afternoon session was even more painful for the home side as his onslaught increased in ferocity, bringing him another 115 runs. He added 89 between tea and the close, to end the day on 309 not out. He was still a few weeks from his 22nd birthday.

Against testing new-ball bowling from Tate and Larwood, he reached 50 at a run a minute and his century in 99 minutes. No one had got there faster in Test cricket and he made them out of a total of 127. He was out the following day for 334, caught by wicketkeeper George Duckworth off Tate's bowling, having batted for 383 minutes and struck 46 fours in a majestic exhibition of strokeplay, nimble footwork and placement through the field.

Some of his team-mates had minor walk-on parts as this drama unfolded. Woodfull made 50 and shared in a second-wicket stand of 192, the cultured Alan Kippax made 77 and helped Bradman put on 227 for the third.

Bradman had reached 1,000 Test runs in only his seventh match; this was of course the highest individual score in Tests; he had become the youngest batsman to reach 2,000 runs in an English season.

As he propelled Australia to 566 all out some of the bowling figures were not a pretty sight, though Tate plugged away to take 5-124, a commendable effort in the circumstances. Larwood went for 139 in 33 overs, an affront to his dignity, and Dick Tyldesley also claimed an unwanted 'century.'

The pitch began to show signs of wear, and England were soon in difficulties, losing half their side for 206. But they were sustained by Wally Hammond, whose batting at this time could stand comparison with Bradman's. He batted for five-and-a-half hours for 113. Leyland made 44 and there were useful contributions lower down the order from the captain Percy Chapman, Duckworth and Tate, but even a total of 391 could not save England from the follow-on.

Five of their wickets fell to the Australian leg-spinner Clarrie Grimmett, who took 29 in the series from 350 overs. Small, wizened and prematurely bald, he bowled his leg-breaks slowly and accurately

*Don Bradman obligingly pauses to pose for the camera before resumiong his record-breaking innings of 334 in 1930.*

and had a wickedly dipping top-spinner. He was nicknamed The Gnome, for obvious reasons, and sometimes the Pimpernel, because his foes sought him here and there without result.

Rain and bad light aided England's escape to a draw and they reached 95-3 in their second attempt with Hobbs run out for 13 in his last Test on the ground. This was his last season in Test cricket, in which he achieved the stunning average of nearly 57 from 102 innings with 15 centuries. None of them, alas, came at Leeds, where he first appeared for England against Australia in 1909. His top score at Headingley was 88 in the 1926 Ashes series.

There was a slightly sour aftermath to Bradman's masterclass, which marked the beginning of his love affair with Headingley. His team-mates were keen to celebrate such a monumental innings in the hotel bar but Bradman preferred, as he so often did, to stay in his room to write letters and listen to music. He was also reluctant to show himself to the crowd, who had gathered to applaud his achievement, or that weekend to walk through the streets of Leeds.

One newspaper reporter lightly took him to task for this aloofness. "Don Bradman is the most elusive man of all, preferring to write letters in his room or get away to a show. He also has the habit of going off sight-seeing alone, or with only one companion. A more level-headed man or one less likely to become spoiled by admiration never wore flannels." We can take it that some of the other Australian players were not quite so understanding.

The tourists had left behind a country in acute economic distress. Signs of poverty were all around them, in the rural areas as well as in the big cities. The players were all amateurs and it was hard enough to find a job, let alone hold on to it while playing cricket. The average wage was less than £5 a week and although even as amateurs they received some cash – Bradman was given 10 shillings a day for playing Sheffield Shield cricket for New South Wales – times were hard.

To be selected for the tour was a huge financial bonus, as they were given a £600 fee, £50 each for their kit and 30 shillings a week expenses. Bradman also found himself £1,000 richer after his Headingley triple-century, a gift from an expatriate Australian businessman and worth about £25,000 in today's values. Bradman quietly pocketed the telegram and the money and firmly turned down the suggestion from his colleagues that he might like to take them out to dinner.

With the series still level, the final Test at The Oval was again played to a finish and Bradman won it for the tourists with a double-hundred to take his series aggregate to a record 974 from seven innings at an average of 139.14. He was making a mockery of the game; Test cricket was not supposed to be this easy.

# Chapter Five

# Yorkshire 1931 -1948

CRICKET'S Golden Age had long since passed but Yorkshire managed one of their own in the thirties, winning the first of three consecutive championship titles in 1931 and suffering only six defeats in that three-year period.

There was a change in the captaincy, which passed to the Huddersfield industrialist Frank Greenwood, and a change in the points system in an effort to reduce the number of drawn games. Fifteen points were awarded for a win instead of eight and five for first-innings lead in a draw and it was not long before Yorkshire were involved in controversy.

Greenwood and Gloucestershire's captain were reprimanded for bringing the competition into disrepute after turning a rain-hit game at Sheffield into virtually a one-innings contest, something that would not raise a murmur these days. Yorkshire lost by 47 runs.

Greenwood held the captaincy for two seasons but because of business commitments made only seven appearances in 1932 and was succeeded on an unofficial basis by Arthur Brian Sellers, from Keighley. Sellers, Hedley Verity and Bill Bowes were to be the dominant figures in a decade of triumph.

In 1923 Sir Edwin Airey had become the chairman of Leeds CF & AC and was to serve for 32 years. In the Yorkshire offices, still in the city centre, John Nash had succeeded secretary Sir Frederick Toone, who died in Harrogate in 1930. Toone, having arrived from Leicestershire in 1903, had

restructured the club in alliance with Lord Hawke, who in 1924 wrote: "It is remarkable that our office is run by only one secretary and a boy when the membership is far over 6,000, yet all is well ahead of time and Toone himself is, without exaggeration, the best friend to all the players.

"Not only is he a good judge of the game, but his foresight as to the possibilities to be developed in a younger player is seldom or never at fault. I am not going too far when I emphatically state that Toone IS Yorkshire cricket to the backbone."

The boy Lord Hawke was referring to in that tribute was John Henry Nash, who had joined the club in 1922 to learn the ropes under Toone's guidance. Born in Farsley and educated at Pudsey Grammar School, he proved to be an able pupil but seven years later there were concerns among the hierarchy, shared by Hawke himself, that at 25 Nash was too young for the post.

But he was given the job and one of his early tasks was to answer a query from Verity's league club, Middleton in Lancashire, who in 1930 agreed to a request to release the bowler for a county match but asked: "What are your intentions regarding Verity?" Nash rarely gave much away and his reply was: "Oh, we think a lot about Hedley."

In fact, Verity, like Rhodes before him, might have been lost to Warwickshire, who gave him a trial at Edgbaston but watched in disappointment as he failed to make an impact on a bland pitch against some fine batting by a youngster called H T Roll.

After 10 minutes Warwickshire's committee decided they had seen enough and Verity was not even asked to bat.

At that time also he was being courted by the Blackburn club East Lancashire, who were offering him between £15 and £20 a week to play for them. He left their letter in his pocket for a fortnight as he anguished over his future before deciding to take his chance with Yorkshire. He wrote back to East Lancashire rejecting their terms and Middleton went along with his wishes by tearing up his uncompleted contract.

Verity was born on May 18, 1905, in Welton Grove, Headingley. The nearby Test ground, just a long throw away, was to be the scene of some of his most memorable performances.

On his 26th birthday and in only his 14th first-class match he took 10-36 against Warwickshire, 17 years after Alonzo Drake had taken all 10 against Somerset at Weston-super-Mare. "It was one of those rare days," he said modestly, "when everything is set right for the bowler at one end but not for the man at the other end."

That was his tribute to George Macaulay, who had bowled 18 overs for 20 runs. In the modern era it would be called 'creating pressure.'

Headingley's wicket at the time was coming in for criticism for being too good, an accusation not levelled at it these days. The fast bowlers had drawn nothing out of the pitch on the first day and when the second dawned dull and raw there were only 4,000 people in the ground to see Holmes and Sutcliffe notch their 59th three-figure stand to take Yorkshire into a lead of 97.

Warwickshire's second innings began at 3.45; by six o'clock the match was over, Yorkshire winners by an innings and 25 runs and Verity's figures 18.4-6-36-10.

The roller had brought some moisture to the surface of the pitch, the sun broke through the clouds and Greenwood soon brought on Verity and Macaulay, bowling medium-pace off-breaks round the wicket. There was an early wicket but in his third over Wyatt launched into a huge swing of the bat to hit Verity for six.

The Yorkshire Post reported: "Verity was not worried. He calmly and cannily went his way, giving the ball the spin the state of the wicket demanded. Now and then he slipped in a faster ball and all the time he used his command of flight to keep the batsmen wondering. Wyatt stepped out twice as though he intended to repeat his earlier stroke, but

each time he changed his mind and played safe."

Wyatt could not restrain himself in Verity's seventh over, attempting a big blow which went into the hands of Holmes in the covers. Then Mitchell, moved to a backward point position about four yards from the bat, showed his athleticism in taking a catch to dismiss Yorkshireman Norman Kilner, brother of Roy, who had moved to Edgbaston in 1926 and was to play some fine innings against his native county, including one of 197 in 1933.

At 5.30 it looked like ending in a draw and some of the spectators made their way towards the exits, pausing to have one last glimpse of the action. Verity took a fifth wicket, so some of them stayed. Curiosity about Yorkshire's chances of forcing a win turned into a frenzy of excitement as Verity took four wickets in his 16th over, described by the bowler as "an avalanche from heaven." He was twice on a hat-trick.

By then, Verity had shown his willingness to put the team's needs first by making a great effort to take a short-leg chance off Macaulay's bowling. He tore the skin on his right arm in the attempt and bowled that 16th over with it bandaged below the elbow.

Verity shared the anxiety and excitement of the spectators in the final overs as he sought the one remaining wicket that would make him famous. "It was the greatest test I could have had. When I caught and bowled the last man, Paine, the walk back to the pavilion seemed to take hours," he said.

The scorecard reads:

### Warwickshire (2nd Inns)

| Wyatt | c Holmes | b Verity | 23 |
|---|---|---|---|
| Croom | c Greenwood | b Verity | 7 |
| Bates | c Mitchell | b Verity | 19 |
| Kilner | c Mitchell | b Verity | 0 |
| Parson | c Leyland | b Verity | 9 |
| Hill | c Wood | b Verity | 8 |
| Smart | c Mitchell | b Verity | 0 |
| Foster | st Wood | b Verity | 0 |
| Tate lbw | | b Verity | 0 |
| Paine | c and | b Verity | 0 |
| Mayer | not out | | 6 |
| **Extras 0** | **Total (all out)** | | **72** |

Verity returned to his home in Rawdon for his birthday party, while the England selector who witnessed these events reported back to the Test selection committee. Yorkshire had to nip in quickly to give Verity his first-team colours before he played for his country. In July he received an invitation from Pelham Warner to play against New Zealand at The Oval, his fee being £20 plus his rail fare (third-class).

*Hedley Verity and Maurice Leyland in 1939.*

The batting of Sutcliffe, who scored more than 3,000 runs in all matches, Holmes and Leyland and the bowling of Verity, Bowes and Macaulay took Yorkshire to the title, which they had sealed by mid-August. Gloucestershire were the only team to beat them, Lancashire the only one to avoid defeat at Yorkshire's hands. Verity took 188 wickets at 13.52 each and finished second in the national averages to Larwood, who missed several weeks of Nottinghamshire's season because of a car crash.

Essex were beaten at Leeds even though Morris Nichols, who fours years later was to produce a stunning all-round display against them at Fartown, became the first bowler to take a championship hat-trick at Headingley. But the ground had now become the stage on which Verity displayed his genius.

Bowes, his great friend and a man who understood Verity better than anyone (including Sellers, the official captain from 1933), described him as a blend of his mentors, Hirst and Rhodes, but sometimes even Verity had to pay for his art.

In 1931, just after his 10-wicket feat against Warwickshire, he was on the wrong end of a ferocious six-hitting barrage by Kent's batting maestro Frank Woolley and in the following season that fine Lancashire and England player, Eddie Paynter (another left-hander) hit him over the rope five times in his side's innings win at Bradford. Even so, Verity finished with eight wickets.

Yorkshire also lost to Hampshire at Headingley by 49 runs, despite another magnificent century by Sutcliffe, who became the first of only two Yorkshire openers to carry his bat at Leeds, making 104 not out in a total of 170. Holmes was ill and unable to bat in the second innings but that only partially excused a poor batting display.

This was the season of the 555 opening stand by Holmes and Sutcliffe at Leyton and when the team came back to Leeds Sutcliffe made 270, the highest individual score in a county match at the venue, against Sussex. It took his aggregate in three consecutive games to 789.

The game was drawn, Yorkshire winning on first innings, but Derbyshire were swept aside in two days at Headingley as Sutcliffe and Leyland hit centuries and Verity took 11 wickets in the match.

In March of 1932 the ground suffered a major setback when, during a rugby league match between Leeds and Halifax, a fire took hold in the packed grandstand. The spectators were safely evacuated but the building was destroyed. For the rest of the year that end of the ground was a building site as work on a new stand began.

It was against this uninspiring backdrop that Verity produced the most lethal bowling performance of his career, eclipsing even his display against Warwickshire the previous year by taking 10-10 against Nottinghamshire, still a world record.

His figures (19.4-16-10-10) surpassed George Geary's 10-18 for Leicestershire against Glamorgan at Pontypridd in 1929. "Verity of Verities, all is Verity," declared one Yorkshire newspaper (you couldn't get away with that nowadays).

It happened on July 12, a thunderstorm having hit the ground on the previous afternoon with Nottinghamshire, thanks to the pace of Larwood and Bill Voce, on top. Play on the third morning began at 12.30 and immediately Sellers, now leading the side in Greenwood's absence, declared to give the visitors a lead of 71 runs.

It was a daring move which marked out Sellers as the captain of the decade. All the component parts were in place in the Yorkshire side of that time but his constantly aggressive leadership turned the gifted individuals into an awesome unit.

Sellers knew that in Verity and Macaulay's off-breaks he had the bowlers to exploit a drying pitch. Bowes, who knew what made Verity tick better than the captain, was wont to appeal to his friend's vanity by telling him that it all depended on him. To some, this would represent intolerable pressure; it rarely failed to bring the best out of Verity.

Arthur Carr, Nottinghamshire's captain, bagged a pair and, not for the first time, picked up all his kit and threw it into the professionals' dressing-room. When he had calmed down and returned later to collect it, the gear had disappeared.

In his 11th over Verity claimed his first hat-trick with Walker brilliantly caught by Macaulay at slip, Harris taken at backward point by Holmes and Gunn lbw when deceived by the flight of a straight ball. This came in a spell of seven wickets for three runs in the space of 15 deliveries. Nottinghamshire had been 38 without loss at lunch and 44-0 shortly after the interval but then all 10 wickets crashed for 23 runs in 65 minutes as Verity turned containment – at one stage he sent down nine consecutive maidens – into destruction.

The completed scorecards were snapped up as fast as they could be printed after the match, which Yorkshire won by 10 wickets as Holmes and Sutcliffe took just 85 minutes to reach a victory target of 139 against demoralised opponents. The ease with which they knocked off the runs added to the wonder of Verity's achievement.

The scorecard, which bears a remarkable similarity to Warwickshire's with eight batsmen caught, one lbw and one stumped, reads:

### Nottinghamshire (2nd Inns)

| | | | |
|---|---|---|---|
| *Keeton* | *c Macaulay* | *b Verity* | *21* |
| *Shipston* | *c Wood* | *b Verity* | *21* |
| *Walker* | *c Macaulay* | *b Verity* | *11* |
| *Carr* | *c Barber* | *b Verity* | *0* |
| *A Staples* | *c Macaulay* | *b Verity* | *7* |
| *Harris* | *c Holmes* | *b Verity* | *0* |
| *Gunn* | *lbw* | *b Verity* | *0* |
| *Lilley* | *not out* | | *3* |
| *Larwood* | *c Sutcliffe* | *b Verity* | *0* |
| *Voce* | *c Holmes* | *b Verity* | *0* |
| *S Staples* | *st Wood* | *b Verity* | *0* |
| **Extras 4** | **Total (all out)** | | **67** |

Exactly what Macaulay, the bowler at the other end in each of the all-10 feats, thought is a matter for conjecture, but he refused to bowl wide of the stumps even after Verity had claimed his ninth victim and said: "If he's good enough to get nine, let him earn the 10th. I shall get it if I can."

The Yorkshire Post's report said: "The achievement proves not so much the possession of technical skill and artifice as the gift of that natural skill which is the indispensable foundation for artifice and for great bowling. Verity does one thing supremely well; he bowls the left-hander's 'going away' ball irresistibly, as none has since the great Rhodes.....There is another aspect of the matter; to take an opportunity with both hands, to make the utmost of it, demands those qualities of resolution and self-certainty on which greatness must be founded."

With Sutcliffe at the height of his powers, Holmes, Barber and Mitchell all passing 1,000 runs and the bowling in the hands of Bowes, Verity, Macaulay and the emerging all-rounder Frank Smailes from Ripley, Yorkshire were unstoppable and won their third title in succession by August 18 of 1933, having started with seven wins and then reeled off 12 in a row in mid-season. Another change in the system, this time from points back to percentages, could not diminish their supremacy, even though Holmes was fading.

In May, 1933, the new grandstand at Headingley was opened for the game against Kent, designed by J C Procter and built by William Airey & Sons, a construction firm headed by the Leeds CF & AC chairman. There are obvious comparisons with the modern-day set-up, though Paul Caddick is not involved in any of the latest developments as a

builder. Perhaps the politics surrounding Yorkshire's tenancy were less complicated in those days.

The stand cost £20,000 and served a dual purpose in providing accommodation for spectators for both rugby league and cricket. It was and remains a remarkable structure but can hardly be described as beautiful. Like Headingley as a whole, it is loved or loathed for its austerity rather than for any grandeur, but is has served its twofold purpose and is still the symbol of Headingley for cricket followers throughout the world.

By the end of 1933, the campaign in which the Keighley-born Sellers, a product of St Peter's School in York, officially took over as captain, Warwickshire were probably wishing that the entire ground could be demolished.

In that season they were back at Leeds on another rain-affected pitch and lost by an innings with Verity and Macaulay taking 18 of the 20 wickets that fell in four hours.

Bob Wyatt, their captain, had made a bet with Verity and Bowes before the season began, five shillings if he could get 50 against Yorkshire. He hung on defiantly for 90 minutes to make 33 not out in their first-innings total of 63.

"They got us on another sticky wicket. Verity and Bowes agreed that as I was not out I hadn't lost the bet and could count 25 towards my second-innings score," said Wyatt. "That wasn't really fair, as my 33 not out on a bad wicket when my side had been dismissed cheaply was worth a good deal more. However, I agreed against my better judgment. In the second innings Hedley got me out for 24, so I lost my bet by one run."

The pace of Bowes, the spin of Verity and the tactical acumen of both forged a potent alliance during the 1930s which forced Cardus to write at one stage that England ought to pick the whole of the Yorkshire team to face Australia, though they might still consider Hammond and Paynter. Between them they took nearly 2,400 wickets for the county and propelled the side to seven championships between 1931 and 1939 with another hat-trick of titles from 1937 to the outbreak of war.

As is the case now, Test calls were always a problem, especially when the Australians were the tourists, and in 1934 they were probably the main reason why Yorkshire slipped to sixth place, their lowest finish since 1911. In the nine years of Verity they won 153 championship games out of 260 and were beaten only 24 times. In each of those seasons

Verity took at least 150 wickets, averaging 185 a year, and in the three campaigns from 1935 he topped 200.

Under Sellers, they developed into a formidable fielding unit, the best the game had seen. He led them from 1933 to 1947 with gusto and a good measure of old-fashioned horse sense. The plain truth is, of course, that Yorkshire at this time boasted better batsmen, better bowlers and better specialist fielders than any other team in the land but such individual riches do not always make for collective success.

With Sellers in charge, they did. Few teams have ever matched the Yorkshire side of this period for the manner in which the whole was actually even more potent than the sum of the parts. Sellers had his problems even with Verity and often had to use his pal Bowes to communicate with him, which suggests that he was not a gifted diplomat or man-manager. But on the field Sellers was the supreme master of his craft and turned captaincy into an art form as few others have done.

Sutcliffe and Verity in particular were, in their approach and demeanour, responsible for changing it into a profession. It was a sign of a changing social order that when the Second World War came Verity and other professionals were commissioned.

It is often said that the hallmark of a truly great cricket team lies in its fielding and in this department Yorkshire were unsurpassed. They exuded menace and aggression and there was tremendous attention to detail, as confirmed by Arthur Mitchell, who fielded at gully to Rhodes and then Verity.

"When fielding to Wilfred I used to stand a little squarer," he said. "For Hedley I varied the position according to the batsman, between square and a foot and a half behind, but mostly I was behind," he said. "I'd be no more than six or seven feet from the bat to start with and usually I finished much nearer – only a yard from the bat when the ball was played.

"But Hedley bowled a marvellous direction and there were few occasions when the close-in fieldsmen were in danger...I could watch him deliver the ball, judge its length and then transfer to the bat. By then, I knew what I expected the batsman to do. In a way it was like batting against him."

In the 1933 season 223,000 people paid through the gates to watch Yorkshire, who were more or less unstoppable at Leeds with innings wins over Kent, Warwickshire and Northamptonshire.

Against Kent Bowes took 12 wickets and against Northamptonshire Leyland made 192, Verity took 13 wickets and Macaulay six. But Yorkshire had the worst of a draw in the Roses match.

The highlight of a draw against Kent in 1934 was an innings of 248 by Wilf Barber, a right-handed batsman from Cleckheaton who tended to be regarded as an understudy to the great artists in the team but a player who often came into his own when Test calls robbed Yorkshire of his more famous colleagues, Sutcliffe and Leyland.

Like his left-handed contemporary Cyril Turner, from Wombwell, Barber had to wait for his chance, making his debut in 1926 after a spell on Warwickshire's groundstaff. As you may have gathered by now, Warwickshire would have had a fine side had they held on to all the Yorkshiremen who came through the gates at Edgbaston. Barber then left to play for Scarborough in 1929 but rejoined the county staff three years later and became one of Yorkshire's most dependable batsmen.

Yorkshire then beat Middlesex at Leeds by an innings and three runs, Mitchell making an unbeaten 102 out of their total of 191-4 declared. Middlesex were bowled out for 65, falling to a combination of Macaulay and Stanley Douglas, a left-arm bowler of just over medium pace who made only spasmodic appearances in his nine-year association with the county – this was to be his last season – but who, as a professional in the Bradford League, had a great influence on the career of Bob Appleyard.

Yorkshire went back to the top in 1935, which was Macaulay's last season. He had served the club magnificently since 1920, with constant fire and fervour. One umpire told him that there was only one person in the world who made more appeals than George – and that was Dr Barnardo.

In 1933 he had taken 12-49 in the Old Trafford Roses match including the hat-trick and four wickets in five balls. He left the field with a face like thunder and when asked what was wrong said: "If only the so-and-sos had to go in again."

He had started his career as a fast bowler but had been encouraged by Hirst to temper his pace and spin the ball. He thus became a devastating dual-purpose performer who could swing the new ball and then switch to off-breaks.

Another bowler of similar versatility had by now come into the side, Frank Smailes who, like Barber and Turner, could ensure that Yorkshire's potency was not diminished when Hutton (who had made

*A man with an insatiable appetite for victory, Brian Sellers led Yorkshire to the championship six times in nine years as captain and continued to tower over the club's affairs in the committee room. After his "resign or be sacked" ultimatum from Sellers in 1970 Brian Close was physically sick.*

*Maurice Leyland hits out at Headingley in 1938.*

his debut in 1934), Verity, Bowes and Leyland were summoned by England.

He was a more than useful left-handed batsman, too, and made 89 in a two-day innings win over Sussex at Leeds in 1935, a match in which Barber hit 191. Leicestershire were the next to suffer at Verity's hands, the spinner taking 8-28 as they were skittled for 55 but Yorkshire, who claimed the extra half-hour, ran out of time and the match was drawn.

Middlesex were also humbled by an innings, this time Hutton leading the way with 131 and Verity taking 11 wickets in the match. It was becoming almost monotonous.

They faded slightly in 1936, when Derbyshire emerged as the new force in the county championship. Smailes took 130 wickets in the season, but with no Macaulay the bowling generally was too reliant on Verity and Bowes, the latter in far from robust health and probably playing on when he should have been resting various strains.

The Headingley matches against Lancashire and Hampshire were rain-hit draws – Yorkshire had 18 of their matches affected by the weather – but centuries by Sutcliffe, his 'pupil' Hutton and Leyland brought an innings win over Surrey and Leyland notched another three-figure score in the win over Worcestershire, completed by a 7-24 return by Smailes in the second innings.

The 1937 campaign developed into a tight struggle between Yorkshire and Middlesex, who would have snatched the title had they been able to win their final two matches, but they were held by Surrey.

Yorkshire won the championship, but the committee admitted in the annual report to being "apprehensive of the apparent and at times patent weakness in the bowling."

Norman Walter Dransfield Yardley appeared for the county while on vacation from Cambridge, where he was a blue in all four years at the university, and so did Ellis Pembroke Robinson, an off-spinner from Denaby Main who took a while to establish himself as Macaulay's successor.

But Robinson took 10 wickets in the 140-run win over Gloucestershire at Headingley and after a draw with Nottinghamshire Verity was on the prowl again against hapless Warwickshire, who must by now have been sick of the sight of him. In their first innings he took 9-43 in 42.2 overs and followed that with 5-49 in a nine-wicket win. Hutton, the Pudsey prodigy, blossomed in this season, hitting 10 centuries and piling up 3,000 runs at the age of 20.

He made a century in a draw with the New Zealand tourists at Leeds.

The championship was won again in 1938, even though Australia were the tourists and Yorkshire were sorely depleted. No fewer than five players were picked for England in Hutton's Test at The Oval in 1938, among them the Bradford-born wicketkeeper Arthur Wood, who was to become Yorkshire's first wicketkeeper to pass 1,000 runs in a season. Smailes's fine form earned him selection for the Old Trafford Test in that Ashes series but it was abandoned with not a ball bowled.

There was a rain-ruined draw with Sussex at Leeds and a fine win over Middlesex by seven wickets in two days during a Test match which took Compton and Edrich out of the visiting ranks as well as Hutton and Verity. Leyland took 4-15 with his left-arm spin, which brought him more than 60 wickets in the season.

On October 10, 1938, Lord Hawke of Wighill Hall died, a Golden Age player and captain who had presided over Yorkshire's own golden age in the thirties. He had shaped Yorkshire cricket like no other before or since and the club exists as it is today because of the principles which he laid down – of smart dress, pride in performance, of integrity as well as ability. "When you are choosing an XI remember to insist on two essentials; good temper and good manners," he told Sir Pelham Warner.

He also held the highest offices at the MCC and, though retaining his belief that the county championship should never be submerged under the weight of Test cricket (modern administrators please take note) he did much to make England more efficient and professional.

In December of 1938 there was a notable first for Headingley when the Leeds-Salford rugby league match, threatened with postponement because of a frozen pitch, was played on the cricket field. Yes, a cricket match has been played on the other side, too.

Throughout 1939 Yorkshire and Middlesex competed again for the championship crown but the game in general had to compete with increasingly ominous reports of the impending outbreak of another world conflict. They lost four matches, twice as many as in 1938, but won 20 of their 28 games.

At Headingley they beat Kent by 101 runs, drew with Northamptonshire after an unbeaten century by Mitchell, hammered Surrey by 177 runs through brilliant batting by Leyland and Hutton and eight wickets from Verity. In the late 1920s Roses matches had become more or less unwatchable because of their dour, no-risk cricket but now Yorkshire were on top, winning the last four matches before the war.

The 1939 encounter at Headingley was one of the most remarkable, with Lancashire falling to superlative batting by Hutton and gripping off-break bowling by Robinson. They led Yorkshire by 54 runs on first innings but Robinson tipped the scales with 8-35, the best performance of his career. He and Verity bowled unchanged throughout the final morning and Lancashire, losing five wickets for nine runs, were all out for 92.

This left Yorkshire to make 147 for victory. Hutton mastered everything the Lancashire bowlers could hurl at him and played an innings which he considered to be probably the best of his career. But the other batsmen struggled and they had lost half their side for 106 with dark clouds building up.

At 129 Sellers should have been run out but the bowler did not notice the captain flat on his face in the middle of the pitch and did not break the wicket, allowing him to get up and scramble to safety.

Yorkshire were six runs short of the target when the heavens opened and the pitch was drenched but to their credit the players continued in a cloudburst, during which Hutton completed an astonishing century in just over three hours before making the winning hit over cover with Cyril Washbrook splashing after the ball in a vain attempt to take the catch.

The final match of the season, in which Verity bowled Yorkshire to victory over Sussex at Hove, was completed in an unreal atmosphere. The Scarborough Festival had been cancelled and Sutcliffe did not make the trip to Brighton as he had become the first of Yorkshire's players to be contacted by the War Office.

By the time Yorkshire started the trip home by coach the roads out of London were so jammed that the team had to break their journey in Leicester, grab what sleep they could and get back on the road at dawn. They parted in City Square.

Jim Kilburn wrote: "It was a sad and silent party...and thence departed their several ways one of the finest county teams in the whole history of cricket. It never assembled again."

Yorkshire's yearbook of 1940 contains a terse reference: "Owing to the War, county cricket in 1940 must be of necessity uncertain" and the committee urged members to keep supporting the club financially.

When a Yorkshire team did assemble again there was no Verity, killed leading the Green Howards in a night action across a blazing cornfield on the plains of Catania below Mount Etna. He was evacuated to Italy but died of his wounds in hospital in Caserta, where he is buried. Smailes erected a monument on his grave. Bowes had suffered for three years as a prisoner of war after being captured in North Africa in 1942 and Hutton had needed an operation on his left elbow, which shortened the arm, after an accident in the Physical Training Corps.

Headingley at least escaped bomb damage, which is more than could be said of dear old Bramall Lane, hit in December 1940. It recovered to stage the second of the Victory Tests between England and Australia in 1945. In 1940 there was a cricket match for the Red Cross at Headingley. In terms of fund-raising and blood shed, Yorkshire's war effort was no less considerable under secretary John Nash than it had been in the First World War under Frederick Toone.

Verity's was the most grievous loss to the game. Douglas Jardine, a fervent admirer, said that he would have made an excellent captain. Like Rhodes before him, he had opened the innings for England and it was said that had he devoted more time to his batting (and had it been more needed by Yorkshire) he would have been a genuine all-rounder. One observer said of his style and technique that it was like watching Sutcliffe slightly out of nick, which most of us would take as the ultimate compliment.

Other counties had similar rebuilding problems, so when the championship resumed in 1946 Yorkshire won it again, probably as much through the psychological advantage they had established over the rest during the 1930s as through their performances.

Hutton and Barber were the only batsmen to pass 1,000 runs but Yorkshire batted effectively lower down the order, Bowes adapted his style intelligently to preserve his strength, Smailes and Robinson were fine off-break bowlers and Yorkshire found another one to use to new ball in Alec Coxon, from Huddersfield, a fiery character both on and off the field who tended to make a few enemies in high places.

Hutton made 111 in a draw with Leicestershire at Headingley and Smailes and Robinson bowled Yorkshire to a six-wicket win over Surrey in a low-scoring scrap. There was a thrilling two-day affair against Worcestershire which the home side won by

*The 1936 Yorkshire vintage: Bright Heyhirst (masseur), Len Hutton, Hedley Verity, Bill Bowes, Frank Smailes, Cyril Turner, Arthur Wood, William Ringrose (scorer), Wilf Barber, Herbert Sutcliffe, Brian Sellers, Maurice Leyland and Arthur Mitchell.*

*The ground, which has always had more character than charm, as it looked just before and after the second World War, the shared cricket and rugby stand making it more instantly recognisable.*

one wicket.

Robinson took 7-41 in Worcestershire's first-innings total of 119, Yorkshire replied with 152 and Coxon then tore through with 8-31 as Worcestershire were bowled out for 121 in their second attempt. But Yorkshire went through agonies before reaching their target, Smailes and new boy Johnny Wardle, from Ardsley, nudging them to 90-9. It was easier against Gloucestershire, who were flattened by nine wickets with Robinson's off-spin the key factor.

In 1947, the last in the reign of Sellers, Somerset were swept aside by an innings, Wardle and Robinson doing most of the damage after Scarborough's Ted Lester had made an unbeaten 85.

The match against Middlesex at Leeds was Bowes's benefit, which contributed to a record yield of £8,000, but it ended in a two-day defeat, watched by 41,000 spectators. Bill Edrich made 70 and 102 on a difficult pitch and Yorkshire found no answer to the left-arm spin of Jack Young and Denis Compton, who took 16 wickets between them.

An exciting tussle with Warwickshire ended in a six-run win with two minutes left, Coxon returning a decisive 4-30 as the visitors fell just short of a victory target of 261, but Middlesex, with Compton and Edrich in full flow, galloped to the title and Yorkshire slipped to their lowest ranking for more than 30 years.

# Chapter Six

# England 1931-48

WHEN you look at Don Bradman's batting average it becomes easy to accept his own statement that he did not believe in the law of averages.

If England thought that his spirit had been broken during the 'Bodyline' series of 1932-3 they were mistaken. England had been spun to defeat in the first Test of 1934 at Trent Bridge by Bill O'Reilly and Clarrie Grimmett but hit back in devastating fashion in the second game at Lord's, which came to be known as 'Verity's Match.'

In England's first victory over the old enemy at headquarters since 1896 the Yorkshire left-arm spinner dismissed Bradman twice on an increasingly responsive pitch and at that stage there were concerns not only about his form but also over his health.

Australia had been made to follow on, with Bradman caught and bowled by Verity in their first innings (a dismissal which he tended to blame on his captain, Woodfull, who had sent out a message for Bradman to 'cool it a bit'). There was heavy rain over the weekend but a drying sun on the last morning, the Monday. Verity's sense of anticipation was disturbed when he ran over a black cat on the way to the ground and spent a long time finding the owner to apologise.

In the second innings Bradman tried to hit the spinner back over his head since there was no outfield but had fallen into the classic slow left-armer's trap and sent the ball spiralling off a top edge high into the air, wicketkeeper Les Ames

taking the catch. Critics, it was said, shook their heads as Bradman departed and he was given a black look by his captain.

Bob Wyatt, England's captain, described it as a "desperation stroke" and Jardine, now an observer, said that the trouble with Bradman was that he felt that scoring at anything below eight runs an over was an insult to his dignity. There were even claims that his morale had been shot to bits by the events of the 'Bodyline' series and would never be the same again, but Bill Bowes exonerated Bradman from blame, saying that it was the Australian method to hit out on such pitches.

Verity ran through the Australian second innings at Lord's to take 8-43 to add to his seven wickets in the first and he took 14 wickets on that last day. "I was not well," Bradman said later. "I didn't feel I had the stamina to play a big innings, my mental outlook on the game was wrong."

A throat infection then swept through the Australian camp and Bradman was ill for much of the drawn third Test at Manchester, a high-scoring affair in which Maurice Leyland and Herbert Sutcliffe shone with the bat and Verity himself made an unbeaten 60.

Various rumours started to spread about the great batsman's health. He was suffering, it was whispered, from pernicious anaemia; he was about to visit a heart specialist; he was having a nervous breakdown; he needed his wife Jessie to come out to England to give him "special nursing and care."

*A poignant portrait of Hedley Verity in net practice at Headingley in 1939. One of the strongest links in the club's chain of spin wizards, he was soon to be in the midst of a war that took his life and robbed the game of one of its finest men.*

The fourth Test match at Headingley started on July 20, with the series level at 1-1 and with Bradman having showed something like his true from a week earlier in the tour match against Yorkshire at Bramall Lane. Bradman, who felt that he had failed in the other Tests, was anxious to make amends. The public were eager to see if he had the mental and physical strength to do so and over the four days an estimated 101,500 packed into the ground with its recently rebuilt grandstand.

England won the toss but batted ineptly against the spinners, O'Reilly and Grimmett taking seven wickets between them as they collapsed from 135-2 to 200 all out. The top-scorer with 44 was opener Cyril Walters, who had joined Worcestershire as secretary after five years with Glamorgan and blossomed into an elegant and wristy right-hander, making 401 runs in this series at an average of just over 50.

Before the end of the first day, however, Bowes raised hopes of an English comeback by taking three wickets without conceding a run. Opener Bill

Brown and Woodfull were bowled and Bert Oldfield caught behind the wicket and Australia were 39-3. The game was nicely poised with Bradman, as ever the key to it all, about to come in.

That evening he declined an invitation to dine with Cardus, explaining that tomorrow was a big day on which he had to make at least 200. Cardus had the nerve to point out that according to the law of averages he had no chance of getting anywhere near 200, to which Bradman replied: "I do not believe in the law of averages."

The following day he played one of his greatest innings, starting with outrageous bravado by hitting Bowes's first two balls off the back foot for straight fours. "I knew he had got me," said Bill, and he was right. He toiled away with his usual gallantry and finished with six wickets but they cost him 142 in 50 overs.

By the end of the second day Australia were 494-4, the one wicket to fall being that of Bill Ponsford, who trod in his stumps in hitting Verity to long-on.

Their partnership of 388 had lasted nearly all day, Ponsford hitting 19 fours in 181 made in 387 minutes of rock-solid batting. His sturdy frame belying quick, nimble footwork, Ponsford had been ruffled and humbled by Larwood in two series Down Under but in 1934 gained his revenge in his last series when he headed the averages with 569 runs at 94.83.

In what was to be his final Test appearance, at The Oval, where the Australians won by 562 runs, Ponsford and Bradman showed that their Leeds partnership was merely a rehearsal for the real thing. They added a record 451 in 316 minutes, Ponsford making 266. In all, the prolific Victorian made seven Test hundreds and averaged more than 48.

Bradman batted with a more sedate approach in this Leeds game, as if aware that at least a part of his reputation was on the line. He made 271 not out in the day (yes, they called that 'sedate' in those days) and another 33 the following morning before being bowled by the persevering Bowes for 304. The innings was described as " a textbook of batting come to life with never a mis-print or an erratum."

Bradman himself admitted that it had been "a very severe strain indeed" and he had again not

endeared himself to his team-mates when he brushed aside their intended toast to him at the end of the second day and said that he would only listen to a toast to victory.

It did not happen. Bradman stumbled in the field during England's second innings and tore a muscle in his right thigh. He was helped off the field by some of his colleagues and took no further part in a match which ended in a draw. At the end of the third day England were 188-4 with Leyland and Hendren defying the spin of O'Reilly and Grimmett. Hendren fell for 42 early on the last day but Leyland was still there on 49 not out when rain came to England's rescue with their total on 229-6.

Bradman was out of action for a month and his brilliant batting in the final Test at The Oval, which enabled Australia to regain the Ashes, was followed by an attack of acute appendicitis so serious that some cricket writers were asked to pen his obituary.

It took him three days to overcome the crisis and he later wrote: "There can be no doubt that for some time I hovered on the brink of eternity." Had he not been such a great batsman, he could have been a poet.

In 1935 South Africa were England's opponents at Headingley for a three-day game which drew an

*This was the scene after a 10-minute cloudburst on the last afternoon of the*
*1934 Ashes Test match, which saved England from almost certain defeat.*

aggregate attendance of about 55,000. Wilf Barber, from Cleckheaton, was rewarded for his consistent championship form with a Test debut but he made only 24 and 14. There was more success for Bradford's Arthur 'Ticker' Mitchell, who made 58 and 72 in a game dominated by the home side.

They were dismissed for a modest 216 in their first innings, Walter Hammond top-scoring with 63. Eric Rowan made 62 for South Africa but there was little resistance elsewhere and they crumbled to 171 all out with Verity taking two for five in 12 overs, nine of which were maidens.

Half-centuries by Hammond (87), Mitchell, who opened in the second innings and made 72, and Derbyshire's stylish left-hander Denis Smith (57) enabled England to declare at 294-7, which put the tourists out of contention, but they held on comfortably enough for the draw, closing on 194-5. This time Verity had figures of 13-11-4-0, indicative of the stalemate.

The next instalment of the Bradman saga, in July 1938, came against the backdrop of unpleasantness in the Australian camp in the previous series, in which he had taken over as captain. England had gained easy wins in Brisbane and Sydney to take a 2-0 lead and Australian disgust at the performances of their side was mirrored in reports of ill feeling between several of the players and Bradman.

But he showed his greatness by recovering his own batting form as well as leading the side with considerable aplomb and Australia won the next three games by a mile to take an astonishing series 3-2.

Much of the criticism levelled at Bradman, that he was too obsessed with his own performances to be a good captain, was echoed later in Yorkshire cricket's prolonged self-mutilation over Geoffrey Boycott. The difference is that whereas Boycott seemed to divide both county and country into two opposed camps, supporters and detractors, the Australian public's adoration of Bradman never wavered.

The 1938 series began badly for the tourists, whose bowlers took a fearful hammering at Nottingham, where Eddie Paynter hit 216 not out and there were centuries for Denis Compton in only his second Test, Gloucestershire's Charlie Barnett (who had become a close friend of Verity) and Len Hutton, whose 100 was his second three-figure score in four Test appearances.

Australia, facing a monumental total of 658-8 declared, were sustained by the brilliance of Stan McCabe, whose double-century was, for Bradman, one of the finest innings ever played, a decent

tribute coming from him.

Australia batted out for a comfortable draw at Lord's and the third game at Old Trafford was a total wash-out, though not without high drama. A dose of typical Manchester weather can hardly have improved Bradman's temper, which was foul because of the Australian Board's refusal of his request to let his wife Jessie join him in England at the end of the tour. It was strictly speaking against the contracts which all the Australian players had signed but was a concession afforded to the previous captain, Woodfull.

Bradman was at least pleased that his players on this occasion backed him and he came out with a startling statement, issued second-hand through a journalist, that he would never again play in a match under the jurisdiction of the Board. In short, he was threatening to quit Test match cricket.

The Board relented, but to show that Bradman was not being given preferential treatment they extended the invitation to all the wives to join their husbands at the end of the tour.

There was lingering ill feeling between the captain and the tour management and as usual he took out his anger on an assortment of English county bowlers between Manchester and the Leeds Test, reaching 2,000 runs in the season in just 21 innings.

This time, it was not so much the law of averages as the weather which made it a safe bet that he would not score his third triple-century on the ground. The stage was wet after a spell of heavy rain and the forecast was for more, so it looked certain to be a low-scoring match.

Sure enough, Bradman made 'only' 103 this time, but in those conditions it was probably worth three times as many and Australia would have been in dire trouble without their captain's masterly innings.

England won the toss and made 223, only Hammond resisting the pace of Ernie McCormick and the spin of Bill O'Reilly and 'Chuck' Fleetwood-Smith for long. The England captain made 76. O'Reilly and Fleetwood-Smith were by now established as the fulcrum of Australia's attacking strategy, 'Tiger' O'Reilly a leg-break bowler with a fast bowler's temperament who did not turn his orthodox delivery much but spun his googly much more and gained abnormal bounce with them both. Fleetwood-Smith was a left-arm back-of-the-hand merchant, his stock ball being the off-break to a right-handed batsman with the leg-break as his 'wrong 'un.' He was generally not easy to bat against, though Hammond several times got

*Johnny Muscroft (Yorkshire Post) and John Hutchinson (Yorkshire Evening News) take their pictures from the pavilion at the 1938 Test match against Australia.*

after him.

Both these bowlers, plus Leo O'Brien and McCabe, all of Irish-Catholic origin, had been hauled before the Board of Control amid reports of insubordination (Jack Fingleton was alleged to be the ringleader of the dissenting group). Bradman had known nothing of this meeting and was furious when he found out about it, but the players suspected that he had set up the whole charade. O'Reilly said just before his death that he never forgave Bradman for it.

Whatever their innermost feelings about their captain, they did not let it get in the way of taking English wickets. Eight fell to them in England's first innings in the 1938 Leeds Test. When Bradman walked out to the crease on the second morning his side were 87-2 and the light was dreadful. It did not hamper Bradman, who 'farmed' the strike with sublime skill to make a chanceless 103, his sixth century in consecutive Test matches and probably the finest of them all. He struck nine boundaries in three hours with Cardus describing the tourists as "lost souls in a November fog, being led about by Bradman's torch."

The innings disproved any notion of the captain playing for himself or for the record books. This was Bradman leading and inspiring Australia, single-handedly steering them through the gloom until he was eighth out at 240. Ken Farnes, of Essex, tall and extremely quick, took four wickets and Bowes three as Australia made 242.

England's second innings also took place in murky light and on a moist pitch and their batsmen could not fathom O'Reilly, who took 5-56 to finish with 10 in the match. He snared them with quickish spin delivered to a packed legside field and this time there was no escape even for Hammond, who was caught first ball at short leg. Fleetwood-Smith claimed 4-34 and England were rolled over for 123, Barnett top-scoring with 29.

This left Australia with a victory target of 105 and they took some getting. Indeed, the tension reached such a pitch that Bradman, one of three victims of Kent's leg-spinner Doug Wright after Verity and Farnes had removed the openers, could hardly bear to watch his side's tortured progress.

They won in the end by five wickets, leaving the Yorkshire public wondering how England might have fared had the dangerous Wright had more runs to bowl at. Despite the penetration of Australia's two slow bowlers, there was no doubt about who had really won such a low-scoring match in such trying conditions.

"What I shall remember most," wrote one journalist, "is the picture presented by Bradman and Bowes as they faced each other. Bradman was all intense concentration, motionless for a full seven seconds as he watched Bowes turn, run up and shoot the ball. Very, very rarely was he puzzled. His footwork was beautiful. He kept the secret of his stroke to the last half-second. There, beyond all question, was a captain of men."

So Australia had retained the Ashes at Leeds, though there was a large measure of revenge for England when they won by a huge margin at The Oval in the final Test with Hutton making his then Test record score of 364. The best of Yorkshire was on display in London with Leyland making 187 and putting on 382 with the 22-year-old as England amassed 903-7 declared. Wicketkeeper Arthur Wood, who made 53, Bowes, who took 5-49 in Australia's first innings, and Verity made up Yorkshire's Test quintet in a victory by an innings and 579 runs. About a year later war was declared.

Such was the public's appetite for sport immediately after the war that almost 90,000 turned up for the Test against South Africa at Headingley in 1947, the Australians having easily retained the Ashes at home during the previous winter.

England won by 10 wickets, Nottinghamshire's Harold Butler, a quick if ungainly bowler, marking his Test debut with 4-34 in South Africa's first innings of 175 and taking another three wickets in their second innings. He had been promoted to his county side when Harold Larwood was partially disabled through his efforts in the 'Bodyline' series and took over as Bill Voce's new-ball partner when Larwood retired. He played in only two Tests.

Bill Edrich, a tearaway bowler who literally hurled himself as well as the ball at opposing batsmen, took 3-46 in the first innings though 1947 was, of course, the season notable for the time he and his Middlesex 'twin' Denis Compton spent at the crease. Edrich scored 3,539 runs in the season, including 12 centuries, took 67 wickets and held 35 catches. He was not quite in Compton's class as a footballer but played for Tottenham Hotspur. Considering that he had four wives (not all at once) it is a wonder how he found the time for it all.

England, under Norman Yardley's captaincy, replied with 317-7 declared, Hutton leading the way with exactly 100 before being run out. He and Lancashire's Cyril Washbrook, now established as one of England's most successful opening partnerships, put on 141 with Washbrook making 75.

England's commanding position was enhanced by another Lancastrian, Ken Cranston, an amiable and forceful all-rounder whose first-class career was short because of the commitments of his dental practice. He was completely new to the first-class game when Lancashire invited him to be their captain in 1947 but he had only two seasons in the job. Biting through South Africa's tail, he took 4-12 in seven overs as the tourists were dismissed for 184 in their second innings and Hutton and Washbrook had no trouble in taking their side to victory. Dudley Nourse, the backbone of South Africa's batting at this time, scored a half-century in each innings but lacked adequate support.

Their most successful bowler in the match was the bespectacled 'Tufty' Mann, a left-arm spinner who specialised in maiden overs and started his Test career in this series with eight consecutive ones to no less than Compton and Edrich at Trent Bridge. At Leeds in the first innings his figures were 50-20-68-4.

Mann had had an eventful war. He was taken prisoner in Italy but escaped and was hidden by peasants. He died in 1952 after being taken ill during South Africa's tour to England the previous summer.

His memory lingers through one of John Arlott's comments after Mann of England had hit the spinner for six, described as "Mann's inhumanity to Mann."

Bradman was a captain more at ease with himself and with his team when he came back to England for the last time in 1948. Suspicions of disloyalty had gone with the departure of Fingleton and O'Reilly, both of whom were in the Press box for this tour. One London newspaper had unsuccessfully tried to get Bradman out of the way in 1946 by offering him £10,000 to cover that winter's Ashes series instead of playing in it.

He was visibly more relaxed with his players, more willing to have a drink with them and to share a joke, even at his own expense. He actually managed to enjoy, or to appear to enjoy, the endless round of social functions on the team's arrival in England.

The Australian players had been warned what to expect, that this was a different England from the one encountered by some of them on the 1938 tour.

The euphoria of the Allied victory had to some extent worn off to be replaced by the harsh economic aftermath of war. The tourists were told

*Len Hutton and Lancashire's Cyril Washbrook come out to open the innings against South Africa in 1947. They compiled the first of their three century opening stands at Headingley in this match.*

*On the right is Norman Yardley, post-war captain of Yorkshire and England, but these wide-eyed youngsters probably hoped that Don Bradman, captain of the Australians, would win the toss and bat so that they could see their idol in action.*

*Leeds was a great centre for cricket photography and here four 'Long Toms' capture the action in the 1947 Test match on the balcony to the side of the Press box.*

*Don Bradman hits through midwicket on his way to his last Test century at Headingley in 1948, helping Australia to a victory which he regarded as the most satisfying of his career.*

that they would be on British rations for the duration, which was perhaps one of the reasons why there was no squabble this time about their wives joining them on the trip. The Britain of 1948 was a poor choice for a holiday destination.

The Australians brought with them food parcels as a gesture of goodwill, which went down well in some quarters while others thought it patronising. But there were no rations or half-measures about the welcome afforded to Bradman from the highest to the lowest in the land.

He had reached that status where his actual nationality did not seem to matter any more. He was a world player and all wanted to take pride in his achievements. Bradman entered into the spirit of things and even managed to delay the BBC's nine o'clock news as an interview was broadcast live and was so good that the editor could not bring himself to cut into it.

But if there was charity in Australian hearts it disappeared when they went on the cricket fields of England. Bradman had made it his ambition to lead them through an entire tour without defeat. Even just winning was not quite enough, it seemed; if possible the opposition had to be crushed like an insect, the county sides gobbled up as a warning to England's Test team about the awesome power and skill of this Australian team. Essex were massacred at Southend, the Australians scoring 721 in a day.

By the time Bradman and his men arrived in Leeds for the fourth Test the Ashes had already been secured thanks to wins at Trent Bridge and Lord's and a rain-hit draw at Manchester. Old Trafford was not one of Bradman's favourite grounds but from his first trip he had of course made a habit of prodigious feats at Headingley.

The fact that the destination of the Ashes had been settled made no difference to the sense of anticipation among the Yorkshire public, who had taken Bradman to their hearts. The ground was packed on all five days, the aggregate crowd being about 158,000. The reserved accommodation had been well over-subscribed after the first post on the first day of applications. Receipts were £34,213, a record for a provincial ground. The spectators were not to be disappointed, witnessing one of the most remarkable run chases in the game's history.

England lined up with Len Hutton, Cyril Washbrook, Bill Edrich, Alec Bedser, Denis Compton, Jack Crapp, Norman Yardley (captain), Ken Cranston, Godfrey Evans, Jim Laker and Dick Pollard. The Australians had Arthur Morris, Lindsay Hassett, Don Bradman (captain), Keith Miller, Neil Harvey, Ian Johnson, Ray Lindwall,

Sam Loxton, Ron Saggers (on debut), Bill Johnston and Ernie Toshack.

It turned out to be a glorious final chapter in Bradman's own Headingley story but it did not look that way as England, who won the toss, reached 423-2 on the second day. Hutton, controversially dropped for the previous Test, returned in triumph to make 81 and put on 168 with Washbrook, who went on to make 143.

Bedser, sent in as nightwatchman, took his duties so seriously that he made 79 on the second day and added another 155 with Edrich, who scored 111. England had cause to be disappointed by a final total of 496, Loxton taking 3-55 in 26 overs.

Australia lost their first three wickets for 68, among them Bradman, who was bowled by Lancashire's Pollard for 33, but they recovered superbly as Harvey, in his first Ashes Test, added 121 in 95 minutes with Miller in a flurry of strokeplay and 105 with Loxton, who played a typically swashbuckling innings, including five sixes, before Yardley bowled him for 93. Lindwall hit a bold 77 further down the order, lifting the tourists to 458.

England's lead was slender on such a pitch, but they batted well again on the fourth day with Hutton and Washbrook putting on 129 for the first wicket. Edrich and Compton also made half-centuries and Evans chipped in with an unbeaten 47 to take them to 362-8 at the close. Everyone was expecting an overnight declaration but it did not come. Yardley batted on for just a few minutes, perhaps to allow himself the use of the heavy roller between innings, which would not have been available had he declared overnight.

The final equation was that Australia were set to make 404 in 345 minutes and Bradman was not optimistic. "It is a colossal task on the last day of a Test match. We are set 400 to win and I fear we may be defeated," he wrote in his diary.

Australia lost Hassett, caught and bowled off Compton's unorthodox left-arm spin, with the total on 57 and when Bradman walked out for his last innings at Leeds at one o' clock he again had to force his way through a line of spectators eager to touch their hero.

He received a standing ovation and later, when presented with life-membership of Yorkshire in September of that year, said that it was the greatest and most moving he had received from any public in the world.

"My thoughts weren't altogether clear," he said of his innings. "We wanted to win. We didn't want to

*Don Bradman is patted lovingly by one of the many boys to whom he was a hero as he walks out at Headingley for the last time in 1948. He did not disappoint his admirers, making 173 not out in a memorable Australian victory.*

*The 19-year-old Neil Harvey is applauded back into the pavilion after making 112 in the first innings of the 1948 Headingley Test.*

lose. What should I do?" Earlier in the tour
Bradman had encountered some problems in being
caught in a leg trap specially set for him with
Bedser the bowler and Hutton the fielder. It had
brought his dismissal a few times but he had
countered by not trying to score off Bedser's
inswinger and instead defending against it, often
letting the ball hit his pad.

On this day it was Hutton's leg-spin bowling, which
brought him useful wickets for Yorkshire but was
rarely used by England – he had bowled only 21.4
overs in 30 Tests before this – that made up
Bradman's mind for him. He conceded 30 runs in
four overs (one of which was a maiden) as Bradman
and Morris scored 62 runs in the half-hour before
lunch. The stage was set for a thrilling afternoon's
play.

The day was sunny, the pitch dry and dusting and
at this time there were no sight-screens at
Headingley. England were crying out for a specialist
leg-spinner and although they were available none
had been picked, so Yardley had to rely on
Compton's interesting but hardly reliable left-arm
unorthodox bowling.

Catching and stumping chances were missed and
gradually England became disheartened. A huge
stand between Morris and Bradman built up but
there was a worry for the Australians as their
captain suffered rib muscle problems and was
forced to ask his partner to take the bulk of the
strike.

Morris, an elegant left-hander who was particularly
good against spin, shouldered the burden with
relish, hitting 33 boundaries in his 182 and the pair
added 301 at a rate of 83 runs a hour. Bradman's
unbeaten 173 contained 29 fours and was scored in
255 minutes. The captain let young Harvey hit the
winning run and Australia had made 404-3 to
triumph by seven wickets with 15 minutes to spare.

Bradman left Leeds with a record of 963 runs in six
innings at Headingley, an average of 192.60. Only
at Melbourne and Adelaide, where he batted more
often, did he score more Test runs. This was his
19th and final century against England and took his
aggregate against them to an unsurpassed 5,028.

Ironically, it was the Warwickshire leg-spinner Eric
Hollies who dismissed him for a duck in the final
Test at The Oval and so prevented Bradman from
making the four runs he needed to achieve a total
of 7,000 Test match runs and end his career with a
Test average of 100.

From 1930 to 1948 Headingley had seen the best of
the best.

*Arthur Morris on his way to 182.*

*Jack Hickes took this picture of the record crowd for the Ashes Test of 1948 which was titled "the crowd within and the crowd without."*

*Don Bradman walks out at Headingley for the last time in 1948.*

# Chapter Seven

# Yorkshire 1949-1965

IN 1948 Norman Yardley, who had succeeded Sellers as captain of St Peter's School in York before going on to lead Cambridge University, inherited the county captaincy from the same man.

He was by then also captain of England and was to go on to become chairman of the Test selectors and president of Yorkshire. He is remembered with respect and affection by all who came into contact with him, notably for the way in which he tried to steer a fair-minded course through the tempestuous climax to the Geoff Boycott row in the 1980s.

As a right-handed batsman, a thoughtful bowler good enough to dismiss Bradman and a fine close fielder, he is the best player among Yorkshire's list of amateur captains.

Len Hutton, his senior professional, was the premier batsman in England and the late 1940s and 1950s was the era of some of the great names in Yorkshire cricket – of Brian Close, Bob Appleyard, Willie Watson, Don Brennan, Vic Wilson, Wardle, Ted Lester, Raymond Illingworth, Frank Lowson and, of course, Fred Trueman.

But a joint championship title with Middlesex in 1949 was to be their last for 10 years, a famine without precedent since they had first worn the crown in 1893 and during the 1950s they even slipped into the bottom half of the table on two occasions. What went wrong?

The decline, hard to take for a public which had come to view even second place as an affront against nature, was the more painful because while Yorkshire failed to turn their undoubted individual talent into consistent winning performances Surrey did exactly that to claim a record seven consecutive championships.

From the first, Roses matches always provided the sharpest rivalry, there were long periods when games against Middlesex also had a special frisson with players and public alike and it is from this period that the 'Brown Hats' from The Oval started to get under Yorkshire's skin. Yorkshire might have felt that they were the better side but they could not prove it.

The 1948 campaign marked the end of the playing career of Sellers, who led the side in Yardley's frequent absences on Test duty. Yorkshire finished fourth, behind champions Glamorgan, Middlesex and Surrey. They had the worst of a draw in the Headingley Roses match, watched by 44,500, with Washbrook scoring 170 in Lancashire's total of 450 and Eric Edrich, the least famous of the four brothers from Norfolk to play first-class cricket, also making a century. Hutton made 100 for Yorkshire but the rest of the batting struggled against the flame-haired work-horse Dick Pollard, who took 5-58, and they were bowled out for 256 to concede first-innings points.

Nottinghamshire were beaten by 204 runs, half-centuries by Coxon and Watson in the first innings followed by 88 from Lester in the second. The visitors were bowled out for 97 in their second innings, unravelled by Wardle in a spell of 4-23 in 20 overs. There were few finer sights in cricket at this time than Scarborough's Lester in full flow or than the graceful left-hander Watson, who brought the same elegance to the wing-half position for Huddersfield Town and England.

Hutton made an unbeaten 144 out for 302-6 declared in the drawn game with Essex at Leeds, in which off-spinner Robinson took 5-29, but the opening batsman's absences, and Yardley's, created a disciplinary void on the field which was to become increasingly apparent after the successes of 1949.

Sellers, though not as good a player as Yardley, had welded the glorious individual talent at his disposal into a near-perfect cricket machine in the thirties, but in this period a similar abundance of ability was to a large extent wasted. Yorkshire's players had still to be careful not to step out of line off the field with Sellers waiting to pounce in the background, as the amiable Lester found to his cost when he boarded a coach having omitted to put on a tie and was forced to ferret through a packed suitcase to find one.

But on the field Yorkshire were not quite the team they ought to have been, probably because Yardley, though a good cricketer and a fine and cultured man, was less disposed to be confrontational than his predecessor with some of the more forceful characters in the side.

There was little hint of this in 1949 as Yorkshire lost only twice to finish alongside Middlesex at the top of the table. Close, a prodigious games player from Rawdon who had already signed forms with Leeds United, had a meteoric first season, making his debut along with Lowson and Trueman at Fenner's, making a Test debut at the age of 18 years and 149 days and achieving the 'double' of 1,000 runs and 100 wickets in his first season in the first-class game before going off to serve in the Royal Signals.

In sporting terms, Close was the C B Fry of his day, the only difference being that had he been offered the throne of Albania he would probably have accepted it and turned them into one of the great cricketing nations.

Off the field, Yorkshire were spending £1,600 on improving the toilets at Headingley, Hull and Sheffield (no sarcasm, please) and on it they hammered Somerset at Leeds by nine wickets in a game that was a personal triumph for Ron Aspinall, a hearty opening bowler from Almondbury who later played for Durham and became an umpire. He took 6-54 as Somerset were skittled for 112 in their first innings and another seven wickets in their second-innings total of 176.

Yorkshire gained first-innings points against Essex thanks to good all-round performances by Close

and Coxon, the former taking 5-58 as Essex were dismissed for 174 and then hitting an unbeaten 88 out of 346-9 declared, Coxon making a breezy 59 to go with his eight wickets in the match.

At this time the main problem with Headingley – hard to appreciate in view of modern trends – was that it was too good a batting square to produce anything other than dull cricket. This was exemplified in a remarkable match against Sussex, who also succumbed to Close and Coxon in their first innings and were bowled out for 181. On a featherbed wicket Yorkshire piled up 520-7 declared with Vic Wilson, a formidable left-hander of Malton farming stock, hitting an unbeaten 157 and Lester 112 – all this after Hutton and Bradford's Lowson had put on 132 for the first wicket.

Sussex were heading for a heavy defeat as they limped to 116-3 in their second innings but James Langridge and George Cox junior then compiled a match-saving stand of 326 for the fourth wicket with Langridge making 133 not out and Cox an unbeaten double-hundred out of a total of 442-3 to save the game. Sussex have always kept their cricket in the family. James's son Richard also played at Hove and his brother John was one of the best batsmen never to play for England. Cox had followed his father, of the same name, into their side in 1931 and scored 50 centuries in a career which ended in 1961. Only wicketkeeper Jack Firth did not bowl for Yorkshire in that mammoth second innings.

The victory over Somerset was Yorkshire's sole success in four games at Leeds in the 1949 season, for they were also held to a draw in the Roses game and lost on first innings. Harry Halliday, a Pudsey batsman and fine slip fielder who had made his debut before the war and held his place until 1953 without ever quite fulfilling his early promise, made 96 and Lester 55 in Yorkshire's 301-8 declared but Lancashire replied with 356 thanks to a century by John Ikin and 71 by yet another of the Edrich family, Geoff. Close persevered to finish with 6-130 and Yorkshire were 8-2 in the second innings when stumps were drawn.

Ikin, from Staffordshire, had made his debut for his native county at the age of 16 before the war, when one of his team-mates was the legendary Sydney Barnes, then aged 61. After the war, in which he served as a 'Desert Rat' he won a place in the England side with only 18 first-class games behind him. A left-handed bat and leg-break bowler, his figures are not startling but he was hugely respected as a good team man. Geoff Edrich was entitled to think that merely being alive to play

*Don Brennan is the anxious wicketkeeper, Harry Halliday is at slip and the batsman is another Yorkshireman, Norman Horner of Warwickshire, here sweeping Wardle to the boundary.*

*Len Hutton is poetry in motion as he crouches to drive another boundary off New Zealand's attack on his way to 101 at Headingley in 1949.*

county cricket after the war was a bonus, for he had fought against the Japanese, was a prisoner of war for more than three years and when liberated in 1945 weighed six-and-a-half stones.

There was a shared title again in 1950 but Yorkshire slipped to third behind Lancashire and Surrey, the latter now moving into top gear. Hutton's benefit raised a record £9,712 but his benefit game against Middlesex at Headingley was badly hit by the weather and abandoned as a draw after the visitors had made 356-4 declared. Even so, 26,000 people turned up.

Sussex were thrashed by an innings and 21 runs, Wardle taking 9-70 in the match as they were bowled out for 108 and 155, and Yorkshire had the better of a draw against Nottinghamshire thanks to half-centuries by Lowson, Halliday and Lester and an unbeaten 44 by Geoffrey Keighley, whose parents came from Bradford but who was born in Nice.

Close missed much of the season through National Service and Watson turned out only in August as he was on World Cup football duty, but he and Lowson hit centuries in a drawn game with Northamptonshire.

The 1951 season was notable for an explosive entry by Appleyard, who achieved the astonishing feat of 200 wickets in his first full season. The Leeds public had plenty of evidence of his outstanding talent of this tall, cunning bowler from Wibsey, who did not make his debut until he was 26.

He had started out as a fast-medium inswing bowler but taught himself off-breaks from his banana-like middle finger with hardly any diminution in pace and none in his accuracy, which was deadly. Bill Bowes had taken one look at him in the nets and declared that he could not teach him anything; Johnny Wardle in that summer of 1951 said that he sometimes bowled like Alec Bedser, sometimes like Jim Laker.

Appleyard, it seemed, could do anything, for like most of Yorkshire's greats his natural ability was harnessed to a keen intelligence. He took 10 wickets in the drawn game with Surrey at Headingley, in which Keighley made 110, and he and Wardle took all 20 Glamorgan wickets between them in an innings win in two days. Yorkshire did not bat well and were grateful for runs low down the order from Brennan and John Whitehead, a fast bowler who made 58 not out at No 10. Appleyard took 9-68 in the match and Wardle 11-58 as Glamorgan mustered 66 and 90.

Yardley made an unbeaten 183 in the 10-wicket win over Hampshire, who fell to the combined efforts of Appleyard, Wardle and leg-spinner Eddie Leadbeater, from Huddersfield. Yorkshire, who finished runners-up to Warwickshire, also played a Yorkshire Past side at Headingley in which Wilf Barber made 116 in a draw.

In the Hampshire game Yardley was assisted by a debutant by the name of Raymond Illingworth, who was stationed as a National Serviceman at Dishforth when he was called up by secretary John Nash. He had been picked to play for the Combined Services along with the Catterick-based Close, but was given the option of playing for Yorkshire by his squadron leader Larry Lamb, later well-known as a rugby union referee.

Vic Cannings had reduced Yorkshire to 40-4 with seam and swing but Illingworth, encouraged to play his shots by his captain, made 56 out of a stand of 96.

It was the start of a journey that was to take Illingworth to fame as one of the shrewdest cricketers and captains this country has seen, to a fall-out with Yorkshire, to success with Leicestershire and thence back to Headingley and to the epicentre of the Boycott storm.

In 1952 they finished runners-up to Surrey, who had embarked on a record sequence of seven championships. It is from this point that Yorkshire cricket starts to look fractious. In truth the side had always contained abrasive characters who, with proper handling, had helped make Yorkshire the team the others feared most. Now, however, the chemistry was not quite right and there were enough strong sides around, notably Surrey with Lock and Laker and Bedser and Loader (plus a groundsman who knew exactly what type of pitch to prepare for the next visitors to The Oval), to knock them off their perch.

It is easy to exaggerate the point, though, and there is no doubt that Test calls, injuries, Appleyard's serious illness and National Service duties at various times crucially tilted the balance against Yorkshire. But there remains the suspicion that even when they were all together physically they were not quite together in spirit.

Actually, 1952 was a good year. Yorkshire's achievement was considerable since Appleyard had been laid low by an attack of tuberculosis which caused him to miss two seasons after his phenomenal efforts in 1951. He featured in only one game and Trueman, the lethally-fast bowler from Maltby who had made his debut in 1949 with Close and Lowson, was either terrorising Indian batsmen for England or was on National Service and missed all but four.

Hutton and Lowson put on 245 in the Headingley Roses game, each making a century as Yorkshire piled up 347-2 declared. Lancashire replied with 260-9 declared, were set a target of 233 and were hanging on at 146-8 at the end, Close having taken 5-36.

Kent were swept aside by 106 runs as Hutton hit a majestic 189 in the first innings, Wardle took 10 wickets in the match and Halliday chipped in with a decisive 5-73 in Kent's gallant second innings of 306. Even the champions were no match for Yorkshire at Leeds as Vic Wilson (121) and Lester (130 not out) put their bowling to the sword and propelled Yorkshire to 423-5 declared. Eric Burgin, a good swing bowler who also played football for York City, took 6-43 to send Surrey sliding to 192 all out and although they topped 300 at their second attempt, Wardle worked his way through to finish with 7-119 and Yorkshire won by nine wickets.

Believe it or not, there was more money spent on the toilets at Headingley in 1953 but Yorkshire plummeted to 12th in the table, their lowest ranking since the championship was officially recognised in 1873. They were well on top in the drawn game against Somerset, big hundreds by Hutton and Watson and 98 from Lester lifting them to 525-4 declared.

But they flopped badly against Northamptonshire, losing by 10 wickets. Wilson was run out in both innings and although Illingworth batted pugnaciously to make 33 not out and 50 Yorkshire had no collective answer to the slow left-arm wiles of Australian George Tribe, a back-of-the-hand spinner who had played three Tests for his country just after the war but was then squeezed out and furthered his cricketing education in the Central Lancashire League.

He gave fine service to Northamptonshire and took nine wickets in this match, Yorkshire's heavy defeat made perhaps the more painful since it was a Yorkshireman, the Kippax-born Dennis Brookes, who made a century for his adopted county.

Surrey again came to Leeds but this time went away with a draw, rain intervening after Lowson and Lester had made centuries.

The following year, 1954, brought more improvements to the ground as Yorkshire sought to increase the capacity to house the sort of crowds being attracted to Test matches and big county occasions. More terracing was built on the popular side and the refreshment huts were replaced by public bars.

Yorkshire were again second to Surrey but performed poorly at Leeds, conceding first-innings points to Warwickshire in a draw as Jack Bannister, now a writer and broadcaster on the game, took 8-54 to bowl them out for 111.

There was hardly any play at all in the Roses game and Derbyshire gained a notable six-wicket win with another one-time York City footballer, Arnold Hamer, who had played a couple of games for Yorkshire in 1938, making an unbeaten 147. Trueman, back in harness for the county along with Appleyard, took 6-109 but a total of 272 put Derbyshire in control, aided by some lapses in the field. Derek Morgan had match figures of 10-78 as Yorkshire were dismissed for 119 and 207.

Trueman, Appleyard and Wardle took nearly 400 wickets between them that season but there was another Headingley defeat in August, this time at the hands of Middlesex, and that paved the way for Surrey to take the title again. Appleyard bowled superbly to claim a match haul of 10-103 but after making 197 in their first innings Middlesex hit back in the field and only Close resisted to any extent, making 52 out of a total of 113.

The visitors managed only 131 in their second innings but it was enough to give them victory by 96 runs as Yorkshire were bowled out for 119, the off-spin of Fred Titmus and Jack Young's slow left-arm, which had sent down 11 consecutive maidens against Australia at Trent Bridge in 1948, doing all the damage.

It was the same story in the hot summer of 1955 – Surrey champions, Yorkshire runners-up. Although Yorkshire were too often having to make do with silver, this was in many respects a golden age for county cricket and this was a magnificent season in which Yorkshire won 21 of their 28 matches and lost five. Surrey were also beaten five times, including a defeat at Leeds, but won 23. This was championship cricket fought to the death.

Yorkshire started out intent on breaking Surrey's monopoly and won their first six matches. Somerset were flattened at Headingley by 163 runs even though Yorkshire mustered only 161 in their first innings. Half-centuries by Hutton, Lowson and Wilson enabled them to declare on 213-4 in their second.

Appleyard was unstoppable in this sequence and he and the magical Wardle took five wickets apiece as Somerset were rolled over for 84 and Trueman and Appleyard finished the job by bowling them out for 127 in their second innings.

*Len Hutton and Frank Lowson walk out to open Yorkshire's innings in 1950.*

By now, the home fixture against the 'Brown Hats' had taken over from the Roses game as the match of the season and it lived up to its billing in the 1955 campaign. Surrey batted first and Trueman and Appleyard reduced them to 119-8 before Lock (55) and Laker (81) fought back tenaciously to lift their side to 268 all out.

In worsening light Yorkshire limped to 166 all out, a seemingly decisive deficit of 102 runs, but then on the second evening, in deepening gloom which would have caused a short-circuit in Dickie Bird's light-meter, made worse by an industrial smog which hovered over the ground, Surrey lurched to 27-7. On the following morning they recovered somewhat to 75 all out, Trueman taking 4-31 and Mike Cowan, a left-arm quick bowler from Leeds, returning astounding figures of 5-15 in 15 overs. In near-perfect conditions on the third day Yorkshire sauntered to victory by six wickets thanks to half-centuries by Lowson and Watson.

But Middlesex triumphed again, this time by five wickets. Middlesex led by just eight runs on first innings, Yorkshire faltering for the second season

running in the face of the spin of Titmus and Young. They made 175 in their second innings to set the away side a challenging fourth-innings target but Jack Robertson, a classy opener who would have played more than his 11 Tests had he not been unlucky enough to be a contemporary of Hutton and Washbrook, made 82 out of 170-5 to steer his team to victory.

All this took place against the backdrop of a remodelled pavilion to allow for better dining facilities for members and players, while the committee proudly declared that Headingley's Press box was now considered the best in the world.

The journalists taking advantage of this luxury had in 1955 witnessed the closing of an era with the retirements of Hutton and Yardley, the former the supreme professional run-maker of his day with 85 first-class centuries in 527 innings for the county and an average of more than 53, a figure which stands as an eternal monument to his skill and temperament in all conditions.

*Johnny Wardle's Yorkshire career ended in bitternesss in 1958, a sad loss of the mesmeric skills of probably the finest left-arm spin bowler of his time.*

Yardley, the quintessential amateur captain of club and country, scored 17 hundreds in 420 innings, averaged nearly 32, took 195 wickets and held more than 200 catches. Questions have been raised about the tone of his leadership, notably by Illingworth, but J M Kilburn summed up: "Yardley's success in captaincy has been limited by the lack of understanding and ambition in some of his players but he has done invaluable work in keeping the good name of Yorkshire cricket at the highest level."

Herbert Sutcliffe, Hutton's mentor, had turned down the captaincy in 1928 but his son Billy, from Pudsey, succeeded Yardley in 1956 at the age of 29. An amateur, he had two tough years in the post before informing the committee that he would be resigning for business reasons.

The committee's report on the 1956 season was one of its most critical. Yorkshire had slipped down to seventh and the hierarchy was clearly becoming fed up with having to include, year after year, its congratulations to Surrey on winning yet another title, which, had they been expressed out loud, would have been done through gritted teeth.

Surrey's fifth consecutive championship was a record, beating Yorkshire's sequence under Sellers in the 1930s, and the verdict from on high was that "it is considered that more matches would have been won had the players played in a more determined manner on all occasions."

Off the field, the committee was in talks with Leeds CF and AC Ltd concerning a lease of Headingley which, you may not be surprised to learn, turned out to be lengthy and difficult. The club also paid money into the Westminster Bank to help finance further improvements to the pavilion.

On the field, it was not a good year for the team at Leeds. This was a glorious period for the Lancashire and former England off-spinner Roy Tattersall, who topped 100 wickets a season seven times in eight years from 1950 to 1957. He wrecked Yorkshire in the Roses game with 14-90, paving the way for a 153-run victory for his side and in the wet summer of 1956 was neck-and-neck with Glamorgan's Don Shepherd in the race to 100. But having reached 91 he was dropped for seven games and when he asked the coach why was told: "Ours is not to reason why." This, he said, knocked the stuffing out of him, and no wonder.

*A young Doug Padgett takes some advice on his grip from coach Maurice Leyland. He was to emerge as one of the club's most technically accomplished batsmen and later recycled his knowledge as coach.*

Against Derbyshire, only Doug Padgett offered much resistance to the pace and rib-crushing nip of Les Jackson, one of the meanest bowlers of his time. He took 7-55 as Yorkshire lost on first innings. They had the better of a draw with Nottinghamshire thanks to an unbeaten 103 by Lowson after the visitors had been dismissed for 113.

The 1957 campaign, in which Surrey claimed their sixth title in a row and Yorkshire under Sutcliffe rose to third place, was Willie Watson's last for the county before he departed to Leicestershire, where as captain (and assistant secretary) he unsuccessfully tried to lure Padgett to Grace Road. Padgett came to conclude that his refusal to take the same route harmed his own England chances.

Watson scored 26 centuries for Yorkshire and passed 1,000 runs in six consecutive years from 1952. His career had brought him national fame at Lord's in 1953 when, with England facing defeat, he and Trevor Bailey defied the Australian attack, Watson batting for nearly six hours to make 109 and save the game. The world seemed to lay at his feet but he never quite sustained a position in the topmost echelon of the game with his native county.

The committee had to report no satisfactory conclusion to the negotiations on a lease, while Yorkshire had too much fire power for Somerset, winning by an innings as Illingworth made 97 and Trueman 63, which was doubtless worth watching. Wardle tied Somerset in knots and took 11 wickets in the match.

Alan Moss took five wickets as Yorkshire were shot out for 98 to concede first-innings points in a draw with Middlesex and they reached only 188 against Kent later in the season, but Trueman blasted through with 5-26 to give them a first-innings lead in another draw. Colin Cowdrey made 58 of Kent's 151 all out.

With Yorkshire still in Surrey's slipstream year after year, it was encouraging to point out at the end of the 1957 season that the Colts, under the leadership of Ronnie Burnet, an amateur from Saltaire and a decent middle-order batsman with Baildon in the Bradford League, had won their championship. His leadership of the second team, in which he nurtured the talents of, among others, Bryan Stott, Ken Taylor, Bob Platt, Don Wilson, Mel Ryan and Jack Birkenshaw, had impressed those in authority.

So instead of appointing from within the established first-team group, a body somewhat tarnished by factionalism during the previous six years or so, they turned to the 39-year-old Burnet in an effort

to find someone who could impose discipline and engender the sort of one-for-all spirit which had existed under Sellers.

He achieved it, but in 1958 it was an excruciatingly painful process. It was as if Yorkshire as a body had gruesome boils to be lanced. This was to be the last season for opening batsman Lowson and for Appleyard, one of the finest bowlers ever to play for the county. By the end of the summer, a damp one, Wardle had been dismissed. So in the space of about a year Yorkshire had lost Watson, Wardle, Lowson and Appleyard, at least three of whom would have walked into any team before or since this year of destiny.

Burnet knew that he had been brought in to "sort things out" once and for all and despite his admiration for Wardle's magical range of skills as a slow left-arm bowler he had, after a series of flare-ups, complained to the cricket chairman that he and his committee had not gone far enough in releasing Lowson and Appleyard, who were officially thanked for their services.

"Had I been consulted I would have included a third party – Johnny Wardle. As long as we have him in the side we shall never have any team spirit," said Burnet.

The decision to sack him was, it seems, made during a game against Somerset at Sheffield, probably when Wardle was actually leading the side to victory while Burnet was off the field meeting the committee. Once the news broke he was signed up by the Daily Mail for a series of articles in which he criticised the club and the captain, which led to his exclusion from the MCC tour to Australia.

Wardle is said to have admitted later to a group of miners in South Elmsall that he had been a fool. 'Tragedy' is a word that should not really be used in connection with sporting careers but it is hard to think of a better one in this case.

At Leeds in 1958 there was another Roses defeat, this time fast bowler Brian Statham wrecking Yorkshire with 6-16 and 3-29 as they made 64-9 declared and 144. Lancashire made 138 and 71-2 to win by eight wickets, Wilson being the only home batsman to reach 50.

Against Gloucestershire rain prevented a result but Derbyshire were beaten by 86 runs with Bryan Stott, a stocky left-hander from Yeadon, making 72 out of Yorkshire's first-innings total of 120.

Jackson was again the main threat, taking 11 wickets in the match, but after Derbyshire had taken a lead of 27 Yorkshire rallied to reach 244-9 declared in the second innings and Illingworth spun the visitors to defeat and finished with nine victims in the game.

Yorkshire emerged from the dark tunnel in 1959 to win the championship under Burnet's leadership and there was relief on the financial front too as a 50-year lease at Headingley was signed and a sum of £16,000, promised by the owners for work done on the pavilion in 1955, was paid up.

Yorkshire were on the wrong end of draws with Northamptonshire and Gloucestershire, Wilson stranded on 99 not out in the latter game, but Kent were beaten by two wickets thanks to a fighting 74 not out by Illingworth. Cowdrey made 108 in Kent's first innings of 365, Padgett hit 71 as Yorkshire declared on 231-5 and Close then stepped in with 8-41 to turn the match on its head. Kent were all out for 109 and Yorkshire reached a target of 244 through Illingworth's heroics, a half-century by Close and a hard-hit 34 by the young Don Wilson. It was a win contrived out of nothing.

They won the title in a thrilling run-chase against Sussex at Hove, led by Stott and Padgett, having been set to make 215 in 105 minutes. They did it with seven minutes of the season left and Burnet, his job done, was supplanted as captain and went back to the Bradford League with the gratitude of all Yorkshiremen (well, most of them) ringing in his ears.

Vic Wilson took over, the club's first professional captain since Tom Emmett in 1882, and in three seasons he led the side to two titles and one second place, behind Hampshire. The 1960 triumph was marred by yet another Roses defeat at Headingley as Geoff Pullar punished the bowlers with a century and Tommy Greenhough, a leg-spinner from Rochdale at this time at the height of his powers, undermined the batting, Yorkshire mustering 96 and 117 to go down by 10 wickets.

Jack Birkenshaw, the off-spinner from Rothwell who in recent times has been the guiding hand behind Leicestershire's rise, took 11 wickets in the draw against Middlesex but Trevor Bailey's seam inspired Essex to a 57-run win with figures of 7-40 and 5-61. Yorkshire, bowled out for 86 in their first innings, recovered to make 237 in the second thanks to half-centuries by the captain and Phil Sharpe but too much damage had been done.

Trueman had a fine all-round match against Leicestershire, who were beaten by 10 wickets later that season. He smashed 52 to add to Padgett's 97 and along with Cowan and Illingworth bowled Yorkshire to victory.

The three Headingley games in 1961 were all drawn, Stott hitting 116 in the first innings against the eventual champions, Hampshire, Close making 103 against Glamorgan and then contributing 51 not out in the second innings of his benefit game against Surrey.

Yorkshire went back to the top in 1962 and ended their depressing home run against their Roses rivals with a seven-wicket success at Leeds. After Sharpe's unbeaten century had kept it close on first innings Trueman was the key figure, taking 5-29 in 22.2 overs as Lancashire were bowled out for 112 in their second.

In the draw against Nottinghamshire there were centuries by captain Wilson and Ken Taylor, like Watson a gifted footballer with Huddersfield Town (and Bradford Park Avenue) and a brilliant cover-point fielder. This season also marked the debuts of Len's son Richard Hutton, Tony Nicholson, who had served as a policeman in Rhodesia, and a miner's son from Fitzwilliam called Geoffrey Boycott.

Close took over from Wilson in 1963 and led the side to the championship again. He would argue that he was pulling most of the strings in Wilson's reign anyway and Illingworth would claim that Yorkshire's success under Close was down to his interventions to prevent his captain from drifting off to sleep when there was not much happening in the field. It doesn't really matter; Yorkshire were a team again.

The ground changed significantly in 1963 as the club offices were moved from the centre of Leeds to Headingley and combined into a new building which also housed the dressing-rooms. It has come to be seen as an eyesore. The project cost £21,500, £5,000 of which came from Leeds CF and AC, another £5,000 from Sir Stuart Goodwin and £2,000 from John Smith's Tadcaster Brewery. Lancashire, all heart, donated the clock and the club launched a centenary appeal which by the end of the year had raised £15,000. Not enough, said the committee.

On the field Yorkshire had limited success at Leeds. Hampshire were still a strong side and hammered them by 130 runs, Peter Sainsbury taking 7-77 in the first innings. Yorkshire did win a low-scoring game against Derbyshire but were stunningly beaten by Middlesex despite bowling them out for 47 to take a first-innings lead of 100 runs. Don Wilson took 4-11 and Nicholson five wickets for seven runs. Boycott made 66 to enable his captain to declare and set a target of 248, which looked out of bounds, but Peter Parfitt made 63 and Middlesex romped to a six-wicket win.

Another £21,000 was being spent on the ground, on the popular side toilets, resurfacing the cycle track and on a new entrance at the Kirkstall Lane end. The owners chipped in £7,000.

Yorkshire slipped to fifth, but won all three games at Headingley. Boycott's 151 and Illingworth's 6-50 were the highlights of a 10-wicket win over Middlesex, Nicholson took 12-73 as Glamorgan were routed by an innings and there was a thumping success in the Roses match as Illingworth took 4-9 in Lancashire's first innings of 101 and Nicholson 7-32 in the second to clinch an innings win.

Worcestershire retained the title in 1965, with Yorkshire fourth. The sides met at Leeds and in a drawn game Illingworth returned first-innings bowling figures of 30-20-20-8, the best of his career on the ground. Northamptonshire's fast bowler David Larter wrecked their batting with 12 wickets as Yorkshire went down by 58 runs despite a brave 62 from Ken Taylor in the second innnings.

Leicestershire were hammered by 148 runs thanks to a fine all-round effort from Illingworth. His innings of 90 meant that the visitors were set 328 to win and they seemed to be on course for a draw as their openers put on 124 but they collapsed to 179 with Illingworth taking eight wickets in the match.

This year also brought a £10,000 donation from a Mrs Frazer to build a new indoor shed to replace the glass-roofed, leaky edifice which had been knocked down for the office block. Yorkshire's aspiring and established cricketers were learning the game in a different building and were also having to learn to play a new game, one-day cricket.

# Chapter Eight

# England 1949-1965

MORE than 1,700 runs had been scored in the Ashes Test match of 1948 and Headingley's reputation as a batting paradise was enhanced when the ground staged its first game between England and New Zealand the following summer.

It was New Zealand's third visit to these shores and all four matches were drawn, the highlight for the first-day crowd being the sight of their favourite Len Hutton scoring the second of his three Test centuries on the ground.

Hutton's had been the name on the lips of every English youngster since his world record 364 against Australia at The Oval in 1938, when he was only 22 years old. He had lived up to Herbert Sutcliffe's summary of him in 1934: "He's a marvel, the discovery of a generation."

An accident with a vaulting horse during the war, when on a physical training course in York, left him with a visibly shortened left arm and there were fears for his future as a cricketer. But Hutton was the fusion of skill with an iron temperament and inner strength and he not only remained the mainstay of England's batting after the war but also went on to become their first professional captain.

He made 101 in this match, putting on 102 with Denis Compton, who was the second century-maker of the first day and went on to make 114 out of England's total of 372. Compton was the smooth operator of his day, an always carefree and sometimes careless genius with boundless charm. Against the awesome Australians in 1946-7 he had

scored 459 runs in the series at an average of 51 and was even more formidable in 1948 with 562 at 62.44.

At Old Trafford in that series he edged a ball from Ray Lindwall into his face, which was not advisable, but returned still bleeding to hit 145 not out. At this time the papers carried frequent bulletins on the 'Compton knee' as an old football injury (like his elder brother Leslie, he played for Arsenal and England) had flared up again but that had not impaired his dash to a three-hour triple-century in an MCC match in South Africa the previous winter.

Trevor Bailey from Essex made his Test debut at Headingley in 1949 and took 6-118 but New Zealand reached a highly-respectable 341 thanks to a typically hard-hit 96 in two hours by Brun 'Runty' Smith and a stylish 64 from Martin Donnelly, who was regarded as the finest left-handed batsman in the world just after the war and, according to C B Fry, as good as any of his era too.

An Oxford blue who also played for Middlesex and Warwickshire, Donnelly had dismembered Yorkshire's bowling to make an unbeaten 208 for the MCC at Scarborough in 1948 but this tour proved to be the zenith of his fine career. He scored more than 2,000 runs on the tour and in the Tests made 462, passing 50 in five out of six innings.

Bailey was to emerge as one of England's most illustrious all-rounders with his lovely high bowling action and barnacle qualities as a batsman, but he was prone to be a little vague. On the rest day of

*Ray Lindwall, the spearhead of Australia's attack after the second World War, played in three Headingley Tests and in 1948 even managed to shine as a batsman, making 77 in a first innings total of 458.*

this match he intended to take his wife to the coast for a spot of sea air and was surprised to find none of it in Harrogate. His wife shared this characteristic and once, as a tour guide in India, he arrived with a party of 30 at Bombay airport with no tickets. She had thrown them away.

Hutton was out for nought in the second innings but England still prospered through an unbeaten 103 by Cyril Washbrook, 70 by Bill Edrich and 49 not out from George Mann, a popular and successful captain of Middlesex and England until forced to retire by the demands of the family brewery.

Mann was able to declare at 267-4 but New Zealand were never in any danger, reaching 195-2 at the close with Smith this time making 54 not out in just 50 minutes after opener Bert Sutcliffe, another high-class left-hander, had stroked 82. Sutcliffe came out of retirement to tour in 1965 but at Edgbaston was hit on the ear when ducking into a ball from Fred Trueman and although he returned to make a brave 53 he missed most of the rest of the trip.

Rain on the last day condemned the 1951 Headingley Test to another draw but it was probably heading in that direction anyway with the batsmen again in command. Local interest was

*Len Hutton leads England out for the first time as captain against India at Headingley in 1952. In India's second innings the scoreboard showed nought for four.*

raised by debuts for Yorkshire's amateur wicketkeeper Don Brennan, from Eccleshill, and Bradford-born opening batsman Frank Lowson, along with Peter May of Surrey.

Brennan's career was cut short by business commitments but his brilliance as a legside stumper rivalled that of Godfrey Evans. He was also a sharp wit and once, in a game against a university side, shouted up to the bowler, Johnny Wardle: "Don't get him out for a moment, Johnny; he smells bloody lovely."

The South Africans piled up 538 after winning the toss thanks to an innings of 236 by opener Eric Rowan, a colourful character who was in the habit of keeping up a running commentary on the play even while he was batting. Rowan added 198 for the second wicket with Clive van Ryneveld, a superb athlete who by the time he was 23 was playing cricket for South Africa and rugby for England. He later became a politician.

Percy Mansell, on debut, made 90 in 70 minutes. A bespectacled, vague-looking player, he was born in Shropshire and developed into a reliable all-rounder for South Africa with his crisp driving, inexpensive leg-breaks and sharp slip catching. Roy McLean, a right-handed strokemaker from Natal, made 67 before being run out. Three England bowlers conceded more than 100 runs, the most successful being captain Freddie Brown with 3-107.

Lowson partnered Hutton at the top of the order and marked his debut with 58 out of an opening stand of 99. Hutton made exactly 100 but the spotlight was taken by May, who launched what was to be a glittering Test career with 138, becoming the 10th England batsman to reach three figures on debut and the first at Leeds.

Bailey made 95, giving no hint of stubborn innings to come as he dominated a last-wicket stand of 60 with the Lancashire spin bowler Malcolm Hilton to lift England to 505. Eric Rowan's brother Athol shouldered the main burden in the South African attack, finishing with 5-174 from 68 overs of slow-medium off-breaks. Because of wounds suffered in the Western Desert he sometimes bowled with his leg in irons.

The tourists reached 87 without loss in their second innings, Eric Rowan taking his tally in the match to 296 with an unbeaten 60.

June 5, 1952, goes down as one of the most significant dates in English Test history, for it was the day on which Frederick Sewards Trueman made his debut against India, the first match of the series and under the captaincy of Hutton. Bowling up the slope from the football stand end he took 3-89 in the first innings of 293 and Surrey's Bradford-born off-spinner Jim Laker removed the tail to finish with 4-39. India's 293 was founded on a fourth-wicket stand of 222 between two of the finest batsmen to represent their country, Vijay Hazare and Vijay Manjrekar, the latter making 133 before becoming one of Trueman's victims.

England were in some difficulty at 92-4 as Hutton, Compton, Reg Simpson and May all failed to make much impact but they recovered through innings of 71 by Tom Graveney, 66 by Godfrey Evans and 48 from the genial all-rounder Allan Watkins, who in 1948 had become the first Glamorgan player to be picked for England.

A first-innings lead of 41 runs did not look decisive but Trueman had other ideas. He was born in one of a row of colliery-owned houses at Stainton in 1931 and was delivered into this world (at 14lb 1oz, by the way) by his maternal grandmother, from whom he takes his second name. The family moved to Maltby when he was 12 and the man who became known throughout the cricketing world as 'Fiery Fred' (the nickname was first used by Norman Yardley) made his Yorkshire debut at 18 in 1949 and became the epitome of craggy Northern ferocity both in his bowling style and his looks. In the view of Bill Bowes, by now an observer of the county and Test scene as a journalist in Leeds, much of his early bluster and over-use of the bumper stemmed from a inferiority complex (well disguised).

At 5ft 10 in he had the ideal physique for a fast bowler, with strong arms, legs and shoulders and a 46-inch chest. Eventually he did, anyway, though Ray Illingworth's first sight of him was of a "pasty-faced, narrow-waisted waif" and his tutors, Bowes and Arthur Mitchell, agreed that at first he presented an unlikely figure for a fast bowler.

But fast he was, at a time when there were not many of them on the world scene, and as such he was soon the subject of massive publicity. He also possessed what is usually termed a 'great backside' (in the cricketing sense, you understand). Darren Gough's rear end was favourably compared to Fred's when he first came into the Yorkshire side. Trueman also had a magnificent action, a rolling approach coming to a long last stride and a classical sideways-on delivery which enabled him to swing the ball away late.

The Indians discovered the potency of this package in their second innings. The 25,000 Saturday crowd cheered wildly as Fred, given the Kirkstall Lane end by Hutton, took three wickets and Alec Bedser one to leave the scoreboard reading 0-4 after 14 balls. Pankaj Roy let the first ball go through to the wicketkeeper, Trueman dropped the next one in short and Roy was caught off a top edge; Bedser had Datta Gaekwad caught in the gully before the Yorkshireman, who could not get hold of the ball soon enough to start his next over, ripped out Madhav Mantri's off stump and next ball did much the same to the talented Manjrekar.

Hazare only just survived the hat-trick ball, which whistled past his off stump and when Trueman was rested after only four overs the spectators knew that they had just witnessed the start of something big – an English fast bowler capable of attacking flat out and literally frightening the opposition into submission.

India were eventually bowled out for 165, their partial recovery fashioned by Hazare, who made 56 before having his stumps scattered by you know who, and all-rounder Dattaray Phadkar, who made 64. Simpson's half-century at the top of the order put England on the road to an eight-wicket victory completed by Graveney and Compton. Trueman had seized the moment – the Saturday of a Headingley Test – to announce his arrival on the world stage.

Trueman went on to claim 29 Indian victims in the four-match series. His 8-31 at Old Trafford remained the best figures of his Test career in which he of course became the first bowler to take 300 Test wickets – many sound judges at the time reckoned that he would be the only one, but that has not been the case – and boasted a sensational strike rate of a wicket every 49 balls. John Snow's strike average was 59.5 balls, Brian Statham's 63.7, Jim Laker's 62.3 and Ian Botham's 57. The Staffordshire thunderbolt S F Barnes had a better strike rate than all of them but did not reach 200 wickets.

Attendances for the visits of New Zealand and India had been good but there was still nothing to match the attraction of the Australians and once again more than 150,000 watched the five days of the 1953 Ashes Test.

Unfortunately, F S Trueman was not on the England team sheet, though 'unfortunately' is not the word he would choose. Indeed, in the 13 years from his debut in 1952 England played more than 120 Test matches and he figured in just over half of them, which is perhaps the most astonishing statistic of his astonishing career. These days, you would not get him out of the England side and would not want to.

Already the notion that Trueman's face did not fit at

Lord's, that given even the flimsiest excuse the selectors would leave him out, had taken root, certainly in his own mind. A wet summer did not aid his cause at county level in 1953 and his chance did not come until the final Test at The Oval, when Hutton's team regained the Ashes amid unforgettable scenes of celebration.

Well over half a million people watched that series and those at Leeds saw a rain-hit but absorbing match in which Bailey came to England's rescue with bat and ball. Not for the first time, either, for he and Yorkshire's Willie Watson had defied the Australian attack in memorable fashion to save the game at Lord's.

In the fourth Test at Headingley, Lindsay Hassett won the toss, as he did in all five games, put England in and saw Lindwall, who reduced the crowd to stunned silence by bowling Hutton with the second ball of the match, take 5-54 to put them out for 167, a tortured innings of 109 overs in which only Graveney shone with 55.

Bedser and Bailey were preferred to Trueman as the opening bowlers and took nine wickets between them, though Neil Harvey's 71 and a half-century by Graeme Hole steered the tourists into a lead of 99. By the end of the fourth day England had limped to 177-5 with Compton on 60 and Bailey on four.

Compton soon fell to Lindwall on the final day, reducing England to a precarious 182-6, but progress had been so laboured that time was running out. Bailey used up 262 minutes of it in making 38, Laker hit a precious 48 and a total of 275 left the Australians to make 177 for victory in 115 minutes.

They adjusted their batting order in the search for rapid runs and for a time looked like winning until Bailey, with some persistent leg theory and frequent changes to a defensive field, employed delaying tactics to perfection and Australia reached 147-4 in 33 overs, a frustrating 30 runs short of the target. Lock and Laker finished the job on their home ground at The Oval in the last Test but Bailey was perhaps the player most responsible for the regaining of the Ashes.

Hutton, with Trueman in his squad, then led England on an arduous, troubled tour to the West Indies and, without Trueman, gloriously retained the Ashes Down Under. But his own heroic efforts as a batsman in the Caribbean and the strains of leadership amid many outbreaks of controversy took their toll on his health and after a couple of victories in New Zealand in 1955 Hutton bowed out with a record of 11 wins and only four defeats in 23

*If any youngster needs a lesson in the ideal position for a fast bowler in the delivery stride it is provided here by Frederick Sewards Trueman.*

Tests as captain.

Hutton felt that some of Trueman's behaviour in the West Indies had, to put it mildly, not been helpful to the collective cause. He did not figure in any of Hutton's last 11 Tests as captain, including the Australian tour of 1954-5 on which Frank Tyson of Northamptonshire – a Lancastrian to boot – was tagged the fastest English bowler ever to tour that country. Trueman was still champing at the bit after Peter May succeeded Hutton, playing in only three of his first 15 games as captain.

He was not in the side when May led England against the South Africans at Leeds in 1955 in the midst of an exciting five-match series which England won 3-2. Trueman had played at Lord's but that was his only appearance in the series, even though he mowed down county batsmen throughout the country that summer to take 153 first-class wickets at 16 apiece and bowled almost 1,000 overs.

England suffered a stunning 224-run defeat in the 1955 Headingley Test even though they bowled out South Africa for 171 on the first day. Statham and Surrey's Peter Loader opened the bowling and took seven wickets between them. South Africa were 38-5 and 63-6 but rallied through Russell 'Endless' Endean and Hugh 'Toey' Tayfield, who made 41 and 25 not out respectively. This recovery was a sign of things to come in their second innings.

Endean had, in the 1951 series, been involved in one of cricket's most unusual dismissals when Hutton had been given out 'obstructing the field' for deflecting a catch to him when he was keeping wicket and in 1956-7 was himself given out for 'handling the ball' when he pushed away a ball from Laker which was bouncing towards his stumps. Tayfield, a high-class off-spinner who was at the heart of South Africa's progress in this period, was not a run-of-the-mill player either. He derived his nickname from his habit of stubbing his toe into the ground before bowling or receiving a ball and was also in the habit of kissing his cap for luck at the start of each over.

Bailey opened England's innings with Lowson but both failed and the only substantial contributions came from May (47) and Compton, who made 61, though Wardle chipped in with a useful 24 low down the order to give his side a first-innings lead of just 20 runs. Peter Heine, a genuinely fast bowler who formed a dangerous new-ball partnership with Neil Adcock, took 4-70, as did spinner Tayfield.

England's slender advantage was rendered meaningless as the South African batsmen hit brilliant form in their second innings to make 500.

*Not a pretty ground, but an awesome sight with the western terrace full to bursting in the 1950s for the visit of India.*

There was an opening stand of 176 between Jackie McGlew, one of the great 'stickers' of the era, who made 133, and Trevor Goddard, a left-handed batsman and bowler who was his country's finest all-rounder of the period. With Headley Keith, another left-handed batsman, making 73, South Africa's second wicket did not fall until they had 265 on the board and Endean, promoted to No 6 in the order, responded with 116 to ram home their supremacy. Wardle was England's star turn with 4-100 from 57 overs.

Taking the new ball instead of Adcock, Goddard wrecked England's batting with his left-arm attack. Lowson was an early victim, bowled for a duck, and he went on to strangle England to death with figures of 62-37-69-5. The main pockets of resistance came in a third-wicket stand of 101 between May, who was lbw to Tayfield three runs short of a century, and Doug Insole, who made 47, and in Bailey's stonewalling for eight runs in two hours. Tayfield took the other five wickets and England were all out for 256, a chastening defeat.

The following summer was wet, Ian Johnson's Australians were the tourists and Trueman was still left out for the first Test. He was recalled at Lord's and retained for the third game at Headingley, where in grim weather he was the only bowler to take a wicket apart from Lock and Laker as England triumphed by an innings to level the series at 1-1. It was their first victory in an Ashes Test at Leeds.

Washbrook was recalled at the age of 41 and with his captain turned the match and the series England's way. After winning the toss they were 17-3, Ron Archer having used the seam alarmingly well to unseat Cowdrey, Peter Richardson (Worcestershire) and debutant Alan Oakman

(Sussex) in nine overs for three runs. Oakman played only one more Test.

May and Washbrook took the score to 204 before the captain fell for 101 to a superb fine-leg catch by Lindwall off Johnson and Washbrook was two runs short of his seventh Test century when he was lbw to Richie Benaud. Bailey and Evans made good runs down the order and England reached 325.

Trueman did England a service by removing that admirable fighter Colin McDonald early in each innings and the spinners did the rest, Laker taking 11-113 including 6-55 in 41.3 overs in the second innings and Lock claiming seven wickets in the match as Australia, despite noble resistance from Harvey, whose 69 occupied four-and-a-half hours, were bowled out for 143 and 140.

While one Yorkshireman (Trueman) fumed over yet another omission from the ranks, another (Laker) bowled himself into the record books and England to another Ashes success with 19 wickets for 90 runs at Old Trafford later in that month of July 1956.

One of the best-known umpires of this period was Syd Buller, who was born in Leeds but because of competition for the wicketkeeping berth from Arthur Wood had only one match for his native county, against Sussex in 1930. He then moved on to qualify for Worcestershire, serving them with unobtrusive efficiency from 1936 to 1947. His subsequent career as a Test umpire was anything but unobtrusive.

His death in 1970, during a rain interruption in a match between Warwickshire and Nottinghamshire at Edgbaston, ended a great umpiring career which had lasted from 1951 and which tossed Buller into a maelstrom of controversy in the 1960 series against South Africa.

In the second Test match at Lord's his colleague Frank Lee, standing at square leg, no-balled the South African fast bowler Geoffrey Griffin for throwing. Buller did likewise in an exhibition game arranged because the Test had finished early, whereupon his exasperated captain told the umpire that he did not see how Griffin could finish his over if he continued to take such a stance.

Buller replied that the only way out was for Griffin to bowl underarm, which he did – and was promptly no-balled by Lee at the other end for not informing the batsman of his change of style. Buller was a fervent guardian of the game's true spirit, but was accused in some quarters of exhibitionism and courting the limelight.

He needed a police escort from the Chesterfield ground (not many can claim that) after no-balling

Derbyshire's Harold Rhodes five years later.

Griffin, who had become the first South African bowler to take a Test hat-trick in that game at Lord's, had his career finished by the controversy and completed the tour as a batsman. His was an unfortunate case in that an accident at school left him with a crook in his right elbow and rendered him unable to straighten his arm.

Buller was one of the umpires at Headingley in 1957 when the West Indians made their first visit to the ground and lost by an innings and five runs. For the West Indies, this tour marked the end of one era and the beginning of a new one.

Two-thirds of the great triumvirate of Ws, Everton De Courcey Weekes and Clyde Walcott, were to announce their retirement from Test cricket in the following year and in all seven players who in the 10 years from 1947 had taken the West Indies further than they had ever gone before were bowing out. In addition, the spin twins Alf Valentine and Sonny Ramadhin were a fading force.

In this 1957 series Ramadhin had taken 7-49 in 31 overs of mesmeric, disguised right-arm bowling with no batsman (nor often the wicketkeeper) sure as to which way the ball would turn. But in the second innings he had a traumatic experience as May and Cowdrey put together one of the most famous stands in Test history, which reached 411. Ramadhin bowled 98 overs and was never as effective again.

Trueman was Yorkshire's sole representative at Leeds that year but the destroyer of the West Indies was Peter Loader, who took 9-86 in the match as the tourists were dismissed for 142 and 132. England's 279 was founded on half-centuries in the middle order from May, Cowdrey and the Rev David Sheppard, of Cambridge University and Sussex, the first ordained minister to play Test cricket.

The other great W, Frank Worrell, took 7-70 and opened the innings with one Garfield Sobers. It was a tour on which the West Indies were forced to split with the past and look forward to a future dominated by the likes of Sobers, Kanhai and Hall.

But this was Loader's match. The wiry Surrey bowler's nine wickets included a hat-trick, the first in post-war Tests and the first in a Leeds Test since Jack Hearne's in 1899. His victims were the captain, John Goddard, Ramadhin and Roy Gilchrist.

The following year brought another innings win for England, this time against the outclassed New Zealanders, who were overwhelmed even though

*Above: Photographer Brian Thomas with the pigeon that settled on his 'Long Tom' to gain a bird's eye view of the 1957 Headingley Test against the West Indies.*

*Left: Peter May, who scored a century on his Test debut at Headingley in 1951, tosses up with Ian Johnson before the 1956 Ashes Test on the ground where he achieved five victories as England captain.*

*Brian Close drives through the off side on his way to a half-century in the second innings of the 1963 Test against the West Indies with Deryck Murray and Lance Gibbs looking on.*

the first two days were wash-outs. This paved the way for the England spinners, Laker and Lock, to wreak havoc.

New Zealand, all out for 67 in the first innings with only the openers reaching double figures, managed less than a run an over off Laker but this time Lock had the lion's share of wickets with 11-65. May was again in sparkling Headingley form with an unbeaten 113 in England's 267-2 declared and Gloucestershire's Arthur Milton followed him into the record books by hitting a century (104 not out) on his Test debut at Leeds. Trueman was the only wicket-taker apart from the spinners.

England made it four consecutive innings victories at Headingley by trouncing India in 1959 with Trueman now in his pomp. They gave debuts to Lancashire's Geoff Pullar and Derbyshire's fast bowler Harold Rhodes, who took 4-50 to go with Trueman's 3-30 in India's first innings of 161 (they were 23-4 early on) but whose international career was blighted by doubts about his action which first came to the fore when he was no-balled in 1960 by the former Yorkshire player Paul Gibb.

Pullar made 75 and put on 146 for England's first wicket with Gilbert Parkhouse, the Glamorgan opener. Cowdrey compiled an elegant 160 and with Ken Barrington making 80 England hit some quick runs on the third and final morning before declaring at 483-8.

Trueman made a couple of early incisions and Close, making his first appearance in a Leeds Test, did the rest in alliance with Gloucestershire's off-spinner John Mortimore, the pair taking seven wickets between them to bowl out India for 149.

These were golden years for England at Leeds, and in 1961 there was another victory over the Australians, who nevertheless retained the Ashes they had won back in 1958-9 under Richie Benaud. This was England's only win of the series and featured some of the most remarkable bowling of Trueman's career.

The winter of 1959-60 had seen Fred at the height of his powers in the West Indies, where he and his buddie Brian Statham engineered the one positive result in the five-match series, an England victory by 256 runs in Trinidad.

Statham had to come home before the tour's end because one of his sons fell ill and Trueman was thrilled to be made senior pro. "T'first thing these buggers'll 'ave to do now is to cut out t'bloody swearing," he told the touring reporters. But he took his duties seriously, enjoyed himself thoroughly, bowled 342 overs in three months and

returned a contented, supremely fit, popular and lethal fast bowler.

At Leeds in 1961 Trueman shared the new ball with Les Jackson, a miner who had come into first-class cricket at the late age of 27 and formed a formidable bowling partnership for Derbyshire with Cliff Gladwin. Jackson could move the ball wickedly off the seam, especially on the green 'uns that were prevalent in his home county. In any subsequent era he would have played far more than his two Tests for England, for he was feared and respected by the best batsmen in the land, the best of whom were wise enough to watch him from the non-striker's end.

Australia won the toss and were sitting pretty at tea on 183-3 thanks to a half-century by their durable opener Colin McDonald and 73 from No 3 Neil Harvey. But Trueman changed the course of events when he took the second new ball and took 5-16 in six overs, aided by fine close catching by Cowdrey and Lock. The tourists collapsed to 208-9 but an unbeaten 22 by all-rounder Alan Davidson took them to 237 all out, a decent total on a somewhat unpredictable pitch.

England were given a solid start by Pullar and Raman Subba Row, the Northamptonshire captain who spearheaded England's batting in this series with 468 runs at 46.8 but at the end of the season retired from the game for business reasons. Cowdrey's 93 took England to a healthy 190-2 but they too suffered a middle-order crisis as Davidson, cutting down his pace, took 5-63 in 47 overs.

He was well supported by that gentle giant Graham McKenzie but Benaud, troubled by a shoulder injury throughout the series, managed only one wicket in 39 overs and came in for some heavy punishment at the hands of Lock, whose 30 runs at No 9 in the order lifted England to 299 and a useful first-innings lead.

Australia reached 99-3 in their second innings, comparative calm before Trueman's storm. David Allen had Peter Burge lbw at 102 and the Yorkshire fast bowler then thrilled the home crowd by taking five wickets without conceding a run, changing his style to off-cutters. Benaud's own discomfiture was complete when Trueman bowled him for nought for the second time in the match and in all he took six wickets for four runs in 45 balls. Australian lost their last eight wickets in less than an hour to be all out for 120 and England won by eight wickets in three days.

Trueman emerged with match figures of 11-88, his best for his country at Leeds, having shown the intelligence and skill to forsake sheer pace for a style of bowling more suited to the conditions.

The following year Pakistan made their first visit to Headingley but were no match for the home team, losing the series 4-0 and this game by an innings and 117 runs, England's sixth consecutive victory on the ground.

Peter Parfitt, whose Trueman impressions have been an integral part of his after-dinner speeches for years, was at this time letting his bat do the talking. His 119 was one of three centuries in five innings in the series by the left-hander who had followed the Edriches from Norfolk to Middlesex.

Opener Micky Stewart made 86 and England's last three batsmen made more than 100 between them, inspired by Allen's 62, so from a disappointing 194-6 at the end of the first day England climbed to 428 all out.

Trueman took the important wickets of Ijaz Butt and captain Javed Burki but it was Ted Dexter who unravelled Pakistan with 4-10 in 9.1 overs, only three batsmen reaching double figures in their first innings of 131. They fared only marginally better following on, Statham claiming 4-50 and Allen 3-47 to bowl them out for 180.

Only about 35,000 had watched the three days of the Pakistan Test but in 1963 the aggregate crowd was back over the 100,000 mark for the visit of the West Indies. And no wonder, for the first three matches had produced cricket of rare drama and brilliance.

Sobers was by now established as one of the stars in a dazzling West Indian batting array, as well as being a brilliant close-to-the-wicket fielder and a bowler who could operate in three styles – with the new ball, as a first-change swinger or as a left-arm spinner.

The selectors had picked two bowlers to fight for the honour of sharing the new ball with Wes Hall and it was the 22-year-old Barbadian Charlie Griffith, a bowler of frightening pace and hostile intent, who came to the fore in this series.

The tourists won the first match easily, Trueman took 12-119 to pave the way for an England win in the third but fresh in the minds of the Yorkshire faithful at Leeds were the sensational events of the second Test at Lord's in which their own Brian Close volunteered to be a human target for Hall and Griffith to fashion an innings of 70 that will stand forever as a monument to courage. With England six runs short of their victory target when their ninth wicket fell, Cowdrey walked through the Long Room and down the steps with his wrist broken and his arm in a sling to allow David Allen to fend off the final two balls from Hall and earn a heroic draw.

At Leeds, Trueman, Derek Shackleton and Dexter, the captain, reduced the West Indies to 71-3 but Rohan Kanhai batted with great responsibility before being yorked by Lock for 92 and Sobers compiled 102, his only century of the series, in 251 minutes during which he also reached 4,000 Test runs at the age of 27. Joe Solomon's 62 lifted the West Indies to 397.

England had started the series with Edrich as Stewart's opening partner, had then used Peter Richardson and for this game gave Brian Bolus, who had left Yorkshire for Nottinghamshire, his Test debut. He fell to Hall, but Griffith blasted through the innings to take 6-36 in 21 overs. England were all out for 174 and that represented a remarkable recovery from 93-8, fashioned by Lock's 53.

Fred Titmus, the Middlesex off-spinner, took four wickets in the second innings but a total of 229, founded on 52 by Sobers and 78 from Basil Butcher, made the tourists impregnable. Everyone waited for Hall and Griffith to do their worst.

It did not happen. With Hall limbering up and Stewart preparing to receive his first ball, Sobers asked Worrell if he could have the new ball as he was sure he could bowl Stewart. His captain agreed and Sobers duly shattered the opener's stumps in his first over.

Close, bowled for a duck by Griffith in the first innings, made a fighting 57, Bolus 43 and wicketkeeper Jim Parks 57 but Sobers and Griffith shared six wickets between them and spinner Lance Gibbs took the other four as England subsided to 231 and lost by 221 runs.

The tourists went on to a glorious series triumph by winning at The Oval. Outstanding individual talent and the captaincy of Dexter and Worrell, now 39 years old and soon to be knighted (after Bradman, Hobbs and Hutton) convinced all who witnessed it that this was how Test cricket ought to be. Hall and Griffith also gave a foretaste of what it would become, a fearsome and fearful contest which would force batsmen to protect their bodies rather than their stumps.

The 1964 Ashes Test was to be Trueman's last at Leeds and was tarnished by a tactical row with his captain, Dexter, which many believed was the key factor behind England's defeat by seven wickets.

His superb bowling against the West Indies in 1963 had taken him to 284 wickets, already past the world record previously held by his friend and partner Statham and he arrived at Headingley for the third match of the series seven wickets short of 300.

Trueman was convinced that he could take Peter Burge's wicket by luring him into the hook shot in the air and on a good batting track he pressed his captain to post a deep backward square leg as part of a trap. Dexter refused and Trueman, determined to prove his point, bowled persistently short.

Burge took the bait but with no fielder in a catching position the results were calamitous for England.

The big Queenslander was eventually caught in that position but by then he had made a match-winning 160 and had figured in stands of 105 with Neil Hawke and 89 with Wally Grout which, after opener Bill Lawry's 78, lifted Australia to 389 in reply to England's 268. The home side, with Geoff Boycott making 38 as Edrich's opening partner, had been strangled by some wonderful fielding and tight pace bowling by McKenzie and Hawke with only Dexter (66) and Parks (68) making any headway.

Spinners Norman Gifford and Titmus did the bulk of the bowling for England but Burge, belting 24 fours, rescued his team from 178-7 and a spurt which brought 42 runs from the first seven overs with the second new ball, propelled by Trueman and Jack Flavell, proved to be the decisive passage of play.

Parfitt's knuckle was broken in England's second innings of 229 in which Ken Barrington made a fighting 85 and both Dexter and Edrich resisted stubbornly but in vain. Titmus took 2-25 in 27 overs of off-spin as the tourists made studious progress to victory on the fourth evening.

Trueman, in his captain's bad books, was dropped for the next match at Manchester but returned at The Oval, where Hawke became his 300th Test victim and consoled himself with the knowledge that he would probably not have achieved such fame on his own.

Trueman's 67-match Test career ended against New Zealand at Lord's in 1965. He took 307 wickets at 21.57 with a phenomenal strike rate of a wicket every 49 balls, a figure bettered only by Malcolm Marshall and Waqar Younis among bowlers with more than 200 wickets to their name. At the time it was thought that his record might stand for all time. Not so, but we can say with more certainty that English and world cricket will never see his like again.

He did not figure in the Leeds Test of 1965 against the New Zealanders, who were no match for England. Edrich made an unbeaten 310, a record score by an English batsmen at the venue, and shared a second-wicket stand of 369 with Barrington, the second highest in history for England's second wicket.

They declared on 546-4 and won by an innings and 187 runs, Illingworth and Northamptonshire's David Larter bowling them out in the first innings and Titmus (5-19 from 26 overs) in the second.

*Garfield Sobers, having scored 102 and 52, bowls England opener Micky Stewart for a duck in the second innings of the 1963 Test which the West Indies won by 221 runs.*

# Chapter Nine

# Yorkshire 1966-1983

WHILE Geoff Hurst was slamming in that fourth goal against West Germany to win the World Cup for England, no one in their right mind could possibly think that it was about to be all over for Yorkshire as the predominant force in county cricket.

In that 1966 season there were no signs of it either as Brian Close, who with opening batsman Geoff Boycott and fellow all-rounder Ray Illingworth as the nucleus of the side, led the county to the first of three more consecutive championships, emulating the feat of Brian Sellers in the glorious 1930s.

Four years later, Illingworth and Close had departed and Boycott was left to lead an inferior team into the first stage of a period of famine which has stretched into the new millennium and the club into a time of unprecedented internecine strife.

Fast-forwarding to 2001 and looking back on it all it is easy to conclude that Yorkshire County Cricket Club was fulfilling some dark satanic death-wish.

All was well with the world in 1966, Close's reputation as a leader of indomitable spirit and courage elevating him to the England captaincy for the last Test match of the summer against the West Indies. Though vehemently opposed to one-day cricket from the inception of the one-day knockout in 1963, he had led Yorkshire to a Gillette Cup triumph over Surrey at Lord's the previous season in which Boycott had played perhaps the finest innings of his career, a commanding 146. Close, of course, claims that he had constantly to coax him to play his shots.

The Duchess of Kent became the club's Patroness and work started on the new winter shed, with seating for 600 above it. Lancashire were thrashed in two days in the Headingley Roses match but defeats at Leeds by Sussex, also in two days, and by Northamptonshire trimmed Yorkshire's lead over Worcestershire to six points by the time they claimed the title by beating Kent at Harrogate.

The Whitsun Roses game was essentially won on the first morning as Trueman tore the heart out of Lancashire's batting by taking four wickets for seven runs as they lost half their side for 15. They were all out for 57 shortly after lunch, Trueman finishing with 5-18. John Waring, a pace bowler from Ripon, took three first-innings wickets and took advantage of Trueman's stranglehold at the other end when Lancashire batted again, taking 7-40.

Yorkshire's 196-9 contained an unbeaten 48 from Close and although Lancashire fared a little better at their second attempt still only three players reached double figures in a total of 144 which left Yorkshire to make just six runs to win.

There was a 65-over limit on first innings in this season, which put a further strain on batsmen but produced an exciting match against Sussex, who made 231-4 in their allotted overs thanks to half-centuries by Les Lenham and the Nawab of Pataudi, an Oxford product who, through a burning desire to be captain of India, had returned to the first-class game despite losing the sight of his right eye in a car crash in 1961.

*An aerial view of Headingley's cricket and rugby league grounds, one of the most famous sporting venues in the world.*

John Snow was Yorkshire's destroyer, taking 10 wickets in the match. They were all out for 202 in their first innings but rallied to bowl Sussex out for 121 with Illingworth claiming 5-42 and Close 4-38. That gave them a chance of victory but the batting failed against Snow's pace and a total of 128 left Sussex winners by 22 runs.

The batsmen also struggled in the Northamptonshire game. Yorkshire bowled out the visitors for 174 but were restricted to a lead of one run as there was not enough support for Hampshire, who made 76 out of their 175. Colin Milburn's bristling 58 took Northamptonshire to 190 in their second innings and it was too much for Yorkshire, who lost by 66 runs.

Harrogate was again the scene of title celebrations in 1967, a campaign notable for Close's censure for employing 'delaying tactics' in the final stages of a game at Edgbaston, which led to the introduction of a mandatory 20 overs in the last hour. Although an altercation with one of the spectators was less lurid than it was made out to be at the time, his days as England's captain were numbered, even though his

record in charge was six wins and a draw. At times he did himself no favours but the feeling was that his face did not fit at Lord's and that the MCC powerbrokers were constantly searching for excuses to get rid of him.

The 1967 match against Surrey at Headingley was the benefit game for Hull-born wicketkeeper Jimmy Binks, one of the finest to have donned the gloves for the county. Yorkshire's consistent batting to 300 – Chris Balderstone made 71 and only Phil Sharpe failed – was the platform for an innings win, spinners Geoff Cope and Don Wilson, a left-armer who flourished under Close's guidance, taking 15 wickets between them.

The batting prospered in Yorkshire's drawn game with the Pakistani tourists, Boycott making 128, Sharpe 197 and Padgett 70 in a total of 414-3 declared. Illingworth was the main threat as the Pakistanis were dismissed for 150 but there was not enough time for Yorkshire to press home their advantage.

*A head wound could not spoil Brian Close's celebration of the winning of the 1967 championship but he looks a little puzzled by the sight of a bespectacled Geoff Boycott pouring Ray Illingworth a glass of champagne.*

In 1968 both the first and second teams won their championships and the Australians were beaten at Sheffield, Fred Trueman leading Yorkshire in one of the most memorable matches of his career, but storm clouds were gathering over Headingley.

It was the end of the great Trueman era: "Your committee regrets that the time has come for the great-hearted Freddie Trueman to retire. He has been one of the outstanding cricketers of all time and will be greatly missed," said the county's official announcement.

Ken Taylor also retired at the end of this season, but the greatest blow of all was the loss of Illingworth, who had the temerity to ask the committee for the security of a longer-term contract than the normal one summer, was told where he could go by Brian Sellers and did indeed go, to Leicestershire, where he was to rise to the England captaincy as well as turning that county into a major force in the land.

Some £6,500 was spent on the toilets at the Kirkstall Lane end and on the field there was a draw against Nottinghamshire and two innings wins over Lancashire and Middlesex. Taylor made 60 out of Yorkshire's 119 all out against Nottinghamshire, one Garfield Sobers taking 4-26, and the Huddersfield batsman hit another half-century when they recovered to make 238 in their second innings. The visitors declared on 203-7 (Sobers was bowled by Trueman for a duck) and were 17-2 at the close.

On a placid pitch Lancashire's batting was a fairly gruesome sight as they were again tormented by Trueman, who bowled Roses debutant Farokh Engineer on his way to 5-45, the only substantive resistance coming from opener Graham Atkinson and David Hughes.

Padgett made his second Roses hundred and was well supported by Taylor with 85, Hampshire with 56 and Illingworth, who hit 49. Yorkshire did suffer a late collapse, losing their last three wickets for no runs, but a total of 348 put them in control.

Facing a deficit of 172, Lancashire never recovered from the first-over dismissal of Atkinson and were bowled out for 116. Trueman contented himself with 3-17 and it was Wilson who did the bulk of the damage with 4-32 in 26.2 overs.

Taylor's consistency brought him another half-century against Middlesex and with Padgett shining with an unbeaten 136 Yorkshire were able to declare on 358-7. Middlesex had no answer to the spin combination of Illingworth and Wilson, who claimed nine wickets in their first-innings debacle of 59 all out. In the second innings they took all 10, Wilson leading the victory romp with 7-36 from 24 overs.

The 1969 campaign brought the advent of the Sunday League and another Gillette triumph for Yorkshire, who had yet to play at Headingley in the competition. They took the semi-final against a Sobers-inspired Nottinghamshire to Scarborough and beat Derbyshire in the final, making a £5,600 profit from the cup run.

The abandoned game against Leicestershire at Leeds brought one noteworthy incident – Close bowled by Illingworth for 69 – and there were other draws against Derbyshire and Somerset.

Against Derbyshire Yorkshire batted consistently, Padgett, Barrie Leadbeater and Binks making half-centuries in a total of 333. Mike Page hit a century and Ian Buxton 97 as Derbyshire replied confidently with 291-6 declared and although Yorkshire tried to force a win, scampering to 118-9 in their second innings, Derbyshire declined to chase the target of 161 and closed on 42-1.

The Somerset game turned out to be a duel between Greg Chappell, who took 7-40 in Yorkshire's first innings of 140 all out, and Richard Hutton, son of Sir Leonard and a good enough all-rounder in his own right to play five times for England, whose 7-39 on a seaming pitch gave his side a lead of one run. Boycott, not one of Hutton's favourite people then or subsequently, made 105 not out in the second innings, enabling Yorkshire to declare on 233-6, and at the close Somerset were hanging on at 141-7. Hutton's accuracy and movement also brought him 7-15 in the team's one Sunday League outing at Leeds, a win over Worcestershire.

But it was a depressing championship season in which Yorkshire slipped to fifth from bottom, then their lowest finish. Supporters in subsequent years would have to get used to that, but in 1969 it was an ignominious fall. Boycott's century against Somerset was Yorkshire's only one in the championship that season, though he, Sharpe and Hampshire all reached three figures in Tests.

Close, already having to rebuild a side shorn of his right-hand man, Illingworth, as well as Taylor and Trueman, was then faced with the retirement of Binks, a wicketkeeper of the highest class who had not missed a championship game since making his debut in 1955 and left the game with hands still in such pristine condition that Ted Lester reckoned he could have walked off the cricket field and played the piano. Close put his departure down to poor relations between the dressing-room and the committee.

It did get better in 1970, Yorkshire rising to fourth to create the impression that Close was pulling things round despite all the difficulties. The year was, however, officially described as a financial disaster. The South African tour was cancelled and the replacement 'Tests' against a Rest of the World side, though producing some fine cricket, were not as well supported. Yorkshire lost £8,109.

To make matters worse, Yorkshire were flattened in the Headingley Roses match on a flat pitch. Yorkshireman Barry Wood, who had played a handful of games for the club in 1964, made 105 and put on 151 with David Lloyd for the first wicket. Engineer chipped in with 70 as Lancashire reached a formidable 381, Tony Nicholson battling away to claim 5-116.

Ken Shuttleworth removed Boycott, Padgett and Sharpe cheaply and Yorkshire never recovered, folding to 121 all out against Shuttleworth and Peter Lever, who took 4-51. Even though Shuttleworth, who had modelled his action on Trueman's, was unfit to bowl in the second innings Boycott (71) and Hutton (51) were the only batsmen to emerge with much credit and a total of 281 left Lancashire to make 22 to notch a 10-wicket win.

Yorkshire were on top against Sussex as Boycott, Close, Sharpe and Hutton all passed 50 but Barbadian Geoff Greenidge made 70 as the visitors reached the safety of 216-4 in their second innings. In the Sunday League Kent were beaten by two wickets as Middlesbrough's Chris Old, one of the finest fast bowlers the county has produced since Trueman but, sadly, not quite so great-hearted, took 1-12 in his eight overs.

Then the bombshell. "After long and careful consideration your committee decided not to reappoint D B Close as captain for 1971 and in view of this decision it was also decided that he should no longer be a playing member of the team," was the official statement.

In his eight years as captain Close had won four championships and the Gillette Cup twice. It could be argued that the sacking of Johnny Wardle had at least had the desired effect on the team as a whole; it is even possible to see both sides of the argument behind Illingworth's departure, though some attempt to meet him halfway would surely not have meant the end of civilisation as we know it. The sacking of Close, however, still looks now what it seemed at the time, an act of madness.

This time, many of the members decided that enough was enough and formed an Action Group, a foretaste of things to come. They brought about some changes, notably the resignation of Sellers as cricket chairman, but Close left for Somerset, the departed Illingworth wrested the Ashes from Australia's grasp with a glorious triumph Down Under in the winter of 1970-1 and Boycott, Yorkshire's new captain, broke an arm on the tour. It was not going terribly well.

The 1971 season brought misery on and off the field and worsened the divisions within the dressing-room and the atmosphere of dissent and disappointment within the club as a whole. Yorkshire collapsed to 13th in the championship and 16th in the Sunday League and the committee, reporting a loss of £12,000, announced a special meeting in order to raise subscriptions.

The campaign began without the injured Boycott and when he returned he became the first English batsman to average more than 100 in a season, though even this remarkable feat was tarnished by the debate as to whether he was more concerned about his own performances than the team's.

There was some comfort for Yorkshire at Leeds. Middlesex were beaten by eight wickets, Boycott leading the way with 88 and 112 not out. Mike Brearley, who could be seen as the mirror-image of Boycott in that his captaincy skills heavily outweighed his own batting talent, made a half-century in the visitors' 258 in which Wilson took 4-53.

Yorkshire made 200 at their first attempt, Boycott run out for 88, but after Middlesex had declared on 153-7 the captain and John Hampshire spearheaded a fine run-chase, the latter making an unbeaten 72 as Yorkshire reached 213-2 in 53 overs.

Boycott was absent again for a spell but again returned in personal glory, fashioning a huge innings of 169 which was the platform for an innings win over Nottinghamshire. David Bairstow, who had usurped Neil Smith as the wicketkeeping successor to Binks, chimed in with 67 not out as Yorkshire piled up 375-5 declared on a good batting track.

Sobers failed twice as Nottinghamshire were skittled for 142 and 102, Nicholson taking seven wickets in the match and Hampshire's leg-breaks doing the damage in the second innings (5-37).

The game against the Indians was ruined by the weather after Yorkshire had bowled out the tourists for 145. Richard Lumb was 57 not out in a score of 137-3, but in the Sunday League Yorkshire felt the full force of Clive Lloyd's batting as he thrashed an unbeaten 97 in a 48-run defeat by Lancashire.

In October of 1971 John Nash retired as club secretary, ending 40 years of service which had begun when he was just 25 years old. Regarded as a somewhat distant and aloof personality, he was the guiding figure behind the team during its most glorious eras in the 1930s and 1960s. He was no doubt relieved to be going, for if he was saddened to be the man to announce the sacking of Wardle in 1958, any thought that this was as bad it it could get proved sadly incorrect. The entire ethos of the club had changed. The committee was increasingly mistrusted, there was a more questioning and critical Press corps to deal with and the departure of Illingworth and then Close led to far more public washing of dirty linen than had been the case in the past.

He was succeeded for the 1972 season by Joe Lister. Born in Thirsk in 1930 and related to George Macaulay, he had played twice as a batsman for Yorkshire in 1954 before joining Worcestershire. There he gained a reputation as a stern and highly-efficient administrator. He never actually said so, but may have hankered after a quieter life in the shadow of Worcester Cathedral as he tried in the ensuing years to steer a sane and civilised course through the mayhem.

That winter also brought the retirement of Padgett, who could be viewed as a peace-making influence in a dressing-room which had Sharpe, Wilson and Hutton as a strong spine of opposition to Boycott's captaincy. Padgett became club coach in succession to Arthur Mitchell and Second XI captain in succession to Bob Platt, who had served the club magnificently in that role, maintaining high standards of performance no matter what was going on in the senior side.

The 1972 season started well. Against Lancashire at Leeds, in Wilson's benefit game, only 1,500 turned up on a cold and windy first day but Boycott scored his fifth Roses century and can rarely have played better. He scored 82 out of an opening stand of 119 with Sharpe and reached his century out of 147 runs on the board before being bowled by Shuttleworth for 105.

*One of Yorkshire's great bowling stalwarts, Tony Nicholson is pictured here in 1973, two years before his retirement. Though his body often seemed to be falling apart, his spirit never wavered and this hugely popular county servant was much mourned when he died at the age of 47.*

Yorkshire declared on 253-8 and good new-ball bowling by Old and Nicholson reduced Lancashire to 21-3 before a sixth-wicket stand of 90 between Engineer, who made 69, and David Hughes lifted the Red Rose side to 190. Nicholson finished with 7-49.

Amid several interruptions for rain and on a deteriorating pitch, Yorkshire struggled against Peter Lever, who took 5-27 as their second innings stuttered on to 95-9, when a declaration left Lancashire to make 159 to win in just under two hours. But hopes of an exciting finish were ruined by the weather.

Andrew Dalton, a gifted batsman from Leeds, made 128 on his home ground against Middlesex but was not to play again after the 1972 season and was one of the talents lost because of a troubled dressing-room. Showing considerable maturity, he also made 49 in the second innings – and this in a game in which no other batsman reached 40. Hutton and Howard Cooper, a steady performer from Great Horton who was to be particularly effective in one-day cricket, took 16 wickets between them as Middlesex were beaten by 98 runs.

Headingley staged its first Gillette tie in this season but it was a nasty experience for Yorkshire, who lost

by four wickets, and for their captain, who had a finger broken by Bob Willis.

This was the first year of the Benson and Hedges Cup and Yorkshire marched to Lord's with a seven-wicket semi-final success over Gloucestershire at Headingley, where fine seam bowling by Old, Nicholson, Hutton and John Woodford held the visitors in check and Boycott guided his team to a small target with an unbeaten 75.

The final turned into a bitter-sweet experience and only added to the acrimony in the club, for Boycott was unfit to play and Yorkshire lost to a Leicestershire side inspired by two Yorkshiremen, Illingworth and Balderstone.

By the end of the season there was more bad news. Cope, a thoughtful cricketer determined to fill the off-spin void left by Illingworth, failed to satisfy the TCCB on the legality of his bowling action and took one-to-one tuition from Wardle to have it remodelled.

Also at this time Yorkshire, standing aloof from the national trend, were suffering painfully at the hands of the many overseas players being employed by the other counties. Early in the 1973 campaign, for instance, they were mauled at Headingley by the West Indian dasher Gordon Greenidge, who smashed an unbeaten 196 out of Hampshire's total of 341.

Boycott made 73 but Yorkshire were bowled out for 168 and although they improved in their second innings, Hampshire hitting 84 to lift them to 259, they were soundly beaten by seven wickets.

Against Leicestershire they crumbled against the seam bowling of McKenzie and Higgs and were rolled over for 113 in reply to 319 but rallied magnificently in the second innings to save the game, Lumb and Sharpe taking Yorkshire to 155 without loss at the close.

But the batting failed horribly against Surrey, whose first-innings total of 184 was founded on Graham Roope's 81. Yorkshire were bowled out, largely by Robin Jackman, for just 90, Edrich then hit a century to enable Surrey to declare at 247-3 and although the home side showed some guts and gallantry in the second innings, Hampshire, Johnson and Sharpe all making half-centuries, they were winkled out by spinners Pat Pocock and Intikhab Alam and lost by 42 runs.

Yorkshire's 14th place in 1973 was their lowest yet and although they did well in the Sunday League they were humiliated by Durham in the Gillette Cup. Cope's standing with the authorities remained a cause for concern, dear old Bramall Lane staged its last first-class game and at Headingley work on the seats in the lower tier of the Main Stand was hampered by a steel shortage.

In the year when sniping off-stage against Boycott's captaincy increased with Burnet, Trueman and Brennan adding their names to the list of his detractors, Wilfred Rhodes passed away, as did Arthur Wood and the President, Sir William Worsley, who had served as captain, committee member and President for 46 years. He was to be succeeded by Sir Kenneth Parkinson.

In the 1973 Sunday League games at Headingley there was the first of a series of ferocious innings from Clive Lloyd, who hit 79 not out in Lancashire's six-wicket win. There was a heavy defeat, too, against Gloucestershire, for whom the rotund David Shepherd made 66 not out.

Bonus points had been part of the scene for some years and in 1974 there was a 100-over limit on the first innings, though teams bowling the opposition out in fewer could claim the unused ones for themselves. No matter how the authorities tinkered with the regulations, Yorkshire continued to tear themselves apart and things had become so bad in 1974 that the official report on the season was

forced to rejoice in the fact that at least the Fenner Trophy (part of the Scarborough Festival) had been recaptured.

Cope found some stability and form after his troubles, Boycott played the unusually high number of 30 first-class innings for the county but Hampshire was injured and missed six weeks of the summer.

The battle-lines were now drawn. Outside observers – and many within the county boundaries – resented the criticism of Boycott as the one world-class player in the side. But the 1974 Headingley Roses match, a tawdry affair, stoked up the argument against his leadership.

Clive Lloyd was at it again in this game, making 69 and 84 not out, but Lancashire batted slowly to make 250 in their first innings and Yorkshire even more slowly in the face of a desultory over-rate to reply with 220-9. Leadbeater was left unbeaten on 92 and Shuttleworth took 7-61.

Lancashire showed more enterprise in making 213-7 declared and Yorkshire made no attempt to go for a target of 244 in 210 minutes. Boycott went his own way, making an unbeaten 79 out of 124-3 as the game fizzled out. The Sussex game was also drawn, Boycott making 117 and 49 not out and sharing in two century stands with Lumb.

Lloyd belted 90 in Lancashire's 32-run win in a Gillette Cup tie at Leeds and the Sunday League campaign was made famous by Middlesex's 23 all out on a mosaic pitch after Yorkshire, fuelled by Boycott's 48 and Hutton's 60, had reached 148. Clive Radley top-scored for the visitors with six and the bowling figures were amazing: Nicholson 3-6, Arthur Robinson 3-9, Graham Stevenson 2-4 and Hutton 2-3. Nicholson, a true lion-heart considering he had fought back from a career-threatening thrombosis and seemed to be held together only by his iron will, also took 4-15 as Kent were beaten by 45 runs

It was to be Hutton's last season. He declared himself unavailable for the following year and so did not have his contract renewed; Sharpe left for Derbyshire and Wilson resigned.

If 1974 was the low point for Boycott as a captain under fire, the following year suggested that his supporters in the shires were right in thinking that he was being unfairly persecuted and was a man capable of taking a reshaped team to a brighter future.

Officially, the committee seemed to agree. Its report on a 1975 season in which Yorkshire rose to be championship runners-up said that it was down to his personal decision not to play representative cricket. The side had unquestionably benefited not only from his batting but also from the continuity of leadership.

By the standards of years to follow, it was a good Yorkshire side. Boycott and Lumb had formed an effective opening partnership; Old was a Test-class all-rounder; Bairstow a wicketkeeper inching his way towards England status. Hampshire and Leadbeater gave daring and durability to the batting, Stevenson was hugely talented, Sidebottom was a clearly gifted all-round sportsman and Cope and Phil Carrick were developing into a formidable spin combination, perhaps not of the sheer quality Yorkshire had been used to but more than adequate for the needs of the time.

Yorkshire could not win at Headingley. Lumb made 82 and Old 77 in a tame draw against Middlesex and the Roses game also ended in stalemate, with more suffering at the hands of Clive Lloyd. It was another no-risk match of sluggish over-rates.

Lloyd made 100 and Frank Hayes 101 in Lancashire's 340-5 and Yorkshire were sent reeling by Lever, who reduced them to 13-4 with some devastating new-ball bowling. But Pocklington's Colin Johnson and Old batted well to take their side to 201-8 declared before Lloyd blasted another 82 and put on 138 with Andrew Kennedy, enabling Lancashire to declare on 191-3.

This left Yorkshire to make 331 in four-and-a-half hours on a good pitch but their start, though solid, was too slow with only 83 runs coming off the first 30 overs. Lumb made 70 and Boycott compiled an unbeaten 105 in a total of 219-1.

There was frustration at Headingley in the Gillette Cup, where Leicestershire's last-wicket pair of McKenzie and Higgs batted their side to victory in a low-scoring affair. In the Sunday League, Lloyd caused more mayhem with 101 not out in Lancashire's seven-wicket win.

If the committee and the supporters thought that this was a new dawn for the team, they were mistaken. In 1976, with Boycott again injured for several weeks and Nicholson no longer on active service, Yorkshire drew a blank at Leeds, where all three championship games were drawn.

Another overseas batting star, Zaheer Abbas, blazed his way to 111 in Gloucestershire's four-wicket win in a Gillette tie. The greatest humiliation came at Barnsley, where they were beaten in a Benson and Hedges tie by a Combined Universities side containing Yorkshireman Steve Coverdale (later

chief executive at Northamptonshire), Paul Parker, Chris Tavare, Peter Roebuck and Vic Marks.

In the championship game against Gloucestershire Zaheer made 188 in a run spree of a match. Johnson and Hampshire both hit centuries for Yorkshire in a total of 344-3 declared but Gloucestershire replied in kind. Boycott made 161 not out and Lumb 132 as Yorkshire piled up 321-2 declared in their second innings and another Pakistan Test player, opener Sadiq Mohammad, scored 107 for the West Country side to take the aggregate of runs in the game to 1,221 for the loss of 15 wickets.

The Roses match was spoiled by the weather, Lancashire making 201-7 declared thanks to half-centuries by the other Lloyd, David, and little Harry Pilling. The accurate medium pace of Bob Ratcliffe proved too much for Yorkshire, who were bowled out for 141 as he took 5-30, but rain ended proceedings with Lancashire on 27-1 in their second innings.

Hampshire led the side against Sussex and led the way with 113 in Yorkshire's 265 all out. Sussex were only five runs adrift on first innings but a maiden century by Middlesbrough's Bill Athey, who was to earn three England caps as a Yorkshire batsman but another 20 after he moved to Gloucestershire, kept his side in control.

Lumb made 75 in the second-innings score of 296-1 declared but Hampshire set a stiff target of 302 in 210 minutes and Sussex showed no interest in it, closing on 100-4. Hampshire's 88 propelled his side to a Sunday League win over Glamorgan but they were beaten by Warwickshire at Leeds where John Jameson hit 61.

Yorkshire slid even further down the table in 1977, to 12th, but for Boycott's supporters it was an annus mirabilis as their hero was lured back into the England fold after a three-year exile, scored a century on his return at Trent Bridge and then, in the next match of the Ashes series at Headingley, completed his 100th hundred amid scenes of mass euphoria.

For Yorkshire, however, there was only more trouble and strife. 'Rocker' Robinson, a strong and willing left-arm seam bowler from Northallerton, took 5-28 as Leicestershire were dismissed for 67 at Leeds before being saved by rain, Hampshire having hit 93 in Yorkshire's 242.

The game against Nottinghamshire was also a rain-ruined draw but with Boycott away on England duty Yorkshire were savaged by Gordon Greenidge, who smote 208 out of Hampshire's total of 332 to

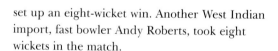

*Above: For 20 years John Hampshire thrilled Yorkshire's crowds with his attacking strokeplay and in 1969 scored a century on his Test debut against the West Indies at Lord's.*

*Right: The awesome power of the batting of Clive Lloyd is captured here as he drives Derek Underwood over long-on for six as Alan Knott and Chris Old look on.*

set up an eight-wicket win. Another West Indian import, fast bowler Andy Roberts, took eight wickets in the match.

There was a rare one-day victory over Lancashire, who were beaten by six wickets in the Sunday League as Boycott, Hampshire and Love all scored half-centuries, but the cricket was increasingly becoming a side-issue and for the media the busy season started in October.

Don Brennan launched another attack on Boycott's captaincy, for which he was officially ticked off, the rift between Boycott and Hampshire became ever more visible and the Reform Group, formed in the wake of Close's sacking, was back in even greater strength in support of what it saw as a persecuted captain.

Then, in November of 1977, through a series of phone calls with a few key members of the

hierarchy, Illingworth was offered the job of team manager with full authority in all cricket matters including selection. He would, however, not be taking up his post until 1979, which left Boycott in charge for the 1978 campaign in which the side rose to fourth in the championship table.

As ever in Yorkshire cricket, nothing is straightforward, and Boycott's critics seized on the fact that Hampshire, as deputy during Boycott's absences, had led the team to as many wins from roughly the same number of matches and was to them the man to restore dressing-room harmony..

At Headingley the highlight was a Roses victory by an innings and 32 runs, a triumph gained without the services of Boycott and Old but tarnished by the reporting of the pitch as unfit for first-class cricket.

Yorkshire's match-winners were the Ackworth all-rounder Graham Stevenson, a cricketer of immense natural gifts but too many flaws to make the most of them, and slow left-armer Phil Carrick. Despite a fighting 58 by Clive Lloyd, Stevenson kept finding the edge and David Bairstow pouched the catches, the bowler claiming 8-65 in Lancashire's 123 all out.

Yorkshire were sent reeling early on by Willie Hogg and slumped to 20-4 but Carrick came in at No 7 and fashioned a superb maiden century, 105 out of Yorkshire's 260 all out. Cooper and Oldham did all the damage in Lancashire's second innings of 105 all out.

Boycott hit an unbeaten 103 and Hampshire 90 in the drawn game against the New Zealand tourists, for whom Bruce Edgar made 92 in the first innings and John Wright a century in the second, but Yorkshire lost in a 10-over slog in a Gillette tie against Sussex, flailing their way to 59-8 when chasing 69 to win.

Cope's action again failed the test of the TCCB scrutineers in the 1978 season but all things to do with bat and ball were increasingly an irrelevance as the Boycott issue divided county and country into two camps. You were either for or against him; professing to be neutral or uncommitted was to be a social outcast and was tantamount to an admission of criminal lunacy.

Hampshire had at Northampton played a 'go-slow' innings in imitation of the way he claimed the captain had batted for years – for himself rather than for the team. Illingworth, though not yet officially employed, was seen by Boycott's supporters as more than a background figure in the picture as in September the committee decided that Hampshire would replace Boycott as captain for the 1979 season.

In a crowded room at Headingley, with TV lights flashing and reporters straining to catch every word of the statement, chairman Arthur Connell famously declared: "It is nothing to do with what Mr Boycott has done or has not done. It is to do with what he is."

There was uproar in the shires. The Reform Group forced a special general meeting but their motion of no-confidence was defeated as was the move to reinstate Boycott, whose eight-year reign had ended. The committee bemoaned the outlay of £11,000 for the meeting on top of costs incurred in fighting Kerry Packer and "the parasite called World Series Cricket."

Hampshire, probably not as good a captain as he was a batsman, found leadership a gruesome business, sensing that the majority of the crowd was willing him to fall flat on his face. Illingworth, in his first year as manager, found some reasons to be cheerful, notably in a run to the Benson and Hedges semi-final in which Yorkshire beat Kent at Headingley thanks to Hampshire's 73 and Oldham's 4-26. They eventually lost to Essex at Chelmsford. Then there was the emergence of Neil Hartley, a Colts all-rounder from Shipley, who led the side to a glorious Roses triumph in a thrilling Headingley run-chase.

Boycott, as usual reacting to personal adversity with a huge pile of runs, was in prime form in 1979, averaging more than 100 again and making 151 not out in the rain-hit draw with Derbyshire at Leeds.

He also produced some penetrative bowling, notably in that Roses win, taking 4-14 in 14.2 overs as Lancashire subsided to 155 all out. Boycott then held Yorkshire together with 94, supported by half-centuries from Hampshire and Arnie Sidebottom, who battled through the years of turmoil to emerge as a valuable all-rounder, an accomplished technician with bat and ball.

Clive Lloyd – yes, him again – had been out for five in the first innings, which only made him angry. He hit a dazzling 103 in the second as Lancashire recovered, the West Indian putting on 135 with Hayes for the fourth wicket. John Abrahams also batted well and at 266-7 and with time running short Lancashire seemed to have saved the game.

Their last three wickets went for four runs but even so Yorkshire needed 104 to win at more than seven runs an over. Hartley sparkled with firm hits, judicious placements and some electrifying running between the wickets to make 53 not out and guide Yorkshire to a six-wicket win inside 14 overs.

Stevenson bowled well in the 1980 Headingley Roses match, taking nine wickets in the draw. Lancashire batted competently to make 234 and Bairstow, having taken six catches, then hit a breezy 61 in Yorkshire's 257, Carrick making a valuable 63 and sharing in a century stand for the seventh wicket. A battling 54 by the stubborn Abrahams took Lancashire to 182-8 at the close.

Stevenson again showed his prowess against Northamptonshire but could not save Yorkshire from an eight-wicket defeat. Peter Ingham and Jim Love made half-centuries in Yorkshire's 200-3 declared and Stevenson took all eight Northamptonshire wickets to fall before they called a halt at the same score. With an all-10 feat beckoning, the bowler left the field to change a sweaty shirt. One suspects that Trueman in the same position would not have done that.

Only Stevenson, with 52, found any answer to the bowling of Jim Griffiths, who took 7-52 as Yorkshire were bowled out for 109 and Wayne Larkins's unbeaten 60 took the visitors to an easy win.

Yorkshire were beaten by the West Indians, for whom Faoud Bacchus made 164 not out in a game in which the tourists lost only four wickets before Colin Croft sealed a 58-run win with 6-80. They had some good wins in one-day cricket at Headingley but the season ended with a distressed Hampshire, whose family had been subjected to abuse from Boycott zealots, quitting the captaincy. A year later he left the club.

In 1981, the year of covered pitches, Yorkshire spent £40,000 on improvements at Headingley but there was no improvement on the field under Old's leadership. Mike Gatting hammered 158 to give Middlesex a big first-innings lead which was turned into victory by Wayne Daniel (6-64). Wrecked by John Lever, Yorkshire followed on against Essex but rallied as Martyn Moxon hit a century on his debut and Lancashire were innings victors in the Roses match as Clive Lloyd went berserk again with 145 and left the execution to Michael Holding and Paul Allott, who took 18 wickets between them.

Lancashire also won in the Sunday League and Yorkshire were simply not doing well enough on the field to quell the turmoil off it. A vast injury list provided some excuse, but there was a row between Illingworth and Bairstow in a Scarborough hotel bar when the manager at one stage promoted Hartley to captain and North Marine Road saw unprecedented scenes of strife at the end of the season against Northamptonshire when Boycott was suspended by Illingworth for a breach of discipline.

In 1982 the committee reported an £11,000 loss and one of the cost-cutting measures was to make the hallowed yearbook a softback edition in 1984. In the context of the conflagration consuming the club this was a mere spit. Yorkshire CCC had become ungovernable and had one side dared to say what day of the week it was there would probably have been counter-claims and court injunctions.

At first the national media were fascinated by all the Illingworth-Boycott intrigue but as the saga rumbled on they contented themselves with having a laugh. The phrase "it could only happen in Yorkshire" was frequently heard. Subsequent rows at Taunton and Derby may give the lie to that theory but when it came to falling out among themselves Yorkshire could do it better than anyone.

It was, sadly, the only thing they were really good at, though Boycott and Athey scored centuries in the draw with Glamorgan and Athey, Bairstow, Boycott and Lumb were all among the runs in a high-scoring Roses draw. Lancashire set a target of 290 in just over three hours but after an opening stand of 144 between Boycott and Lumb the middle order was wrecked by Croft, so Yorkshire batted out time.

Midway through the season the wheels came off at Middlesbrough (against Northamptonshire, who were often key witnesses to Yorkshire's strife) and Illingworth, now turned 50, took over the captaincy from Old, who left for Warwickshire at the end of the season.

Illingworth's first success in the role was against Warwickshire at Leeds, where a truce patched up between the leading figures paid off as Boycott made 152 not out. Simon Dennis, a left-arm seam bowler from Scarborough and nephew of Len Hutton, took 5-42 to give Yorkshire a big lead and despite 94 from Dennis Amiss and 55 by Geoff Humpage Yorkshire won by nine wickets.

Yorkshire were also pressing for victory against Kent thanks to a century by Athey but the visitors held out at 142-9 in the second innings with Chris Cowdrey making a stubborn 51 not out in fading light. Bairstow, with 92, led a tremendous recovery, completed by Old and Stevenson, in the NatWest Trophy tie against Worcestershire after Yorkshire, needing 287, had been reduced to 38-4 in a tie spread over two days and Essex were beaten by nine wickets, also at Leeds. Worcestershire won there in a depressing Benson and Hedges campaign and in the Sunday League Yorkshire finished second bottom.

The 1983 season was Athey's last and all four championship games at Headingley were drawn. By this time more county cricket was promised for Leeds under the terms of the recently-signed lease. But there was no more league cricket, the Leeds club being disbanded.

Against Sussex they needed 227 in 250 minutes but struggled to 162-7 in a game with 14 lbw decisions, a record for a Yorkshire fixture. Against Lancashire Moxon, his cover-drive in full flow, hit a superb 153 and Yorkshire, set a stiff victory target of 296, had to scramble to avoid defeat at 90-7.

By now Yorkshire had even set up a peace-keeping triumvirate (Burnet, Trueman and Billy Sutcliffe) and they were needed after a big but slow Boycott innings at Cheltenham, though as usual the principle characters could not even agree on whether he had been reprimanded.

Illingworth was fed up and threatened to quit and although Bairstow batted brilliantly to make 86 and 100 not out against Middlesex Yorkshire finished bottom of the championship for the first time in their history.

Lamb, with 76, and Griffiths (5-33) propelled Northamptonshire to a NatWest success at Leeds and Lancashire were winners on run-rate in the Benson and Hedges Cup but since Yorkshire managed to win the Sunday League title for the first time, beating their Roses rivals by four wickets at Headingley, the members did not know whether to laugh or cry.

When the committee decided in October 1983 to sack Boycott (while also awarding him a testimonial), appoint Bairstow as captain and confirm Illingworth as manager the Reformers, now re-styled as Yorkshire Members 84, decided to cry and forced a special general meeting which eventually took place at Harrogate at a cost of £30,000.

The motion to reinstate Boycott was passed, as were votes of no-confidence in the committee and the cricket committee. Many did stand for re-election but the casualties included Trueman, Burnet, Platt and Sutcliffe while president Norman Yardley and chairman Michael Crawford did not seek office again. Illingworth, seeing the writing on the wall, went on holiday, where he was told by the new chairman, Hull's Reg Kirk, that his contract would be paid up.

Illingworth had viewed Hartley as potentially the next captain, which is probably one reason why it was Bairstow who led a reformed Yorkshire into the 1984 season with Close as his cricket chairman.

# Chapter Ten

# England 1966-1983

ENGLAND had witnessed nothing like it since the Bradman years.

In 1966 Garfield Sobers, the 30-year-old West Indies captain, proved himself to be not only the supreme cricketer of his generation but probably the finest all-rounder to have played the game.

He had just led the West Indies to a glorious series triumph over the Australians in the Caribbean, marred by the suggestion from Richie Benaud and Keith Miller, now cricket correspondents, that Charlie Griffith threw his yorker. Suspicion stuck to him like a shadow for the rest of his career.

Headingley saw Sobers at his most imperious and Griffith was barely needed. Geoffrey Boycott, with 20 Tests already behind him, had met the West Indians for the first time earlier in the series at Lord's, where his 60 and 25 were overshadowed by one of the epic partnerships of Test cricket between Sobers and David Holford.

At Nottingham, Griffith was the executioner, though Boycott gave evidence of things to come with a patient and technically impressive 71. His future battles with the battery of West Indian fast bowlers, especially with Michael Holding at the height of his powers, were to be the essence of the greatness and brutality of Test cricket in this era.

And so to Leeds for the fourth Test with the tourists already two up. Sobers won the toss for the fourth time and declared at 500-9. Seymour Nurse made 137 and the captain played one of his greatest innings, making 174 out of 265 runs scored while

he was at the wicket and offering not the hint of a chance in striking 24 fours.

He hit 103 between lunch and tea on that first day, a display that will live in the memory of all who witnessed it and sent the scribes back to the Bradman era for suitable superlatives.

As if that were not enough, Sobers then tore through the second half of England's batting after Wes Hall had done the initial damage. He took 5-41 in 19.3 overs as England were dismissed for 240. Basil D'Oliveira top-scored with 88 and at No 9 Ken Higgs smote a lusty 49.

An inspired Sobers took the new ball when England followed on and took three more wickets before leaving the demolition to spinner Lance Gibbs, who took 6-39 to give the West Indies victory by an innings and 55 runs and the series. Any doubts about where he stood in the pantheon of all-rounders had been settled. England summoned Brian Close to captain the team at The Oval and won.

For the Test against India in 1967 England gave a debut to the Essex leg-spinner Robin Hobbs. A glance at the scorecard suggests that it was Boycott's finest hour, for he made 246 not out in England's total of 550-4 declared. But the selectors decided that he had spent too many hours compiling the runs for their liking and he was dropped for slow scoring.

At the time it was a sensation, but in the light of later controversies in Boycott's career can be viewed

as a minor hiccup. India had a quartet of fine spin bowlers – Chandrasekhar, Prasanna, Bedi and Ventakaraghavan – but Venkat was not picked for this Test and Bedi was injured on the first day and bowled only 15 overs in the match.

Edrich fell early on but Boycott then figured in a series of huge stands with Ken Barrington (run out for 93), Tom Graveney (59) and D'Oliveira (109) before Close declared. A quick execution seemed likely as India slumped to 86-6 at the end of the second day but an innings of 64 by their captain, the Nawab of Pataudi, lifted them to 164, spinners Hobbs and Illingworth claiming three wickets each.

As the sun came out India showed how attractively they could bat. Engineer, opening the batting, made 87, the tall left-hander Ajit Wadekar 91, Hanumant Singh 73 and 'Tiger' Pataudi, who later played under the name Mansur Ali Khan having been stripped of his title by the Indian Government, stroked a masterly 148. As a result, India took the game into the final day by reaching 510, Illingworth finishing with 4-100 from 58 overs. Boycott did not bat in England's second innings,

Barrington taking over as opener and making 46 in the six-wicket win.

The series was an uneven contest. The wet conditions in the first half of the season did not suit India's strengths, which lay in spin, and they were poorly treated by their Board. One player said that he had to save from his £1 daily allowance to buy a bat as no cricket kit was provided and they never had enough to eat.

For the visit of the Australians in 1968 England gave debuts to Keith Fletcher of Essex and Roger Prideaux, the Northamptonshire opener. The former was to play 59 times for his country, the last seven as captain, but the place and timing of his debut was unfortunate. Yorkshire folk reckoned that their own Phil Sharpe should have been chosen and when Fletcher put down three slip chances there were derisory cries of "give 'im a bucket." He was also out for a duck in his first Test innings.

Barry Jarman and Graveney led the teams because Lawry and Cowdrey were injured. Jarman won the toss and Australia's 315 was founded on substantial

*Far left: Geoff Boycott raises his arms in triumph and relief as the crowd roars its approval.*

*Centre: The old manual scoreboard, later to be replaced by an electronic model, tells the story of Geoff Boycott's feat as on the evening of August 11, 1977, he became the first batsman in history to score his 100th century in a Test match.*

*Right: Garfield Sobers, the world's finest post-war cricketer, stands and delivers four more of his 8,032 Test runs.*

contributions by a trio of young batsmen, the dogged Ian Redpath (92), Ian Chappell (65) and the dashing Doug Walters, who made 42. Underwood was England's most successful bowler with 4-41.

A good contest developed in fine weather as England replied with 302. They were sorely troubled by the movement of the Victorian Alan Connolly, who took 5-72 after Prideaux, making 64, had aided Edrich in an opening stand of 123. After Barrington's 49 the innings fell away until Underwood, the last man, entertained the crowd hugely by hitting 45 not out and dominating a last-wicket stand of 61 with David Brown.

Illingworth shone with 6-87 from 51 skilful overs in Australia's second innings but half-centuries by Chappell and Walters and another resolute innings from Redpath took them to 312, which left England to make 326 at 66 runs an hour. The risks involved in chasing such a target were too great, England were not tempted and Australia retained the Ashes.

In June, 1969, Illingworth arrived at Brighton for a Leicestershire match – he had broken his journey to visit the injured Colin Milburn in hospital following the car crash in which he lost an eye – to be greeted by a gaggle of reporters. He had completed the journey from Wesley Street School and Farsley's second team to the England captaincy.

It did not take him long to show that although he was not the greatest off-spinner the world has seen – and certainly not the greatest batsman – his various talents welded to an innate cricketing intelligence made him a great captain.

Illingworth regards the 1969 Test against the formidable West Indies as his finest hour, even though in the previous game at Lord's he had scored his maiden Test century and with John Hampshire had dug England out of a hole to draw the match.

The pitch was green early on. Boycott was out for 12, but Edrich made 79 and hearty innings from Alan Knott and D'Oliveira in the middle order took England to 223, Vanburn Holder claiming four of the wickets. The captain's Leicestershire team-mate

*His daughter, Mrs T H Burnley, leads the 90-year-old Wilfred Rhodes into the Headingley ground in 1968.*

Barry Knight, who had joined that county from Essex, took 4-63 as first-change bowler, his victims being the top three in the order plus Sobers, who was caught by Sharpe in the slips for 13. The West Indies were all out for 161.

Apart from Boycott, who fell to Sobers without a run on the board, all England's players reached double figures in their second-innings total of 240 in which Sobers finished with 5-42. The tourists needed a daunting 303 to win but the pitch was easing and their batting line-up full of menace.

At one stage, with Steve Camacho and Basil Butcher in full cry, they were 177-2, but Camacho was out for 71 and in came Sobers. Illingworth had laid a plan to dismiss Sobers which involved Knight giving him a wide half-volley, the reasoning being that Sobers would be unable to resist attacking it.

It had worked in the first Test at Old Trafford and again in the first innings at Headingley. Sobers moved right across to avoid edging the ball into the slips but so far across that he inside-edged it into his stumps and was out for nought.

Illingworth took Underwood out of the attack and came on himself to get rid of Clive Lloyd for 23 and with the gate open England waltzed through it to win a thrilling match by 30 runs. Sobers had been outmanoeuvred by a master tactician.

In 1970, with the South Africa series cancelled for political reasons, England played matches against a Rest of the World XI, one of which was at Leeds. It was a fine contest in which England made 222 thanks to 89 by Fletcher and 58 by Illingworth. Sobers smashed 114 to take the Rest to 376-9 declared and when England batted again the Kent opener Brian Luckhurst fell eight runs short of a century and Boycott, Fletcher and Illingworth all passed 50 in a total of 376.

The Rest squeezed home by two wickets, led by Sobers with 59 and Intikhab Alam with 54, but even Sobers was eclipsed by the South African Eddie Barlow, known as 'Bunter' because of his spectacles and stout frame, whose 12 wickets in the match included a hat-trick and four wickets in five balls.

Illingworth, aided by the brilliant batting of Boycott, led England to a magnificent Ashes victory in a tempestuous six-match series in Australia in 1970-1 and in the summer of 1971 presided over another win at Headingley, this time against Pakistan.

Boycott made 112 and figured in a big stand with D'Oliveira, who made 74, to take England to 316 but the tourists took a first-innings lead of 34 though consistent batting led by Zaheer Abbas and Mushtaq Mohammad and cemented by wicketkeeper Wasim Bari's 63 at No 8. Richard Hutton was also in the England side and bowled well to take three wickets along with D'Oliveira and Norman Gifford.

Both Boycott and Luckhurst failed in the second innings but Amiss and the reliable D'Oliveira made half-centuries and 45 from Illingworth proved crucial to the outcome as England lost their last five wickets for 16 runs to be all out for 264. Salim Altaf, a lively fast-medium bowler from Lahore who made two trips to England, did the damage with 4-11 from 14.3 overs.

The game was wide open and drifted away from England as the tourists reached 160-4 but spinners Illingworth and Gifford bowled effectively, D'Oliveira claimed the vital wicket of opener Sadiq for 91 and Lever ripped out the tail to finish with 3-10 from just 21 balls. England had won by 25 runs with Illingworth again holding his nerve in a crisis.

Illingworth was 40 when the 1972 series against Australia began and it produced some fine cricket as he held on to the Ashes with a 2-2 draw. Australia moaned about the pitch at Leeds for the fourth Test and when it ended at just after five o'clock on the third day bitter arguments ensued.

There were claims that it had been deliberately doctored to suit England's spinners, notably the lethal left-arm attack of Underwood, but the problems were put down to the fact that the pitch had fallen victim to an attack of fusarium disease, having been kept under covers because of heavy rain in the days leading up to the match.

Illingworth was not complaining. He was bowling in harness with the Kent man before lunch on the first day. He felt that it was a grafter's pitch, one well

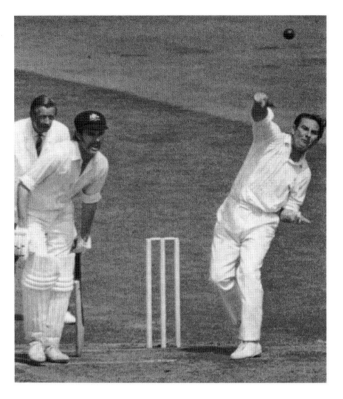

*Ray Illingworth led England to victory over Australia in the Headingley Test of 1972, taking four wickets with his off-breaks and top-scoring with 57 in the first-innings total of 263. Greg Chappell is the batsman awaiting developments.*

*A lucky escape for Keith Fletcher in the Headingley Test of 1974 as he edges to slip where Majid Khan not only misses the chance but seems to smack Shafiq Ahmed on the nose.*

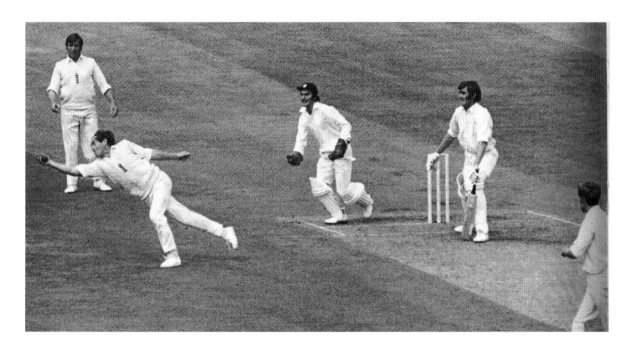

*Ray Illingworth shows his prowess as a fielder in the 1972 Ashes Test , pivoting to hold a superb one-handed catch to get rid off Paul Sheahan for nought, one of Derek Underwood's 10 wickets in the match.*

suited to the talents of Herbert Sutcliffe and Len Hutton in former times and to Boycott's at this time.

But Boycott was out injured and it was left to Illingworth himself to play the key innings of the game, toiling for four-and-a-half hours for 57 and adding an unlikely 104 with John Snow (48) for the eighth wicket. This lifted England to 263 in reply to Australia's 146, the disgruntled tourists having collapsed from 79-1 at lunch.

Australia were given little chance against the spinners in their second innings and so it

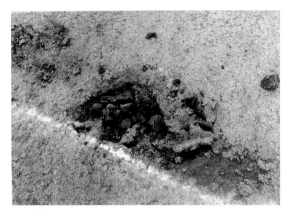

*There were always plenty of people ready to suggest that Headingley's Test pitch should be dug up but in 1975 'Free George Davis' campaigners took matters into their own hands, forcing the Ashes Test to be abandoned as a draw.*

transpired. After Ross Edwards had bagged a pair and their captain, Ian Chappell, had been caught behind the wicket for nought Underwood ripped through with a spell of 5-118, pushing the ball through quickly and gaining turn and lift. Paul Sheahan stood firm and played straight to make 41 not out but there was a resigned air about the rest of the batting and they were all out for 136, England winning by nine wickets.

Illingworth was put through a Test trial against Glamorgan's Tony Lewis before being confirmed in the post for the visit of New Zealand and the West Indies in 1973. The Leeds Test was against New Zealand and resulted in an innings win for the home side, for whom Boycott was in majestic form with 115. Fletcher made 81, Illingworth himself 65 and there were runs lower down the order too as England reached 419 in reply to New Zealand's 276.

Chris Old was their top bowler with 4-71 in the first innings and Geoff Arnold took over in the second with 5-27. New Zealand were shot out for 142 despite a fine 81 by their classy opener Glenn Turner and failed by one run to make England bat again.

This year also brought the first one-day international at the ground, against the West Indies in the Prudential Trophy, and after Old dismissed Sobers for a duck England scraped home by one wicket at 182-9 with Willis and Underwood at the crease. Rohan Kanhai top-scored for the West

*One of the more unusual pitch inspections in cricket history as hundreds of early arrivals mill around to view the damage in 1975.*

Indies with 55 and Mike Denness was England's best with 66.

Illingworth's 61-match Test career, 31 of which had been as captain, ended with a 2-0 defeat in the three-game series against the West Indies in that summer of 1973 and for the visit of Pakistan to Headingley the following season Denness was in charge. Boycott had played one Test against India in June and was not to be seen again for three years, leaving Old as Yorkshire's sole representative.

The weather, which took out the whole of the last day, ruined an evenly-poised contest. An innings of 75 by Majid Khan and 53 by No 10 batsman Sarfraz Nawaz lifted Pakistan to 285 and England struggled against Sarfraz and his new-ball colleague Asif Masood, who had a moustache and long black hair and was once referred to as Masif Asood by the BBC's Brian Johnston. They were all out for 183, David Lloyd top-scoring with 48.

The England seam trio of Old, Arnold and Mike Hendrick did the damage in the second innings, taking three wickets each as Pakistan made only 179. After both Lloyd and Amiss had failed, Edrich held his side together with 70, Denness made 44 and Fletcher was actually threatening to endear himself to the Leeds crowd as he reached 67 not out when the rain came with Old also at the crease and England needing 44 to win with four wickets intact.

Edrich, batting in the middle order, was at his

unruffled best in making 90 to steer England to a four-wicket win over India in the one-day Prudential Trophy game at Leeds that year after Old, Arnold and Jackman had bowled tidily.

The 1975 Ashes Test was also uncompleted but this time the last day was lost because of one of the most bizarre incidents in the history of the game. Yorkshire's committee felt that "outrage" was not too strong a word to describe the affair. With the match on a knife-edge at the end of the fourth day – Australia needed another 255 runs to win with seven wickets standing – the early-morning arrivals next day were dismayed to find that vandals had gouged the pitch and poured oil over it. It soon emerged that this was an act of protest against the imprisonment for armed robbery of one George Davis.

The pitch was beyond immediate repair and the match was abandoned, the only consolation being that the weather closed in anyway and would have prevented a positive result. Edrich found an equally steely partner in Northamptonshire's silver-haired David Steele, who had made 50 and 45 on his Test debut at Lord's in the previous Test and here added 112 for the second wicket with Edrich.

Gary Gilmour, a left-arm swing bowler and naturally gifted all-rounder, took 6-85 but a half-century by captain Tony Greig took England to 288. Australia had attacked with a four-pronged pace attack including Lillee and Thomson; England took a different route and Phil Edmonds, the Zambian-

*George Cawthray came to Headingley from The Circle, Hull, where he was both club professional and groundsman, and endured the trials and tribulations of a diseased pitch and a vandalised one before overseeing the preparation of his last Test match strip in 1978.*

born Middlesex left-arm spinner making his Test debut, took 5-17 in his first 12 overs.

So England took a lead of 153 and thanks mainly to Steele, who followed his 73 in the first innings with 92 before being one of three more victims for Gilmour, they reached 291, an apparently match-winning advantage.

But by the end of the fourth day no one could be so sure. After an opening stand of 55 Ian Chappell showed his class by peppering the boundary in a century stand at a run a minute with opener Rick McCosker. Though Chappell fell lbw to Old before the close, McCosker was still there with 95 and Walters was looking ominously assured.

Gilmour had already been England's destroyer that season in the first World Cup, though Australia had no answer to Clive Lloyd in the final. Headingley staged three games, Australia beating Pakistan and India accounting for East Africa before the semi-final between England and the Aussies.

The 'fusarium' Test and the George Davis affair had been freakish mishaps but on this occasion the pitch was not up to standard for a one-day international. Gilmour took a stunning 6-14 as England were shot out for 93 in 37 overs and the Australians were 39-6 before Gilmour joined forces with Walters to win the tie.

There was nothing wrong with the pitch for the 1976 Test against the West Indies. Roy Fredericks and Gordon Greenidge gave their side a magnificent start with a stand of 192, both making centuries. Viv Richards hit 66 and Lawrence Rowe 50 as the tourists raced to 437-9 on the first day on their way to 450 all out. Snow was England's best with 4-77.

This year was the first unveiling of the West Indian pace attack which was to terrorise world cricket. Roberts and Holding reduced England to 80-4 and Greig was struggling desperately, but at the start of his second spell Holding went lame and left the field.

Greig seized his chance, Alan Knott batted vivaciously and both hit centuries to take England to 387 and it looked as if this might be enough as England's own pace attack, spearheaded by Snow and Bob Willis, flattened the West Indians, who were all out for 196.

*West Indian jubilation at Headingley in 1976 as the slip cordon leaps to salute the dismissal of Alan Ward, caught behind the wicket off Michael Holding for a duck, as the tourists close in on victory.*

*Confusion and despair in the England ranks as Frank Hayes (foreground) misses a chance to run out Australia's Gary Gilmour (on the ground) in the Prudential World Cup semifinal at Headingley in 1975. Gilmour survived and with Doug Walters (far left) steered Australia to victory.*

*The Saturday of the Headingley Test of 1977 and huge queues form down Cardigan Road (left) and down towards the turnstiles in Kirkstall Lane.*

In the end, Collis King's 58 in that second innings proved decisive, for although Greig countered with a brave unbeaten 76 only two other English batsmen reached double figures against Roberts, Holding and Wayne Daniel and the West Indies clinched the series with a 55-run win.

In 1977 Boycott ended his self-imposed Test exile and returned to face Australia at Trent Bridge. There he batted for more than 12 hours in all, the only blemish being that in the process he ran out local hero Derek Randall. The Yorkshire Post's cricket correspondent Terry Brindle wrote that immediately after this error the Nottingham crowd were ready to throw Boycott in the River Trent; by the end of his innings they were convinced that he could have walked across it.

He made 107, his 99th century, and 80 not out. It is a measure of the greatness of his batsmanship that when fate beckoned in the next Test at Headingley he answered the call. No matter what the controversies surrounding his captaincy of Yorkshire, there was room for nothing but unbounded admiration for the supreme achievement of fashioning his 100th century in a Test match against the oldest enemy in front of his own crowd.

They had queued since early morning in the hope of seeing it and expectations rose when Mike Brearley won the toss. He had taken over at the helm from Greig, who stayed in the side but was stripped of the captaincy when it was discovered that he had been a 'secret agent' for the Packer Circus, formally called World Series Cricket.

The gates were shut well before the start on the first two days. Brearley was caught behind off Thomson without a run on the board but Boycott wrapped himself in a cast-iron shell of concentration, reaching the landmark with a trademark on-drive. The reaction around the ground was a mixture of pride, sober but heartfelt admiration and wild jubilation.

Though the ball quite frequently beat the bat it was England's first day. Boycott was 110 out of 252-4. Surrey's Graham Roope, later to live in Yorkshire and become a club cricketer, had a fine career of his own but will best be remembered in these parts for being the man at the other end when Boycott did it.

Progress was sedate on the second day as Knott joined the Yorkshireman in another productive stand. Boycott tired and scored only 30 between lunch and tea and was eventually last man out for 191 having batted for more than 10 hours, a triumph of skill and will under a weight of expectation that surely ought to have been too much for a mere mortal.

While Boycott's star reached its zenith, a meteor called Ian Terence Botham was about to hit an unsuspecting world. Born in Cheshire but a Somerset lad from the age of three, he had made his Test debut in Boycott's comeback game at Nottingham and taken five wickets in the first innings.

He and Hendrick wrecked Australia at Leeds and they were 67-5 at the end of day two, McCosker having been run out by Randall when he backed up too far. Botham completed the job the following day to claim 5-21 in 11 overs. He was unsuccessful in the second innings, but Hendrick took four more wickets, Willis captured his 100th in Tests and, after a defiantly aggressive 63 from Marsh, Australia were all out for 248, losers by an innings and 85 runs. The Ashes had been recaptured in Jubilee year and for the first time at Headingley.

Old and Botham shared eight wickets in the rain-ruined draw with Pakistan in 1978. Sadiq made 97 of Pakistan's 201 and Sarfraz took 5-39 as the home side struggled to 119-7 in the action that was possible.

It was even worse against India the following year, when two entire days went down the drain, though there was time for Botham to show the batting prowess that would make him one of Headingley's heroes. With the game going nowhere, he thrilled the small band of spectators by smashing 99 runs in a pre-lunch session and went on to make 137 out of England's 270. Sunil Gavaskar, the brilliant Indian opener, and the tall, elegant Dilip Vengsarkar, made 78 and 65 not out respectively to take the tourists to 223-6.

Leeds staged three games in the 1979 World Cup but not this time a semi-final, which went to Old Trafford. England reached the final but were blasted to defeat by Viv Richards as the West Indies retained the Prudential Cup.

At Headingley Pakistan were easy winners against Canada and New Zealand beat India by eight wickets thanks to an unbeaten 84 by Bruce Edgar. England were engaged in a low-scoring affair against Pakistan, grinding their way to 165 in 60 overs but then bowling their opponents out for 151, Hendrick taking 4-15 and gaining support from an unusual source, Boycott, who took 2-14.

David Bairstow joined Old and Boycott in the one-day side for the Prudential Trophy match with the West Indies at Leeds in 1980. The tourists, fuelled by Greenidge's 78, reached 198 and England lost by 24 runs despite a fine unbeaten 82 from Kent's Chris Tavare, who was to develop a reputation as a solid if rather dull opening batsman but in fact was

capable of devastating one-day innings, as Yorkshire found to their cost.

In a break from normal tradition, Headingley staged the final Test of the West Indies series but the occasion was again spoiled by bad weather, which took out the first and fourth days. The groundstaff worked wonders to get play started on the second day but England regretted it as they were put in and shot out for 143. The pace personnel had changed – now it was Holding, Colin Croft, Joel Garner and Malcolm Marshall – but the outcome was the same. The spectators were cheered, however, by an innings of 40 from Bairstow.

Only Desmond Haynes did any better for the tourists, who were restricted to a lead of 102 as Graham Dilley, a 6ft 3in blond-haired fast bowler from Kent, took four wickets. England were 22 without loss going into the last day and occupied the crease to reach 227-6 at the close, Boycott and Graham Gooch putting on 95 for the first wicket and Brian Rose, the Somerset left-hander, finishing unbeaten on 43.

Wherever and whenever Headingley is mentioned the figures 1981 are bound to follow in the next breath. Thanks to Botham, cricket grabbed the headlines on front as well as back pages. If

*Some spectators were unable to contain their excitement over Geoff Boycott's 100th century and invaded the pitch to mob their hero, while others shouted from the rooftops.*

*Above: With the BBC's Peter West poised for an interview, Geoff Boycott raises his glass to acknowledge the cheers of the crowd following his 100th hundred in 1977.*

*Right: Boycott watches the replay of his moment of destiny, the stroke which took him to his 100th century.*

*Below: They gathered in their thousands in 1977 to salute Boycott's moment of destiny as he became the first batsman in history to score his 100th century in a Test match, his monumental 191 paving the way for an innings win over Australia.*

*Below Right: A man for whom success brought with it intense personal problems, Boycott found it hard to sustain a sympathetic relationship with the public and media but the Yorkshire crowd left him in no doubt about their feelings in 1977.*

everyone who claims to have witnessed the denouement had actually been there the final-day crowd would have been about 120,000.

At about 3pm on the fourth day you could have 500-1 against England winning. Indeed, some of the Australian players did just that, in a fascinating side-issue which may have been entirely innocent at the time but which 20 years later would have had Sir Paul Condon knocking on a few doors.

England, following on, were 135-7 and still 92 runs adrift. John Dyson had scored a maiden century, captain Kim Hughes 89 and Graham Yallop 58 in Australia's 401-9 declared. Botham kept going to take 6-95 but the rest of the English seam attack performed poorly on a pitch offering them some encouragement. This was highlighted when England folded to 174 all out against Lillee, Geoff Lawson and Terry Alderman.

Gooch was out for the second time in the day and on the fourth afternoon the home team drifted into worse trouble. Boycott fought the good fight, resisting for three-and-a-half hours in making 46 before falling lbw to Alderman, but when Bob Taylor was seventh out England were on their knees. The spectators – and indeed the players – were resigned to a humbling defeat inside four days.

Dilley came in with only one theory, that there was nothing more to lose, and belted away to smite 56 in the next 80 minutes. By the time he was bowled by Alderman, England were 25 runs ahead. Statistically, this was still a palsied state to be in, but Dilley's belligerence in that partnership of 117 seemed to convince Botham that he had it in his power to reinvent the game.

He found another ally in Yorkshire's Chris Old, who could count this as his finest hour as an England batsman. He scored a modest 29 runs, but his resistance allowed Botham to take full command. The game was now beyond figures, for the psychological balance was shifting. Even the all-rounder's miscues reached the boundary, at times Australia seemed to have only three fielders, one of whom might as well have been posted in the confectionery stall.

His second 50 came in 40 minutes, his century from 87 balls. On a grey Leeds afternoon this bare-headed batsman drove, pulled, carved and hooked to bring some sunshine back into English cricket. The Australians did not know what to do, so they just waited and hoped. When Lawson bowled Old the lead was up to 92. When stumps were drawn at the end of one of the greatest cricketing days Botham was 145, having hit 106 in the final session.

*Yorkshire's great batting triumvirate of Geoff Boycott, Herbert Sutcliffe and Len Hutton meet up at Headingley during the 1977 Test match.*

When Willis was out early on the last morning Botham was left untamed on 149 with a six and 27 fours and Australia needed 130 to win. It should in all logic have been a formality even on a testing batting pitch but they were a mentally scarred team.

The fourth-day crowd had witnessed batting display of sheer genius. The few thousand who turned up on the final day, more out of a sense of duty than with real hope for England, were to see one of the great exhibitions of fast bowling.

Australia were 56-1 when Willis began bowling with the wind from the Kirkstall Lane end. He ran down the slope like a man possessed, bowling fast and straight and achieving wicked lift. In a few minutes before lunch he had Trevor Chappell, Hughes and Yallop caught, England responding to his all-out attack with some inspired fielding.

Australia, most of their batsmen either frozen or in a blind panic in the face of this force of nature, crashed to 75-8 but Lillee and Ray Bright clubbed 35 off four overs. Then Lillee chipped a ball from Willis to mid-on where Gatting plunged forward to hold the catch. Nearly making a crisis out of the drama, Old missed two chances offered by Alderman off Botham but Willis finished it with a yorker.

*Ian Botham displays the sweet power that made him one of the great all-rounders and entertainers in cricket, notably at Headingley in 1981.*

*Dennis Lillee took 39 wickets in the six-Test series of 1981 and at Headingley claims that of Ian Botham, caught by wicketkeeper Rodney Marsh for 50 in the first innings. Botham exacted glorious revenge in the second innings.*

England had won by 18 runs, only the second team in Test history to do so after following on. Sadly, with the whole country wanting to celebrate, their immediate reaction was one of surly hostility to the Press, who had dared to draw attention to the side's inadequacies in the first three-and-a-half days.

It was Boycott's last Test appearance at Leeds. He made an immaculate 137 in the last match of that Ashes series, and another century, his 22nd for England, in Delhi on the following winter's tour to India. But he returned home early, apparently ill, only to re-emerge as one of the leading figures on a rebel tour to South Africa which brought a three-year ban from the TCCB. His 108-match Test career was over. It was as brilliant and as controversial as his relationship with his county. Boycott was never better than when he felt personally attacked and his ability to respond with big innings was a measure of the man.

In the sporting context it was a tragedy that he was so often enmeshed in webs of intrigue and in-fighting, sometimes spun by his own well-meaning supporters.

Botham, meanwhile, disproved the notion that his Headingley heroics were a one-off by doing something similar in the next two games at Edgbaston and Old Trafford.

In the Prudential Trophy game that same year Australia trounced England by 71 runs. Graeme Wood's century was the backbone of their 236-8, spiced by Yallop's 48, and Peter Willey with 42 was the only home batsman to make any impact as Rodney Hogg took 4-29.

England were much too good for India in the one-day international of 1982. Botham took 4-56 as they were dismissed for 193, the one pocket of Indian dominance coming in an innings of 60 by Kapil Dev. England won by nine wickets with nearly five overs to spare as Barry Wood and Tavare put on 133.

The 1982 Test match was a tense affair against a Pakistan side led by another of the world's great all-rounders, Imran Khan, and packed with gifted batsmen.

Headingley was by this time increasingly a pitch for seam, which nullified the threat of leg-spinner Abdul Qadir. Willis, the new captain, used it efficiently with Botham and Jackman to bowl out Pakistan for 275, their innings sustained by unbeaten 67 by Imran after opener Mudassar Nazar (with the slowest Test hundred already behind him) had made 65 and Javed Miandad 54.

Imran bowled beautifully in the conditions to take 5-49 (Qadir had 1-87 from only 22 overs) as England struggled in reply. They lost their first four wickets for 77 before David Gower, who had failed to get beyond 39 on his previous three Test appearances at Leeds, countered with 74 and shared in a rescuing stand with Botham, who hit 57.

That took England to 256 all out and having seen Botham's batting at its destructive best the previous year the Leeds crowd now saw the bowler in action as he took 5-74 in 30 overs. Willis removed both openers and although there was resistance from Javed (52) and Imran (46) they both fell to Botham as the tourists crumbled to 199 all out.

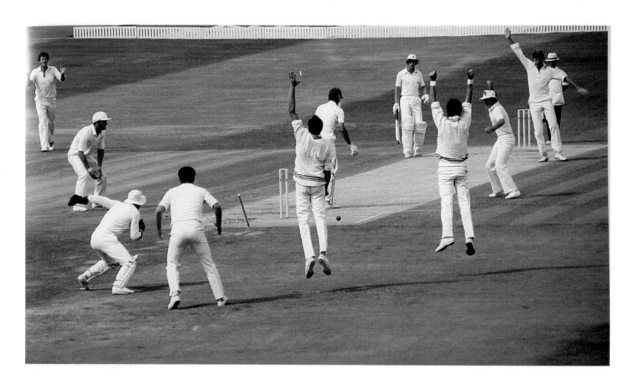

*Chris Tavare is bowled by Ewen Chatfield during New Zealand's first Test victory in England.*

That left England to make 219 to win, a testing assignment on such a pitch, and their three-wicket success owed everything to Test debutant Graeme Fowler, the jaunty and adhesive Lancashire left-hander who had taken advantage of the TCCB bans imposed on Boycott, Gooch and others to force his way into the side.

Fowler made a fine 86 and shared in an opening stand of 103 with Tavare to give England the ideal platform. Once they had been parted the home team struggled desperately against Imran and the medium-pace swing of Mudassar, who took 4-55, but were steered to victory by wicketkeeper Bob Taylor and another debutant, Somerset's off-spinner Vic Marks.

From the early stages of the match Pakistan were a bowler short, Ehtesham-Ud-Din having been summoned into the Test match from the Bolton League. He was overweight and unfit and after bowling 14 overs pulled a muscle in the field, taking no further part.

Since the mid-60s the West Indies (twice) had been the only Test team to win at Leeds but that changed dramatically in 1983 when New Zealand gained their first Test victory on English soil at the 29th attempt, by a five-wicket margin.

This was a strong New Zealand side inspired by their prodigious fast-bowling all-rounder Richard Hadlee, but this match belonged to the less gifted but equally determined Lance Cairns. With his open-chested action and hopping approach, Cairns ripped through England's first innings to take 7-74 in 33.2 overs, only Tavare (69), Allan Lamb (58) and Botham (38) coming to terms with his swing and cut. They were bowled out for 225 after losing the toss.

Edgar was injured early on in his innings but returned to hit a brave 84; Wright, his opening partner, made 93; Hadlee, though wicketless in 47 overs in the match, showed what a punishing No 7 batsman he could be with a priceless 75. Cairns chipped in with an unbeaten 24 and all this gave New Zealand a lead of 152.

Ewan Chatfield, who had nearly died on his Test debut against England in Auckland in 1974-5 when he was struck on the temple by a ball from Peter Lever – he was given heart massage and mouth-to-mouth resuscitation by England's physio Bernard Thomas – removed both openers early in England's second innings but the home side were sustained by a superb unbeaten 112 by Gower.

Sadly, he had no support as Chatfield went on to take 5-95 and Cairns claimed another three wickets for a 10-wicket match haul. They were all out for 252 and although Willis bowled venomously to take all five wickets to fall in New Zealand's second innings at a personal cost of only 35 runs there was to be no repeat of his 1981 heroics as the tourists reached their holy grail at 103-5.

The 1983 World Cup, the last sponsored by Prudential, was again 60 overs a side but the teams played each other twice in the group stages. India emerged as shock winners over the West Indies in the final and Headingley staged three games.

Winston Davis, a lithe and whippy fast bowler from St Vincent who would have played more Test cricket but for the depth of talent in this department in the 80s, demolished Australia with 7-51 to set up a 101-run win for the West Indies, for whom Larry Gomes made 78. Imran Khan made a

brilliant 102 not out for Pakistan, who were nevertheless run close by Sri Lanka before Abdul Qadir clinched an 11-run win.

England hammered the Sri Lankans by nine wickets, bowling them out for 136 and knocking off the runs in 24.1 overs thanks to an unbeaten 81 by Fowler. But for some time there had been growing anxiety about the state of the square at Headingley, where low, slow pitches of uneven bounce were with other factors such as poor spectator facilities and crowd behaviour problems on the Western Terrace to threaten its future as a Test venue.

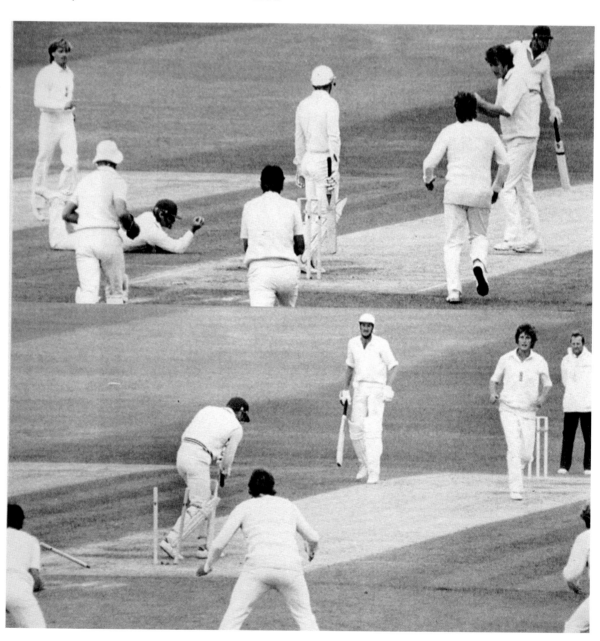

*Allan Lamb plunged forward to hold a bat-pad catch to dismiss Martin Crowe and give Bob Willis his 299th Test wicket at Headingley in 1983 and later, with New Zealand pressing for their first win in England, Willis uproots Jeff Crowe's middle stump to reach 300.*

*Martin Crowe, in the white helmet, turns away in delight after taking a short-leg catch to dismiss Norman Cowans off Lance Cairns to end England's second innings at Headingley in 1983, their first Test victory on English soil.*

*More New Zealand joy as Bob Taylor is bowled by Cairns for nine in England's second innings in 1983.*

# Chapter Eleven

# Yorkshire 1984-2001

JUST as Ray Illingworth could claim that the course of his reign as manager would have been different had Yorkshire won their 1979 Benson & Hedges Cup semi-final at Chelmsford, so David Bairstow's fate as a captain probably hinged on one incident in his first season.

The new captain found himself in the bizarre position of having a committee man in his team, Geoffrey Boycott having taken his share of the plunder from the revolution by winning the Wakefield seat from Dr John Turner, who was thought to be in his camp anyway. One setback to the pro-Boycott faction was the election of Close, never as far as we know a paid-up member of the fan club.

Off the field, the club had two years previously committed itself to a 40 per cent share of the £130,000 needed for a new bar, named after Sir Leonard Hutton, at the back of the football stand and in 1984 the committee announced that in the following year nine hospitality boxes would be built atop the winter shed.

These were belated efforts to drag Headingley into the modern era of corporate sponsorship and spectator comforts, for in this year also the TCCB informed Yorkshire that its status as the only permanent Test venue outside London would be removed and that it would not stage a Test match in 1990.

On the field Yorkshire gave a tantalising hint that their troubles might be over by storming to the

Benson & Hedges semis, where they met Warwickshire in front of a full house at Headingley.

On a fine batting track the visitors piled up 276-4 through Alvin Kallicharran's rapier thrusts, which brought him 85 runs, and some beefy blows from Geoff Humpage, who clubbed an unbeaten 58. Graham Stevenson was the bowler to suffer most, conceding 70 runs in his 11 overs.

Boycott went early but Martyn Moxon held the innings together with a half-century, Kevin Sharp made a scintillating 83 and when Bairstow and Stevenson joined forces to add 71 in 10 overs Yorkshire had Lord's in sight. The captain then swung Gladstone Small into the outfield where Paul Smith emerged from a headlong tumble with the ball in his hands. Warwickshire's players screamed their delight; the home crowd groaned and fell silent. Yorkshire lost by three runs.

In the Sunday League they lost to Essex despite Ashley Metcalfe's 71 and were also beaten by Glamorgan but the championship season at Leeds had started well with an exciting six-run win over Nottinghamshire. Boycott, Sharp and Bairstow all made half-centuries in Yorkshire's 301-5 declared, bad weather forced both captains into further declarations and Nottinghamshire were set to make 301 for victory in 77 overs. They had reached 294 when Simon Dennis bowled last man Kevin Cooper, he and Arnie Sidebottom taking four wickets each.

Cracks were appearing in the side's make-up by the time Lancashire arrived for the Roses match at the

*Improvements at Headingley have taken place on a piecemeal basis in recent years, one example being the extensive refurbishment of the new pavilion, the design of which has drawn as much criticism as praise.*

end of May. Yorkshire were bowled out for 188 as Paul Allott kept the new ball well up and took 6-31, Bairstow managing a counter-attack with three sixes and eight fours in his 62.

Graeme Fowler made his second Roses hundred a year to the day after the first and put on 159 for the first wicket with Alan Ormrod (60) but after the loss of the second day to rain Lancashire showed little enterprise. They eventually declared at 288-7, Sidebottom taking 4-50, but left themselves too little time to drive home the advantage. Yorkshire closed on 16-2.

A month later Yorkshire, sorely hit by injuries, suffered their biggest hiding at Leeds – by an innings and 153 runs – at the hands of a strong Essex side. They were rolled over for 183 and 188, John Lever taking eight wickets and West Indian Norbert Phillip seven. Graham Gooch with 131 led Essex's charge to 524-7 declared, backed up by Ken McEwan's 68 and a century from Keith Fletcher. No one took liberties with Steve Oldham but Paul Jarvis and left-arm spinner Paul Booth were flogged.

Old boy Chris Old returned to torment his native county later in the season as Warwickshire won by 191 runs. Old hit 52 to supplement Humpage's 112 as the visitors reached 285 and in 29 overs of high-class bowling he took 5-53 as Yorkshire folded to 153 all out.

Humpage then blasted another 77 to enable his side to declare on 242-7 and Old ripped through them again with 6-46, though even he was unable to dislodge Boycott as the opener carried his bat for 55.

At the end of October Close resigned as cricket chairman. He was opposed to Boycott's dual role (though at one stage he suggested that he should be reinstated as captain for 1985 under his direction), at loggerheads with chairman Kirk and suspicious that Bairstow was clinging too firmly to Boycott's coat-tails. He claimed that he was being outvoted at every turn by a pro-Boycott committee and quit after a move to persuade Bairstow to give up the gloves failed, the result of which was that richly-promising Bradford wicketkeeper Steve Rhodes left for Worcestershire.

Close returned to the committee but layman Tony Vann took over as cricket chairman in 1985 while Viscount Mountgarret filled the presidential vacancy. A landowner near Ripon, he had been educated at Eton and served in the Irish Guards. Some members may have been inclined to regard him as a "posh twit" but he succeeded in marrying the need for leadership with due regard for democracy and became a firm favourite with the membership, if not ultimately with his committee.

There was more spending at Headingley, £23,000 on a club shop behind the scoreboard and £70,000 on replacing the remaining wooden seats, but revival on the field remained wishful thinking.

They started with another thrilling win, this time by two runs over Middlesex. With Boycott injured, Sidebottom opened and showed good technique to make 55 and Phil Robinson, a strong and attack-minded strokemaker from Keighley, hit 62 in their 304-9 declared.

Wilf Slack and Paul Downton replied strongly with an opening stand of 116 before Middlesex pulled out at 225-2 and then Wayne Daniel with 3-19 and Norman Cowans sent Yorkshire crashing to 135 all out. Middlesex needed 215 in 60 overs and Slack, out for 99, put them on course, but Sharp gave Yorkshire hope by running out Mike Gatting and Sidebottom and Jarvis each took three wickets to give them the verdict in a tense finale.

The other games were drawn, Moxon and Richard Blakey, a stylish top-order batsman from Elland, putting on 223 against Somerset, a match in which Boycott and Viv Richards also made centuries.

Moxon showed his class with 127 spanning more

than six hours in a mundane Roses match in which Keighley's Peter Hartley took 5-91 and there were rain-hit stalemates against Northamptonshire and the Australian tourists, for whom Graeme Wood made 102 not out and whose side included fast bowler Craig McDermott, later to be Yorkshire's prime target as an overseas professional.

The NatWest tie against Somerset produced a four-wicket defeat and nasty repercussions. Neil Hartley made 69 to lift Yorkshire to 208-8 and with Somerset on 83-4 Richards appeared to walk for a catch behind the wicket. He came back to hit a match-winning unbeaten 87 and in a radio interview after the tie Ian Botham accused a section of the crowd of racial taunts against the West Indian.

It provoked a row between chairman Kirk and president Mountgarret, who had differing views as to how it should be settled, and their fall-out became permanent when Kirk opposed, and then resigned over, the package of rule changes overseen by the president, which after more legal wrangling was passed overwhelmingly by the membership at the 1986 annual meeting. One of the new rules was that no player could serve on the committee once present contracts (ie Boycott's) expired.

The following year, 1987, would be a benefit year for the club to raise money towards the estimated £500,000 cost of a new eight-lane indoor school to be built over the road in St Michael's Lane, with backing from local authorities. While more and more attention was devoted to Headingley – since 1982 the club had spent £325,000 on improvements with a similar amount from Leeds CF & A Co Ltd – Bradford Park Avenue had fallen into such

*Youngsters take advantage of Yorkshire's new indoor school facility in St Michael's Lane in 1987.*

*Keith Boyce, who became used to back-breaking spadework in his time as Headingley groundsman, goes to work on the Test pitch in 1986 before relaying it with specially-treated soil. "I am glad to see the back of it," he said, but his troubles were not over.*

disrepair that in 1986 its fixtures were transferred to Leeds.

With Close back in the cricket chair the side made a heady start to the 1986 season, beating Sussex by one wicket at Headingley. Neil Lenham made 75 out of Sussex's 195, Yorkshire forfeited an innings, Sussex then declared on 55-1 and the home side, needing 251 to win, were heading for defeat at 100-6 and 140-7.

But Carrick, now vice-captain, made 51 and Stevenson a quickfire half-century off 36 balls. Yorkshire were 219 when their ninth wicket fell and Jarvis marched in to join Stevenson. The winning hit was a boundary that was a chance to wicketkeeper Ian Gould.

Jarvis, a slim fast bowler from Redcar who on his day could test the best but whose achievements were curtailed by frequent breakdowns, took early wickets in the Roses match as Lancashire slumped to 47-5. They recovered to 296 thanks to a maiden first-class century by wicketkeeper Chris Maynard and a lusty 65 from Allott after being 131-7.

Yorkshire batted solidly in reply, Carrick fashioning another 50 in their total of 314. Gehan Mendis held Lancashire's second innings together with 62 and, set to make 251, the home side settled for a draw at 90-1.

Carrick came to the rescue against Warwickshire, putting on an unbroken 98 with Peter Hartley (61 not out) to take Yorkshire to a draw after they had been reduced to 56-7 in search of a target of 287. Earlier, there were centuries from South African Brian McMillan, opener Andy Lloyd and Kevin Sharp.

Boycott scored his 150th century at Middlesbrough to surpass Herbert Sutcliffe's total but Yorkshire as a team remained stubbornly mediocre, though Surrey were beaten at Leeds by seven wickets. Alec Stewart made 90 in Surrey's 269 but Boycott, in his last match-winning innings for the county, made 135 not out with a broken bone in his hand.

He and Sharp, who made 76, gave Yorkshire a handy lead which Jarvis turned into victory with 7-55, Surrey's shining success being Grahame Clinton, who carried his bat for 84. There was plenty of 'Ash panache' against Glamorgan as Metcalfe celebrated the award of his cap with 149 in a draw and Dennis and the wholehearted Stuart Fletcher took all 10 Middlesex wickets in another rain-ruined game, though not that of Slack, who opened and walked off unbeaten on 105.

Gould, the Sussex captain, complained about a 'dangerous' pitch used for a NatWest Trophy tie and did so from a position of strength having made

88 of his team's total of 213-7 in 60 overs. The umpires agreed and reported it as unfit. The target was well out of Yorkshire's range, though Carrick followed his 0-22 in 12 overs with 54 runs.

In the Sunday League, Jarvis took 4-13 in the win over Worcestershire, Bill Athey returned to make a match-winning 74 for Gloucestershire and there was a tie against Warwickshire, Yorkshire failing to get six off the final over.

It was the last season for Boycott, who was re-elected to Yorkshire's committee. The gods refused to smile on his last game at Scarborough. He was run out for 61, which to some was the supreme irony, to others just plain funny. It left him eight runs short of 1,000 for the season and Northamptonshire, forced to follow on, batted through September 12 to deprive him of a second chance to get them.

Lord Mountgarret was wont to sign his addresses to the membership 'Floreat Eboracum' and in 1987 it looked as if at last he might see that wish fulfilled.

Bairstow, his mind sometimes in a whirl, his hands in a mess but his bristling enthusiasm undiminished, had led a series of uphill cavalry charges for three years but was replaced as captain by Carrick, a less ebullient but more thoughtful cricketer. Bairstow took on a supporting role with admirable gusto.

The result was that Yorkshire won the Benson & Hedges Cup, which at the turn of the millennium remained their last trophy. For quite a chunk of the season it looked as if they might win the championship, too, but it proved beyond their staying power and the season ended in anticlimax.

"There has been much excitable comment about the pitch, some of it bordering upon the hysterical," said chairman Brian Walsh. Perhaps so, but Yorkshire were worried enough about the Test pitch that in mid-season they gave the square a bit of a hammering with a heavy roller which, along with the bore-draw pitches at Scarborough, blunted the attack in the second half of the campaign.

Headingley was their Cup fortress. After winning at Edgbaston, they trounced Lancashire there by 75 runs with Metcalfe stroking 84, Worcestershire were squeezed out by 12 runs with Sidebottom bowling beautifully for 4-15 in 11 overs and in the last eight Hampshire were swept aside by nine wickets, Metcalfe again blazing the trail with 93 not out.

The semi-final against Surrey was a protracted three-day affair, Moxon contributing 97 to Yorkshire's 238-7 and Love dishing out a fearful

flogging to David 'Teddy' Thomas, who went for 70 in eight overs. The formula for success was based on a seam attack of Jarvis, Sidebottom, Peter Hartley and Fletcher supplemented by Carrick's slow left-arm, which may not have been in the same class as some of his predecessors but which he had honed to the demands of one-day cricket.

Pitches were left open to the elements in 1987 but as the bowlers' run-ups were still covered it was a half-cock experiment which was soon abandoned.

By the time Yorkshire beat Northamptonshire in unforgettable tension at Lord's on July 11 they had just suffered two away championship defeats which spoiled a start which brought victories over Hampshire and Essex at Leeds.

Moxon made 98 in Yorkshire's 286-8 declared and on a pitch of unreliable bounce Hampshire were skittled for 148 despite a half-century by Greenidge. Yorkshire in turn struggled, Malcolm Marshall and Cardigan Connor bowling them out for 124, which left Hampshire to make 263 to win. Their attempt was gallant in the conditions but Jarvis and Fletcher, with seven wickets apiece in the match, worked their way through to seal a 15-run win.

Peter Roebuck broke a finger on another pitch of uneven bounce but hit a brave and classy 112 for Somerset. Blakey retired hurt when 16 but resumed his innings only to fall lbw to Vic Marks one run short of a century as Yorkshire took a lead of 70. Marks made 63 not out in Somerset's 229-9 declared and Yorkshire had a dash at making 160 in 17 overs but closed on a frantic 74-7, Adrian Jones having taken 5-31.

Essex were beaten by nine wickets, failing to reach 200 in either innings. To show that it was not all down to the seamers, Carrick took 4-10 in 12.3

*At the start of the 1987 season President Viscount Mountgarret presented Ted Lester with a pair of binoculars to mark 40 years of service to the club as player, Second XI captain and scorer*

*Headingley's groundsman keeps this 'Boyce belter' under covers in preparation for the Ashes Test match of 1989.*

overs in their first innings and 0-8 in 16 overs in the second. Moxon put his side in control with 104 and near the end of June Yorkshire were top of the table.

Despite being 91 adrift on first innings, Glamorgan escaped with a draw thanks to two unbeaten innings by Rodney Ontong and Lancashire arrived to find a pitch that had been flattened under 15 tons to eradicate uneven bounce. It succeeded, but Yorkshire couldn't despite a 6-64 return by Hemsworth's Chris Shaw. Only 12 wickets fell in the match and none at all on the last day as Mendis, Atherton, Moxon and Metcalfe proved how effectively the pitch had been tamed.

A sequence of draws was broken by a 44-run win over Gloucestershire but each side forfeited an innings after the loss of the first day to rain. The square was under official scrutiny from the TCCB's pitch inspector, who at the end of the season gave it the nod for Test cricket. Blakey became the club's youngest player to score a double century as he made 204 not out but Gloucestershire, inspired by Athey's unbeaten 101, looked capable of reaching a target of 364 as the former Yorkshire batsman and Jeremy Lloyds took them to 269-4. Then Jarvis tore through in fading light to take 7-82.

Metcalfe hit 73 and Sharp 50 in the NatWest Trophy quarter-final against Leicestershire but had little support and Phil DeFreitas took 5-34 in his side's 36-run win. In the Sunday League Love again took a liking to Thomas's bowling for Surrey, thrashing an unbeaten 118 as the bowler this time went for 64 runs in eight overs.

The 1988 season marked the start of an experiment with some four-day matches, a foretaste of things to come. Yorkshire did not take to it and made their worst start to a championship season in their history.

Derbyshire took only three of the four days to win by five wickets on another unpredictable pitch. Moxon was the only Yorkshire batsman to top 50 in the match and Paul Newman was their destroyer in the second innings with 8-29 from 16.5 overs.

The batting was no better in three-day cricket and Yorkshire followed totals of 161 and 192 against Derbyshire with 163 and 123 against Warwickshire, who completed the double for the first time since 1951 with a seven-wicket win set up by South African Allan Donald's nine wickets and ensured by Asif Din's composed 77 in the second innings after the visitors had collapsed to 81 all out in their first.

There was some respite with a four-wicket success

over Leicestershire but this was another result created by forfeitures. Peter Willey made a painstaking 104 in Leicestershire's 253, in which Carrick strangled them with 5-46 in 33.5 overs. The captain had tried Ian Swallow, an off-spinner from Sheffield, as an opening batsman and Blakey had been dropped, but he returned in this game to make 51 and a half-century from Love took Yorkshire to the target.

The highlight was a thumping 10-wicket win in the Roses match as Lancashire crumbled twice against the accurate seam bowling of Sidebottom, Hartley, Fletcher and Shaw. At one stage Sidebottom took 4-4 in 21 balls. Lancashire lost the menacing Wasim Akram, their Pakistani overseas star, with a groin strain but Allott bowled well despite a foot injury to claim five wickets, not enough to prevent Yorkshire from taking a substantial lead thanks to 77 by Love and gritty batting own the order from Sidebottom and Carrick.

Lancashire batted ineptly in their second innings and Yorkshire claimed the extra half-hour to complete an easy two-day win and end a sequence of 12 Roses draws since the 1982 season.

The four-day game against Middlesex produced a high-scoring draw with only 18 wickets falling while 1,285 runs were scored. Metcalfe accepted the riches on offer from an uncommonly good batting track with 216 not out in the first innings and an unbeaten 78 in the second. Slack made 75 and 83 for Middlesex and, set to make 334 to win, they seemed to be cruising at 285-4. But panic manifested itself in rash shots and bad running between the wickets and they ended 12 runs short with the last pair, Cowans and Keith Brown, at the crease.

Moxon and Sharp hit centuries in another draw against the Sri Lankan tourists but there was more NatWest misery at Leeds as Middlesex, with 74 from Gatting and 4-34 by Angus Fraser, won by 37 runs despite Shaw's fine 4-29 and Love's 67 for Yorkshire.

The 1989 season, Carrick's third and last as captain, started with an injury crisis which forced Oldham, who had been leading the Second XI, to return to first-team duty. The efforts of those who refused to see Park Avenue's cricket field go the same way as the football ground, notably Bob Appleyard, were rewarded when an Academy of Excellence was opened on the eve of the Headingley Test match.

Yorkshire, though now go-ahead in their schemes to develop young talent, remained steadfastly traditionalist in their attitude to first-class cricket and came out strongly against four-day cricket and

in favour of a return to three-day games on uncovered pitches.

Even three-day cricket seemed like wishful thinking as Nottinghamshire won at 2.23pm on the second day at Headingley where the genial West Indian Franklyn Stephenson, who at the end of the previous season had scored a century in each innings and taken 11 wickets in Yorkshire's win at Trent Bridge, this time took 13 wickets as Yorkshire folded to 92 and 109. Young seam bowler Ian Priestley took 4-27 on emergency debut as Nottinghamshire were shot out for 86 but Chris Broad and Tim Robinson could not be parted in the second innings.

Yorkshire batted more solidly against Derbyshire, with half-centuries by Moxon, Metcalfe, Sharp and Swallow, but rain and an innings of 70 by John Morris enabled the visitors to escape with a draw. Metcalfe hit 113 and Blakey 97 in the drawn game with Glamorgan but Middlesex were three-wicket winners, despite another fine innings of 81 from Metcalfe. They did not reach 200 in either innings and Mark Ramprakash's 128 proved decisive, though on a deteriorating track Middlesex were grateful for Gatting's nerve and experience in steering them to victory at 75-7.

Metcalfe made another century in the draw with Warwickshire and 95 by David Byas, a farmer from Kilham, near Driffield, who had joined the club in the turbulent year of 1985 and made a duck on first-class debut against Glamorgan at Leeds the following year, took the total to 426-9 declared. Warwickshire were made to follow on but saved the game easily on an easy pitch as Neil Smith made 161 and Asif Din 82 not out.

The NatWest Trophy win over Scotland, by just three wickets, was notable for an entry which read 'Sidebottom c and b Snodgrass 0' and in the Benson & Hedges Cup, where Yorkshire failed to qualify from their group, they lost to a Somerset side inspired by Jimmy Cook and Tavare but beat Derbyshire, Metcalfe answering Kim Barnett's 101 with 77.

They won all three Sunday League games at Headingley that year but lost in a one-day game against the Australians by 109 runs, only Moxon (55) and Bairstow (46) making any riposte to a brilliant 172 by David Boon and 89 not out from Dean Jones.

As if to show that old habits die hard, in January 1990 there was a night of the long knives at Headingley as Viscount Mountgarret was ousted from the presidency by his committee, who had taken against his 'hands-on' approach. He was

*Black clouds overhead, but on the field this was one of Yorkshire's brightest moments as*

*...xon puts an arm round a drained Ashley Metcalfe after their record unbroken stand of 242 in the NatWest Trophy win over Warwickshire in 1990.*

hugely popular with the membership to the end. Sir Leonard Hutton took on what was, briefly, a figurehead role, but died just over six months after taking office.

Moxon was appointed captain in place of Carrick, who took his removal with the same dignity with which he had led the side, and in another modernist move Oldham was appointed the club's first manager.

The 1990 season was Bairstow's last of 21 and the list of Second XI capped players included D Gough, a fast bowler from Barnsley who had made a promising debut at Lord's in 1989, and C White, Morley-born but reared in Australia.

White came back through the connection between Bob Appleyard, the prime mover behind the Bradford Academy, and Jack Potter, who had run the national Academy in Australia, and went straight into the first team.

Another significant move was the announcement that youngsters born outside the county but who had learned their cricket in it (ie Salford-born Michael Vaughan) could be signed. Thought was even given to making the club a limited company, but this was resisted by members. A suggestion of a move to a single ground owned by the club was also rejected but resurfaced later.

On the field, Yorkshire were flattened by Northamptonshire, for whom Allan Lamb made 235, the highest individual score made against them, and put on 393 with Alan Fordham, who made 206 not out, the biggest partnership in any form of cricket on the ground.

Yorkshire lost their first four games, including the one against Hampshire at Leeds, and later in the campaign were beaten by 64 runs by Middlesex, for whom Cowans and Chas Taylor took all 10 wickets in the second innings after Desmond Haynes had hit 131. Moxon was in fine form in two draws with the touring teams, scoring 130 against the Zimbabweans and 45 not out and 93 against the Indians, for whom the dapper Sanjay Manjrekar plundered a weak attack to make 158 not out.

The Roses clash produced an exciting draw after steady batting and a quickfire 66 by Phil DeFreitas lifted Lancashire to 369-9 declared. Michael Atherton then purveyed his seldom-used leg-spin to great effect to claim his best figures of 5-26 and Yorkshire, all out for 188, had to follow on. Metcalfe hit back with a magnificent 146 but with the exception of Chris Pickles, a high-class league all-rounder from Mirfield who never quite made a success of the transition to county cricket, he had

little support and a total of 328 left Lancashire to make 148 in 13 overs.

They nearly got them as Graham Lloyd went berserk to smash four sixes in 70 from 38 balls, adding 74 in six overs with Atherton. Yorkshire ringed the boundary and Lancashire finished on 133-7.

Though Moxon and Metcalfe sometimes showed why they had developed into one of the most prolific of Yorkshire opening partnerships the batting too often failed, particularly on roguish pitches at Headingley, and although the side possessed a high-class spearhead in Jarvis he was too seldom on his feet.

Moxon and Metcalfe were never better than in making 242-0 to fashion a stunning 10-wicket NatWest win over Warwickshire at Leeds that year but there was more humiliation in the Benson & Hedges Cup, where they lost to the Combined Universities by two wickets. Mike Smith, later of Gloucestershire (and England) hit the winning runs and the side also included Rob Turner, Steve James, James Boiling, Mark Crawley, Adrian Dale and Chris Tolley.

Yorkshire were not good enough against Lancashire in the same competition but Jarvis took 5-18 in a Sunday League win over Derbyshire.

Yorkshire's choice for the vacant presidency was Sir Lawrence Byford, who had risen from the West Riding beat to become Her Majesty's Inspector of Constabulary and had led inquiries into the Yorkshire Ripper murder hunt and the Brighton bombing. He at once made it known that he was to be no figurehead.

He wasted no time in setting an agenda, bemoaning the declining membership, the increasing financial losses and the absence of a ground Yorkshire could call their own. At once he was elected chairman of the committee, too, and so became the club's most powerful figure since Lord Hawke. He made 1991 one of the most eventful years in Yorkshire's history.

There was no sign that the rule limiting other counties to one foreign player was helping Yorkshire and the club opened its doors not only to an overseas professional but also to English players from outside the county. His timing was good. The members, though muttering under their breath about the abandonment of heritage, were too fed up with the continuing lack of success to revolt in any numbers.

Following the death of Joe Lister, who had been

secretary since 1972, Chris Hassell was brought over from Old Trafford to be the first chief executive with David Ryder taking over as secretary. There was a proposal to cut the size of the committee, the Press were moved from the top of the old pavilion to a new state-of-the art box behind the arm in the Main Stand. The club also revealed plans for an extensive refurbishment of the old pavilion after the 1992 Test match and the old system of paying the outgrounds to play there would be phased out.

On the field, not much changed. Allan Donald wrecked Yorkshire at Headingley with a match haul of 10-96 and Tim Munton took six wickets in Warwickshire's 30-run win. There was a draw against Nottinghamshire and against Northamptonshire, Moxon hitting 108 in the first innings. The visitors hung on at 138-8 in their second innings as Carrick took 4-25 in 19 overs.

Forfeits and more good bowling by Carrick brought a welcome win over Worcestershire, who were set to make 292 but were bowled out for 176, the former captain taking 5-13. In the draw against Glamorgan Metcalfe made 123 and Hugh Morris 156 not out for the Welsh county.

This was the last season for Sidebottom, Shaw, Neil Hartley, Fletcher and Phil Robinson but the first for Mark Robinson, a Hull-born seam bowler who had developed with Northamptonshire. Phil Robinson made a century in the draw with the Sri Lankans, a game notable for innings of 82 and 109 not out by Simon Kellett, an opening batsman from Mirfield.

In the Benson & Hedges Cup Byas made 92 against Hampshire, who were then routed for 50 as Sidebottom took 4-19. In the quarter-finals Moxon turned into a star medium-pace bowler with 5-31 as Warwickshire were bowled out for 111, Yorkshire winning by 122 runs before going out at Old Trafford, something they would grow used to.

In the Sunday League Blakey hit an unbeaten 71 in the win over Northamptonshire and Metcalfe's 96 and Carrick's 5-22 set up victory over Glamorgan, but the main talking-point was the proposed arrival of Australian Test fast bowler Craig McDermott for the 1992 season.

In the end he withdrew from the contract because of a groin injury and after hasty committee gatherings on the pre-season tour to Cape Town, Sir Lawrence, through Sunil Gavaskar, obtained the services of the young and prodigiously gifted Indian batsman Sachin Tendulkar. It was a major coup and since Yorkshire had been involved in several racist slurs his nationality muted the criticism of those who felt that a batsman for a

bowler was not really what the side needed.

Tendulkar was run out at the bowler's end for seven on his debut, a Benson & Hedges tie against Kent, an inauspicious start to a season which was by no means a failure but in which the Indian did not have the desired dynamic effect.

Jarvis and Moxon were injured in the first championship game, Tendulkar then made 86 in the draw with Hampshire but Yorkshire were demolished on a reported pitch by Gloucestershire. Courtney Walsh smote a quick 51 to add to a century by Dean Hodgson and 88 not out by Mark Alleyne and then took 4-77 and 7-27 in 20 unplayable overs. Tendulkar was out for 92 in the first innings.

The Indian made 93 and White 69 to set up an innings win over Essex, clinched by Mark Robinson, who took 9-68 in the match, and Yorkshire won the Roses match by four wickets in a game settled by declarations. Fairbrother made 166 not out in Lancashire's 399-8, Moxon and Kellett made 90 and 91 for Yorkshire and Lancashire's 182-3 declared left Yorkshire to make 282 in a minimum of 55 overs. Kellett made 89 to lead a well-paced chase, with support from Blakey and Tendulkar.

Kellett shone again with an unbeaten 118 in the Sunday League win over Derbyshire and Tendulkar thrilled the Leeds crowd with 107 before being run out in the defeat by Lancashire in that competition.

For 1993 Yorkshire signed the West Indies captain Richie Richardson but this was to be the last season for Carrick, who was awarded a testimonial for 1994, and for Jarvis, who joined Sussex. Ted Lester retired as scorer to be succeeded by John Potter, who had been 'away' scorer for some years. J M (Jim) Kilburn, the former Yorkshire Post cricket correspondent who had witnessed some of the county's greatest moments, died a couple of years after officially opening the new Press box at Headingley.

The new committee, trimmed from 23 to 12, was in place in 1993, the most notable absentee being Boycott, who had lost by a few votes to Bob Platt in West district, one of four new areas. There were plans to move the players to share the rugby league dressing-rooms below the Main Stand with a viewing gallery next to the Press box.

On the field, there was to Yorkshire's dismay a full programme of four-day cricket and coloured clothing on Sundays. Richard Stemp, a left-arm spinner from Birmingham, was signed from Worcestershire to take over from Carrick and Pontefract's Chris Silverwood also made his debut.

With home-and-away games now a thing of the past, a pre-season first-class friendly was organised against Lancashire and Yorkshire won it at Headingley with Stemp taking nine wickets in the match.

Still there was no success. Moxon led a recovery to a draw against Kent with 171 and White hit 146 against Durham, who held out through centuries by that formidable Headingley adversary Fowler and Phil Bainbridge. Richardson made 52 on his debut in the Benson & Hedges tie against Northamptonshire but the rest of the batting failed and Yorkshire lost. They did beat Northamptonshire in the Sunday League, Moxon and Byas making big scores and Robinson taking 4-23 against his old mates.

The NatWest quarter-final against Warwickshire went into two days. Jason Ratcliffe made 105 in Warwickshire's 245 and Yorkshire seemed intent on suicide as Byas was run out going for a second off the last ball of the first day, reducing them to 69-5. Blakey and White put on a bristling 105 to revive hopes but Paul Smith's 4-37 took his side to victory.

Richardson's second season ended prematurely when he was diagnosed as suffering from "acute fatigue syndrome." This was a posh way of saying that he was tired, which Yorkshire's players knew already since he tended to nod off in the dressing-room. Oldham was now made director of coaching and was steered more towards the Second XI, leaving Moxon in sole charge of the senior side.

Gough and White were picked by England's chairman Ray Illingworth for the Test side and Stemp was also in the squad, while back at the ranch Brian Close captained the Academy side in their first Yorkshire League game against Rotherham at Headingley.

Still no success, though the innings win over the New Zealanders, in which Byas, Richardson and Blakey made half-centuries and White took 5-42, was Yorkshire's first victory over a touring side since 1968. White was outstanding with 108 not out and 5-40 in the draw with Essex, Gough took 6-70 in another drawn game with Hampshire, for whom Paul Terry carried his bat for 141, but Yorkshire crashed to a seven-wicket defeat in the Roses match.

They gambled by batting first on a tricky pitch and were all out for 214, Moxon and Paul Grayson, a batsman and left-arm spinner from Ripon, reaching half-centuries. Nick Speak's 143, including three sixes and 18 fours, took Lancashire to 404 and a lead of 190. Byas made his first Headingley century and Grayson again batted compactly to score 95 but Peter Martin bowled skilfully throughout the match

to claim nine wickets and Jason Gallian's 50 ensured victory for the Red Rose men.

Byas was in terrific one-day form, scoring 101 not out in the Sunday League win over Nottinghamshire and an unbeaten 87 against Derbyshire on his was to a record 702 league runs in the season. Metcalfe returned to the side to make 65 not out against Lancashire in the league but Yorkshire, strangled by tight Lancashire bowling, lost by 43 runs.

Byas also made 71 in the NatWest tie against Somerset, but Yorkshire lost by three wickets as Andy Hayhurst took 4-29 and Richard Harden, later to join Yorkshire, compiled 64 before Graham Rose hit the winning runs off the penultimate ball. Somerset also edged them out in the Sunday League, with Marcus Trescothick making 74.

In 1995 Moxon made a superb unbeaten 203 and 65 not out in an eight-wicket championship win over Kent. Gough smashed 60 in the first innings and did the hat-trick in taking four wickets in five balls, while White did the bowling damage in the second innings with 4-40. But Yorkshire were humbled by Middlesex by an innings, finding no answer to the style and class of Mark Ramprakash, who made 235. Moxon batted well to make 104 and 78 but the Middlesex spinners were irresistible, John Emburey claiming 12 wickets and Phil Tufnell six.

Lancashire were easily beaten in the pre-season game as Byas made 193 in the first innings and Australian Michael Bevan, Richardson's replacement as overseas batsman, followed a duck with 108. Gough destroyed Lancashire with 7-52 in the second innings.

Bevan was a huge success but still Yorkshire failed to rise to the big occasion. They fought their way through to the semi-finals of the NatWest Trophy, centuries by Kellett and White being the highlight of a win over the Irish and Bevan's unbeaten 60 steering them to a two-wicket win over Lancashire which looked as if it might be a vital psychological breakthrough.

But they were hammered by Northamptonshire one step from Lord's. Rob Bailey, a prolific scorer against them, made 93 not out and Lamb hit a quick 63 in a formidable Northamptonshire total and Yorkshire pressed the panic button, losing Vaughan, White and Bevan to run-outs on their way to an 87-run defeat.

The home Benson and Hedges quarter-final against Worcestershire was also a bitter letdown, especially as they had been beaten in the group stage with

Bevan fashioning a measured 83 not out in reply to Graeme Hick's century. Bevan was also a key figure in the win over Northamptonshire, making 64 and then running out the dangerous Bailey for 61 to set up a 10-run win.

But on a damp pitch Worcestershire bowled them out for a dismal 88 with Stuart Lampitt taking 4-16. Moxon played in only four Sunday games where Yorkshire's form at Leeds was mixed. They beat Glamorgan and Middlesex but made only 75 in losing to Kent and were also well beaten by Durham. Bevan was in brilliant form in the league, compiling a record 704 runs in the season.

Yorkshire beat the Young Aussies in a one-day game in which Vaughan made 76, Byas 73 and Alex Morris, a Young England left-handed bat and right-arm seam bowler in his first season, took 5-32. But at the end of it all Moxon quit the captaincy, saying that he had done all he could and that his message was not getting through any more. There was talk of Bevan becoming captain, but the honour went to Byas with the Australian as his vice-captain.

Yorkshire also advertised internationally for a manager-coach but made no appointment. Bob Platt took over the cricket chair from Brian Close for 1996 and stated that he wanted the new groundsman, Andy Fogarty (from Old Trafford), to be the team's unofficial 12th man.

By this time Headingley's existence as a cricket ground came under threat as the committee probed the possibility of building a new ground. Sir Lawrence was the driving force and it became clear that the favoured option was a site just off the M1 motorway at Durkar, near Wakefield, whose council would be partners in the scheme. The cost was something in the region of £50m but with help from the local authority and funding from the Lottery, Europe and other sources Yorkshire could end up owning their own state-of-the-art stadium for nothing.

The 1996 season on the field was encouraging – sixth in the championship, third in the Sunday League and semi-final appearances in both knockouts. Gough hit a maiden century in the 10-wicket championship win over Warwickshire and took eight wickets in the Roses match, in which White made 181 and Blakey 109 not out before rain prevented Yorkshire from forcing the win they deserved.

Bevan had to go home early to join the Australian squad but Richard Kettleborough, a left-hander from Sheffield, came in to make a superb 108 and with emerging all-rounder Gavin Hamilton turned the game against Essex, which Yorkshire won by 98

runs after Nasser Hussain had made a classy 158 in the first innings. Stemp finished them off with 5-38 in 24 overs and the spinner also took five in the draw with South Africa A.

In the NatWest Moxon's century and Stemp's four wickets accounted for Nottinghamshire and Middlesex were beaten with 16 overs to spare. In the Benson & Hedges Cup burly seamer Alex Wharf, whose maiden first-class victim had been none other than Brian Lara at Scarborough, claimed 4-29 and Chris Silverwood, another in an impressive array of young fast-bowling talent, was too good for the Scots. But Old Trafford was Yorkshire's graveyard in both competitions.

In the Sunday League Byas hammered an unbeaten 111 to set up victory over the Roses rivals and White took 4-21 in the win over Essex on a dreadful one-day pitch.

The 1997 annual meeting approved in principle the move to Wakefield but by now an action group had been set up to defend Headingley and the ground's new owner, Paul Caddick, had made it clear that he would do all in his power to keep Yorkshire at the venue. His power turned out to be considerable and he used it ruthlessly, dishing out writs in the sum of millions of pounds against Yorkshire and Wakefield Council.

Bitter rows ensued behind closed doors between Caddick and Sir Lawrence and in the open as Yorkshire's members fell out over the proposal. In the following months the scheme collapsed as the Minister called in the planning application for inquiry, some elements of the funding package disappeared and Caddick showed his determination to hold Yorkshire to the lease signed in 1982.

In 1998 Yorkshire shifted their stance to forging a better deal at Headingley. Even this was a fraught business and only proceeded when the two main protagonists, Sir Lawrence and Caddick, mutually agreed to let others to the talking. They had already decided to ditch all the outgrounds except Scarborough from the 1997 season. Harrogate fought on in defence of its festival week but to no avail.

In 1997 Yorkshire voted for two divisions in the championship but lost and, needing a replacement for Bevan, who was on Ashes duty, went for Michael Slater but had to change tack and instead signed Darren Lehmann from South Australia. Bevan was supposed to come back for the following season and accused the club of a breach of promise when they stuck with Lehmann, who was not only a fine batsman but was hugely popular with players and supporters.

At Headingley there was a rain-hit draw with Glamorgan and a heavy defeat by Gloucestershire, who had emerged as a real 'bogey' team for Yorkshire. Dewsbury-born left-armer Mike Smith took 10 wickets in a match in which Vaughan was injured.

Yorkshire staged a fine recovery to beat Northamptonshire after being 120 runs adrift on first innings, another left-armer, Paul Taylor, taking 6-45. Yorkshire rallied to make 332 and then bowled out the visitors for 176, White taking 5-31 and a substitute fielder, Gareth Clough, holding a magnificent and crucial catch to dismiss Kevin Curran.

White hit seven sixes, five of them off Richard Illingworth, on his way to 172 not out against Worcestershire. Anthony McGrath, an exciting, attack-minded batsman from Bradford who had made his debut in 1995, scored 141 and a diving catch by Stemp to remove the menacing Tom Moody was crucial to a 66-run win.

Silverwood, whose style seemed ideally suited to Headingley, took 7-93 and 5-55 against Kent, who escaped with a draw. In other first-class games Graham Lloyd's massive 225 set up Lancashire's win in the pre-season friendly but Moxon, though increasingly troubled by back pain, made 155 as Yorkshire fought back to beat Pakistan A with Paul Hutchison, a left-arm swinger from Leeds, taking 7-38.

In the NatWest Trophy the side had a scare against Ireland but recovered from 55-6 through White, Hartley and Gough, who then took 7-27 including another Headingley hat-trick. The Benson & Hedges Cup campaign ended with defeat by Northamptonshire – again inspired by Bailey and David Capel – at the quarter-final stage after McGrath had made an unbeaten century against Minor Counties.

In the Sunday League Australian Shaun Young hit a murderous 146 not out in Gloucestershire's win under the new Duckworth-Lewis scoring method for rain-hit games, Alamgir Sheriyar took 4-18 in the defeat by Worcestershire but Yorkshire deprived Kent of the title with a win fashioned by Lehmann's unbeaten 78, though the Australian was robbed of the chance to finish as the season's top run-maker in the league when Bradley Parker came in to dominate the scoring at the end of the innings.

Five consecutive wins at the end of the 1998 season, Moxon's first in his new role of director of coaching following his retirement as a player, lifted Yorkshire to third and raised hopes for the future.

Headingley became a fortress as Byas reeled off a series of centuries and shared in some big stands with Matthew Wood, a compact right-hander from Huddersfield. Yorkshire also managed to finish in the top half of the Sunday League and so qualified for the First Division in 1999.

This year also saw the first day-night match, against Lancashire, which drew a crowd of some 10,000. They saw Gough take another hat-trick but the hired floodlights, for which the club gained sponsorship, put the side batting second at a big disadvantage and Yorkshire were bowled out for 81 with Glen Chapple eclipsing Gough with 6-25.

The batting of Byas and Wood and White's 4-13 brought a big championship win over Somerset and Derbyshire were brushed aside as Byas and Wood hit centuries with Silverwood taking nine wickets in the match. Byas hit his third Leeds century in the draw with Leicestershire and a masterly 108 by Wood put them well on top against Hampshire, who were skittled by Silverwood (5-13) but held out for a draw. Adrian Aymes made a fighting 73 when they followed on and Peter Hartley, controversially released by Yorkshire at the end of the 1997 season, was at the crease at the close with nine Hampshire wickets down.

The one big blemish at Leeds was defeat in an intriguing Roses battle notable for the fact that Lancashire had 12 batsmen, Richard Green replacing Ian Austin after the game had started when the all-rounder was called up by England. Austin's departure was delayed when he was collared for a drugs test and struggled to provide a urine sample.

Matthew Hoggard, another in the batch of fast bowlers who had made his debut in 1996, was caned by John Crawley in the morning session. Crawley made 180 but another century from Byas kept Yorkshire in contention and Hutchison took 5-39 as Lancashire were dismissed for 215. A good cricket pitch turned in favour of the Lancashire spinners and Yorkshire were bowled to a 59-run defeat by Gary Yates and Gary Keedy, who had played one game for his native Yorkshire in 1994.

White was promoted to open against Surrey and succeeded with 55 and 104 not out to set up a 164-run win sealed by Hamilton's 11 wickets and Silverwood's 5-30 in the second innings, while Wood hit a memorable double-century in the innings win over Warwickshire, who were dismissed for 84 in their first innings as Hutchison swung in with 6-25. Nick Knight carried his bat for 130 in the second.

Vaughan captained Yorkshire in a draw when

Cambridge made a rare trip to Leeds. In the NatWest Trophy they again lost at Old Trafford but Lehmann shone in steering them to the semis of the Benson & Hedges Cup where there was another Headingley flop, this time against Essex. Hussain made 78, White turned up not fit to bowl his full quote of overs and Yorkshire folded to 163 and a 95-run defeat.

The side's Sunday League record at Leeds was poor, for besides the Lancashire defeat they were bowled out for 93 by Leicestershire and also lost to Warwickshire, for whom Knight made 92 not out. Gough took 5-25 in a Duckworth-Lewis win over Surrey.

Greg Blewett was signed as temporary replacement for the World Cup-bound Lehmann in 1999 and Richard Harden was recruited from Somerset on the basis that his technique would be ideally suited to Headingley's pitches, but an early-season fracture prevented him from testing the theory.

Blewett was the first outright failure as an overseas player, amazingly so in view of his record at international level, so even though Yorkshire did reach Lord's, in the straight knockout Benson & Hedges Super Cup, where they were humbled by Gloucestershire, it was another season of under-achievement.

Doug Padgett retired after nearly 50 years of service in various capacities, the name Phoenix rose out of nothing for National League games and Sir Lawrence stood down after overseeing the £9.9m Headingley redevelopment scheme to the stage where a Lottery funding bid was ready. He had been president for nine pioneering but latterly controversial years, seven of them as chairman.

Hamilton excelled with bat and ball in the championship win over Gloucestershire and there were also big victories over Durham and Worcestershire, who were destroyed by Hutchison's 6-35 in the first innings and then hammered by Hamilton, who made 94 not out. But Yorkshire's grip at Leeds was loosened by Middlesex despite an unbeaten 142 by McGrath, the visitors winning thanks to a superb 127 not out from Aussie Justin Langer in the second innings. There was a chastening innings defeat by Glamorgan, for whom Matthew Maynard scored 186, Michael Powell 70 and Mark Wallace, a 17-year-old wicketkeeper dragged away from his school desk, an unbeaten 64.

Blakey made 123 in Yorkshire's second innings and Ryan Sidebottom, curly-locked son of Arnie and a left-arm seamer of real zip, not for the first time showed his batting prowess with 48 not out but

Steve Watkin and Owen Parkin worked their way through.

Blewett made nought in the NatWest win over Leicestershire on the way to the semis but contributed 3-26 as a bowler, Vaughan and McGrath batting brilliantly to rescue the side from 14-3 to a 230 target. Blewett did hit some form in the Super Cup win over Hampshire, making 71 to go with Byas's 104 not out.

In the National League White took 4-25 in the win over Gloucestershire, scored 67 to help defeat Hampshire and had runs and wickets in the triumph over Warwickshire, but Hussain was imperious with 114 to set up a win for Essex, Gavin Haynes bowled Worcestershire to victory and there was another day-night defeat by Lancashire.

Their experiences through the 1980s suggested that when Yorkshire did go into the overseas market it would be to strengthen the bowling. When that plan fell through they settled on a succession of batsmen and, since the 1990s produced a plethora of homegrown bowling talent, it should have paid off.

But the 2000 season, under the presidency of the club's former lawyer Robin Smith, was typical in that Lehmann shone too brightly and lacked adequate support. The search for a successor to Moxon at the top of the order was not completed. The introduction of central England contracts may have cured some of England's problems but exacerbated Yorkshire's as one of the main suppliers.

So high hopes remained largely unfulfilled. White took 5-25 in the Benson and Hedges Cup win over Lancashire and Byas saw them through against Leicestershire with 71, but Surrey prevailed in the quarter-final as Alec Stewart survived an early lbw appeal to make 97 not out. Hoggard attracted national attention with 4-39 but Yorkshire's batting, despite half-centuries by Lehmann and Wood, buckled under pressure and three run-outs contributed to a seven-run defeat.

The championship season started well. Yorkshire steam-rollered Derbyshire and Hampshire by an innings but against Derbyshire Vaughan broke a finger and retired hurt for 155. Wood hit an unbeaten 100, which sadly remained the high point of another forgettable season, and Lehmann 95. The Australian made 85 against Hampshire, who were floored by Hamilton's 125, and Shane Warne bagged a pair for the visitors.

After a rain-ruined draw with Leicestershire there was a six-wicket win over Kent on a pitch which came close to incurring an eight-point penalty. Kent were destroyed by Sidebottom, who took 5-27 and a sensational 6-16 as they were shot out for 82 in their second innings.

A draw against Durham, in which Yorkshire suffered the indignity of following on, was a bitter blow to title prospects, though Sidebottom took 5-66 in 33 overs and Yorkshire rallied impressively to close on 386-4 after Lehmann's first century on the ground. Vaughan also reached three figures.

In the Roses match Warren Hegg counter-attacked splendidly with 75 after Lancashire had been reduced to 128-6 and fine batting by Lehmann (83) and Byas (81) gave Yorkshire a lead of 109 only for rain to wash out the final day with Lancashire on 127-2.

Hoggard broke the club wicket-taking record for a one-day league campaign as Yorkshire, at one stage threatened with relegation, surged up the table with five successive wins but results at Headingley were mixed, the low point being a crushing 60-run defeat by Northamptonshire, for whom off-spinner Graeme Swann took 4-14, and the highlight a demolition of relegated Lancashire so swift that the floodlights were not really needed. White and Hoggard did most of the damage as Lancashire were bowled out for 68 inside 24 overs and Lehmann's unbeaten 54 off 43 balls completed the rout.

'Pommie' Mbangwa took 6-14 in the first innings and 10 wickets in all in the 32-run defeat by the Zimbabweans, though Yorkshire were encouraged by an unbeaten 66 by left-hander Michael Lumb, the South African-born son of former opener Richard. Lesroy Weekes, also qualified for county cricket by the end of the year, thought that he had bowled his way to a full-time contract with 6-56 on a shocking pitch against the West Indians but when that fell through he signed for Northamptonshire. Bowled out for 126 and 94, Yorkshire lost heavily despite 53 by Harrogate left-hander Vic Craven, one of several new faces in the first team during the season.

Hopes for a peaceful winter of bricklaying at Headingley were rudely interrupted by Moxon's resignation as director of coaching and the search for a man to apply some cement to a team within touching distance of silverware led Yorkshire to Western Australia's coach Wayne Clark.

# Chapter Twelve

# England 1984-2001

NEW ZEALAND'S famous 1983 triumph was a sign of England's decline as a Test force and of things to come at Headingley, the one exception to their sequence of failure at the ground for the rest of the decade being a crucial Ashes victory two years later.

Although they went on to win the series against New Zealand 3-1, they lost the following winter's three-match series through an innings defeat at Christchurch, were beaten in Pakistan a month later and were then wiped out at home by the rampant West Indies, then the undisputed if unofficial world champions.

In 1984 at Leeds England gave a debut to batsman Paul Terry but for him it was a poisoned chalice against a pace attack spearheaded by Joel Garner and Malcolm Marshall. He made eight and one but managed to avoid becoming a one-Test wonder, making seven at Old Trafford before being discarded.

Allan Lamb did succeed against the pace battery, making exactly 100 out of England's first-innings total of 270, the next best being Ian Botham with 45. Michael Holding, coming on as first change, took 4-70 and Roger Harper represented the spinners' union gallantly with 3-47 including the wickets of Lamb and opener Chris Broad.

Lancashire's Paul Allott responded superbly for England with his Test best figures of 6-61 but the West Indies took a lead of 32 thanks to a brilliant unbeaten 104 by Hilary 'Larry' Gomes, a left-hander who timed the ball with natural ease, was a

fine foil for the bigger hitters in the side and had honed his technique on this trip with hours of batting against a bowling machine to ensure that his bat came through straight.

England lost their first two second-innings wickets for 13 but rallied through a half-century by the dogged Lancashire left-hander Graeme Fowler, a heavy scorer in Roses matches too, and 43 from captain David Gower. But the rest had no reply to devastating bowling by Marshall who, despite operating with a broken bone in his left wrist, took 7-53 in 26 overs as they were bowled out for 159. A century opening stand between Gordon Greenidge and Desmond Haynes paved the way for an easy eight-wicket win.

England's sole success in this period was an 1985 Ashes victory by five wickets in a high-scoring affair. This was the first Test of the series and, bolstered by the return of Graham Gooch and John Emburey after a three-year TCCB ban for touring South Africa, they went on to regain the Ashes.

It was a first Ashes Test for Nottinghamshire's studious opener Tim Robinson and he emerged as the hero with a calm innings lasting almost seven hours in which he hit 27 fours in 175 against a seam attack comprising Jeff Thomson, Geoff Lawson, Craig McDermott and debutant Simon O'Donnell.

Mike Gatting gave him fine support in a third-wicket stand of 136 and England batted solidly right down the order with Paul Downton making a half-century and Botham pounding 60 of 51 balls. It all lifted England to a massive 533, their highest total against Australia at Leeds and a first-innings lead of 202.

Gooch and Emburey had taken two wickets each in support of the front-line seam bowlers in Australia's 331, founded on an untypically brisk 119 by opener Andrew Hilditch, who hit two sixes and 17 fours off 182 balls.

Hilditch was also the backbone of their second innings with 80 but despite his long stand of 139 with Kepler Wessels, who reached 64, the tourists lost six wickets in wiping out the deficit. Both fell to Emburey, who finished with 5-82 from 43.4 overs in the second innings.

Botham, who had taken three wickets in four balls at the end of Australia's first innings, claimed four more to go second behind Willis in the list of England wicket-takers in Ashes games but the home side were held up by an elegant and pugnacious 91 by Wayne Phillips, a left-hander with a liking for the square cut who had succeeded Rodney Marsh as wicketkeeper.

On a pitch of treacherous bounce Phillips, in his first Ashes Test, batted beautifully and had gutsy support from O'Donnell to take Australia to 324. O'Donnell then gained enough movement to trouble England's batsmen, he and Lawson taking five wickets between them before Lamb and Peter Willey took their side to victory. Australia's bowling and catching had been unusually unreliable with Thomson suffering the indignity of conceding 166 runs in 34 overs in the first innings.

England were then beaten 5-0 in the Caribbean, but the Press were optimistic enough to view the defeat by India in the first Test at Lord's in the summer of 1986 as an aberration. After all, in more than 50 years of Test cricket India had not won outside London.

After Lord's Gower had been sacked as captain and replaced by Gatting. Botham was suspended for admitting to smoking cannabis and on the eve of the Leeds Test Gower was injured, so for the first time since 1978 England went into a game without either their best all-rounder or their most gifted batsman. The pitch was not expected to be reliable enough to last for five days.

India suffered a late blow when Chetan Sharma, a bustling, aggressive cricketer who was alleged to have punched an autograph-hunter in the face during their game at Leicester, broke down and Madan Lal, then playing in the Lancashire League, was summoned to Headingley.

Kapil Dev won the toss and gambled by batting first. He seemed to have been vindicated as they reached 203-4 but ended the first day on 235-8, the Essex all-rounder Derek Pringle using the conditions effectively. There were useful runs the following morning from Madan Lal and Kiran More, India's accomplished wicketkeeper, which took the total to 272 but England had cause to be satisfied.

Friday's play turned out to be one of the most dramatic in India's Test history, wiping out memories of some horrendous collapses such as their 0-4 at Leeds in 1952. Madan Lal bowled Wilf Slack and Chris Smith in quick succession and when all-rounder Roger Binny, who had come to the fore in India's World Cup triumph of 1983, dismissed Gatting, Pringle and Emburey the home side were reeling at 63-7.

Bill Athey survived a run-out chance to make 32

*A packed Headingley and a parched outfield for the 1984 Test against the West Indies.*

*Malcolm Marshall returns to the crease at Headingley in 1984 with a damaged wrist and bats one-handed to give Larry Gomes the chance to reach his century. He even managed to hit a four and then bowled the West Indies to victory.*

*Wicketkeepr Jeff Dujon takes the catch and the West Indian fielders rush to congratulate spinner Roger Harper after he dismissed David Gower for 43 in the Headingley Test of 1984, which the tourists won by eight wickets.*

and save the follow-on but with Binny, regarded by some sections of the Press as a bit of a joke bowler, going on to take 5-40 and Madan Lal 3-18 England were all out for 102. In the past they had occasionally been bamboozled by Indian spin but to be routed by Indian seam was unthinkable.

There was anger in the crowd that English cricket should have come to this. They sought solace in repeated Mexican waves, which brought a protests from India's manager. Not even the noisiest of Indian crowds behaved like this, he said.

The spectators were then treated to a masterclass from Dilip Vengsarkar, who overcame the vagaries of the pitch and protected the Indian tail to fashion a superb unbeaten 102 from No 4 in the order. No other batsman in the match reached 40.

India reached 237 through Vengsarkar's excellence and by the end of the third day England were on

their knees at 90-6, unravelled by the left-arm spin of Maninder Singh who, like his mentor Bishan Bedi, bowled with his head swathed in a patka. Not only was the pitch untrustworthy in bounce, it also took spin and only 75 minutes of the fourth day were needed for India to win by 279 runs, Maninder finishing with 4-26.

India won the three-match series and so did New Zealand, who were also victorious in the Texaco Trophy one-day international at Headingley. Jeff Crowe made 66 and an unbeaten 30 from Evan Gray lifted the tourists to 217-8, a challenging total on the sort of pitches being produced for one-day cricket at Leeds. England folded to 170 in the 49th over, the running out of Lamb for 33 proving crucial, and lost by 47 runs.

In 1987 Pakistan gained their first win at Headingley and in grand style, by an innings and

135

18 runs in a little over three days. Apart from debutant David Capel, who made 53, England's batting never came to terms with the bowling of Imran Khan, Wasim Akram and Mohsin Kamal, who each took three wickets as the home side were bowled out for 136 after winning the toss.

Salim Malik was out one run short of a century and punishing innings lower down the order from Wasim and Ijaz Ahmed, who made 50, lifted Pakistan from 152-5 to 353 all out, despite a magnificent bowling stint by Neil Foster, whose 8-107 from 46.2 overs was the third best Test return at Leeds behind Willis's 8-43 against Australia in 1981 and Colin Blythe's 8-59 against South Africa in 1907.

Imran turned the lead into a winning advantage with a prodigious 7-40 in England's second innings. Gower made 55 but there were to be no heroics from Botham this time and England were all out for 199, Imran finishing with a match haul of 10-77.

It was the familiar dismal story against the West Indies in 1988, a match notable for the fact that umpire Dickie Bird and his colleague David Shepherd had to suspend play when water started to well up over Curtly Ambrose's boots as he prepared to run up at the rugby stand end. The drains had been blocked to prevent cracking, though Yorkshire insisted that they were working properly before the start of play and put it down to the volume of rain. Unaware of the circumstances, many spectators settled for blaming Bird, since this was one of the rare occasions when the government could not be held responsible, and his plaintive cries of "It's not my fault – nowt to do wi' me" fell on deaf ears.

England, with Tim Curtis and Robin Smith on debut, were thumped by 10 wickets, bowled out for 201 and 138 by a four-pronged attack of Ambrose, Marshall, Winston Benjamin and Walsh. This was the fourth Test and already England were on their third captain, Chris Cowdrey. His face was not familiar enough to a gateman who refused him entry to the car park on the Wednesday.

At the end of day one England were 137-4 with Lamb and Smith in residence. On Friday morning the West Indies started to look worried as Lamb reached 64, but he then tore a calf muscle in his right leg and retired hurt. England were all out 47 minutes later.

These were dark days for Headingley. The pitch and now the drains were being criticised, the weather was grim enough to keep the aggregate crowd below 45,000 and to cap it all Viv Richards was again at the centre of allegations of racial abuse.

The West Indies, after a half-century by Haynes, reached 275, the innings prolonged and substantiated by a long innings of 56 by Roger Harper. Derek Pringle returned 5-95. England wiped out the arrears of 74 for the loss of only one wicket to get back into the game but the dismissal of Gooch for 50 sparked a collapse and only a brave knock by Lamb, batting at No 8, took the game into the last day. Had it not been for rain and drains it might have been over by tea on the Saturday.

England did have the satisfaction of a Texaco Trophy series win over the West Indies, including a 47-run win on a sub-standard one-day pitch at Leeds. Pringle took the man-of-the-match award for the top score of 39 in England's 186-5 followed by 3-30 as the West Indies were dismissed for 139 in the 47th over. Strangely, Ambrose and Marshall were not given their full quota of overs.

The first Test of the 1989 Ashes series, for which Gower was reappointed captain after a three-year gap, provided Australia with their first win on the ground since Peter Burge's match of 1964.

England had retained the urn under Gatting in 1986-7 but here the Aussies, though starting as underdogs, established command on the first day which was to last throughout the series. Gower suffered the mortification of sending them in and seeing Australia pile up 601-7 declared, then the highest total made by any Test side at Leeds.

The pitch, needless to say, was far better than Gower suspected and the English bowling poor with Phil DeFreitas, Neil Foster, Pringle and Phil Newport all conceding more than 100 runs. The one man with cause for satisfaction was wicketkeeper Jack Russell, who did not concede a single bye.

Mark Taylor announced his entry into Ashes conflict with an innings of 136 spanning six-and-a-half hours. With his captain Allan Border, who made 66, the opener put on 117 and his stand with Dean Jones (79) added 99 before Taylor fell lbw to Foster.

Jones and Steve Waugh then put England to the sword with a stand of 138, Waugh completing a maiden Test hundred. He went on to make an unbeaten 177 with 24 boundaries and English suffering reached its height when Mervyn Hughes came in to hit 71 and share in a seventh-wicket record stand of 147.

England, without the injured Gatting and Botham, batted well enough to avoid the follow-on. Again,

*A group of Scottish supporters from the St Boswell's club in the Borders gather on the balcony of one of the Cardigan Road guest houses for a panoramic view of Australian dominance in the 1989 Ashes Test, a 210-run defeat for England.*

Lamb was the leader with 125, achieving the highest proportion of boundaries of any century-maker in the history of England-Australia matches. Kim Barnett at No 3 made a thrilling 80 off 118 balls and Robin Smith's 66 took England to 430 all out.

Taylor made 60 and Border 60 not out as Australia built briskly on their lead on the final morning before declaring at 230-3 and England, by now on their knees, were bowled out with almost two hours to spare. Apart from Gooch, who made 68, the batsmen showed poor technique against the probing accuracy of Terry Alderman, who followed his 5-107 in the first innings with 5-44 in 20 overs.

Headingley's declining reputation was reflected in the absence of a Test in 1990 and although the one-day pitches were good England lost both Texaco Trophy games, by four wickets to the New Zealanders and by six wickets to India.

Smith scored 128 as England reached an imposing 295-6 against New Zealand but Mark Greatbatch paced his response to perfection with an undefeated 102 to supplement half-centuries by John Wright and Andrew Jones and they won with a ball to spare. Lamb and Gower made fifties against India

but England were bowled out for 229 and Sanjay Manjrekar's 82 and Mohammad Azharuddin's 55 not out took the tourists to victory with two overs left.

For the next two years Headingley was the stage on which England's captain Graham Gooch showed that he was a batsman at the height of his powers, playing two of the finest innings witnessed at the venue. The first created England's first win in a home Test against the West Indies for 22 years and the second set up a six-wicket win over a powerful Pakistan team.

Against the West Indies it looked like being the usual bleak tale as Viv Richards won the toss, sent England in and saw Ambrose, Marshall and Patrick Patterson bowl them out for 198, Smith making a fighting 54 before being run out.

With Steve Watkin on debut alongside Graeme Hick and Mark Ramprakash, England bowled well to claim a lead of 25 runs, DeFreitas leading the way with 4-34 and Pringle and Watkin chipping in with two wickets each. Richards threatened to take control with an innings of 73 but the West Indies were undermined by run-outs which robbed their captain of support from Richie Richardson and Carl

Hooper and the last six batsmen scored only 20 runs between them.

In conditions offering the bowlers help through the air and off the pitch, the contest still looked evenly balanced but Gooch single-handedly shaped it in England's favour. He alone resisted and overcame a fearsome onslaught from Ambrose, whose 6-52 in 28 overs would in nearly all other circumstances have been match-winning figures.

Gooch's unbeaten 154 out of a total of 252 – Ramprakash and Pringle were the next highest scorers with 27 each – made him the first batsman in Test history to carry his bat at Headingley. Needing 278 to win, the West Indies lost half their side for 88, their batting rarely looking solid enough to cope with the conditions.

Although fading hopes were sustained by Richardson, who made 68 before becoming one of four more victims for DeFreitas, they folded to 162 all out and defeat by 115 runs. Watkin did his side a great service by removing Hooper, Richards and Gus Logie before they could get established.

In 1992 Pakistan were waylaid by a pitch which lived up to its reputation for wickedness. It was a triumph not only Gooch's batsmanship but also of his leadership, for he made his team plans to suit the conditions, omitting Jack Russell to accommodate an extra batsman and on a 'horses for courses' basis giving a Test debut to Neil Mallender, a Yorkshireman who had learned his cricket at Beverley Grammar School and Hull CC but had joined Northamptonshire and then Somerset.

In the belief that the pitch would not last for five days, Javed Miandad elected to bat on a low, slow pitch and their only batsman to prosper was Salim Malik, who with occasional flurries of aggression moved to 57 out of Pakistan's 165-8 at the end of the first day. He went on to make a superb unbeaten 82 but much of the rest of the batting was reckless and simply provided Hick with slip-catching practice.

In clearer overhead conditions on the second day Gooch and Michael Atherton, who made 76, put on 168 for the first wicket. Gooch, surviving against the best Pakistan could hurl at him and attacking lustily when the bowling wavered, went on to make 135 in seven hours with 19 fours and a six, which completed a full set of centuries against the six countries he had faced.

But he was bowled by spinner Mushtaq Ahmed just before lunch on day three and England lost nine wickets for 50 runs as Waqar Younis's radar

*Groundsman Keith Boyce digs for victory over the vagaries of the Test pitch, which was relaid in 1992.*

suddenly started to function. He blasted out five men for 13 in 38 balls and England were all out for 320.

Mallender, using all the know-how he had accumulated on the county scene, turned the lead of 123 into a match-winning one with 5-50 (eight wickets in the match) with steady support from Pringle. Ramiz Raja held out for two hours to make 63 and there was another masterpiece from Salim Malik, who again could not be shifted and made 84.

England's search for the 99 runs needed for victory became a fraught business as Pakistan bowled like cornered tigers. There was controversy when umpire Ken Palmer shook his head when they were convinced that Gooch had been run out for 13. The Pakistanis, who had been in trouble with Palmer's brother Roy at Old Trafford, could not conceal their frustration and the climax to the game was noisy and argumentative, leading to a fine for Rashid Latif for throwing his cap down in anger after another appeal was rejected.

After these two heady triumphs England were back on the ropes in the 1993 Ashes series, which had begun with Shane Warne's "ball from hell" to Gatting and with two emphatic Australian victories. They retained the Ashes with another rout at Leeds in the first £1m Test at the ground and in making 653-4 declared achieved the highest total ever made on the ground in any form of cricket, surpassing Somerset's 630 in 1901.

England's seam attack was Kent's Martin McCague (Ulster-born but raised in Australia), Essex's left-armer Mark Ilott, Andrew Caddick of Somerset and Surrey's Martin Bicknell, who was on debut. It was a sad, meek end to Gooch's reign as captain. He resigned within minutes of the defeat by an innings and 148 runs, having said some weeks earlier that he would go if there was no improvement in England's form. He had celebrated his 40th birthday during the match, spending the day watching his team take just one wicket.

Having flourished as batsman and captain in 'typical Headingley' conditions in the previous two Tests, Gooch was disgusted to find that after the 1992 win over Pakistan Yorkshire, perhaps with encouragement from the TCCB and fearing for the ground's Test status, had told groundsman Keith Boyce to dig up the traditional pitch. The new one was an unknown quantity.

England's bowling was a pitiable sight and Gooch must have been planning his resignation speech after the team was booed off at the end of the second day with Australia on 613-4. Tasmanian David Boon's 50th first-class hundred was his third in successive Ashes Tests, matching Bradman's feat in 1938, and took him past 1,000 runs in England. Getting Mark Waugh out for 52 turned out to be a major triumph as Border and Steve Waugh, with an unbroken stand of 332, broke England's will to survive.

Border batted for 570 minutes before declaring as soon as he drove his 200th run and carried on running to the dressing-rooms, eager to attack an England side whose spirit, he knew, had been shattered hours ago. He had become the fifth batsman to score a double-century in Leeds Tests and Waugh was left unbeaten on 157.

Gooch and Atherton made half-centuries but these were mere pin-pricks to the Australians and both fell to Paul Reiffel, ironically the nearest approach to an old-fashioned English seamer in the Aussie ranks. He took 5-65 as they were bowled out for 200 and when they followed on Atherton's dogged 63 and Alec Stewart's counter-attacking 78 only delayed the inevitable, which included Hughes's 200th Test wicket.

Although Yorkshire continued to be worried by outbreaks of bad crowd behaviour on the now notorious Western Terrace, a high-scoring draw against South Africa, playing their first Test at Headingley since 1955, suggested that they were on the right track with the pitch, though many

hankered after the more gripping contests produced in less favourable batting conditions.

Atherton, the captain, became the second batsman after Salim Malik in 1987 to be out for 99 in a Leeds Test as England made 477-9 declared after winning the toss. Graham Thorpe, the Surrey left-hander, made 72, Stewart 89 and Bradford-born wicketkeeper Steve Rhodes an unbeaten 65. Darren Gough, who had made his Test debut along with Craig White in the series against New Zealand earlier that summer, was run out for 27 on his first England appearance on the ground.

Gough's bowling fell way below his and the crowd's expectations as South Africa replied with 447, founded on a maiden Test century by the 39-year-old Peter Kirsten, one of the clearest victims of his country's international exile, and a pile of runs from the last five of Jonty Rhodes, Brian McMillan, Craig Matthews (once a candidate as Yorkshire's overseas professional), Fanie de Villiers and even Allan Donald. They forged a recovery from 105-5 and Gough had figures of 2-153 in 37 overs.

A century by Hick, only his second in his 28th Test match, and 73 from Thorpe took England to a declaration at 267-5 and Kirsten's half-brother Gary, a durable left-handed opener, made 65 as they closed on 116-3.

Atherton lost the toss in the first Test of a six-match series against the West Indies in 1995 and he alone stood firm against the pace of Ian Bishop and Benjamin, making 81 out of England's total of 199. Bishop, a soft-spoken, thoughtful man and a devout Christian, was as lethal as the best of his compatriots when bowling but had his career interrupted and cut short by a stress fracture of the lower back.

Gough, fresh from a bristling all-round display in Sydney the previous winter (51 runs and 6-49), came in to a tumultuous reception from his home crowd and promptly stunned them into silence by hooking Bishop into the hands of Ambrose at wide long leg.

The West Indies, though coming into the game short of batting confidence, hit on a policy of aggression, especially against Gough and Devon Malcolm. It paid off, for although Malcolm removed opener Hooper for a duck the next three in the order all made half-centuries, including 53 off 55 balls by Brian Lara. They ended the second day on 236-5 with Keith Arthurton settled, but England bowled better on the third morning to limit the West Indies to a lead of 83.

England's second attempt followed the same

pattern as their first with no judicious balance between caution and aggression. Thorpe fought it out for 61 but Ambrose and Walsh did most of the damage as they were dismissed for 208, Gough being the next highest scorer with 29.

The West Indies took only 19 overs to score 129-1 and win by nine wickets. Debutant Peter Martin, who had taken 1-48 in 27 overs in the first innings, conceded 49 in just eight overs and DeFreitas and Richard Illingworth also took some hammer as Hooper crashed 73 not out and Lara an unbeaten 48.

In the 1996 draw against Pakistan centuries by Ijaz Ahmed and wicketkeeper Moin Khan which took the tourists to 448 (Dominic Cork took five wickets but Chris Lewis none for 100 runs) were matched by Stewart's 170 at the top of the order and 113 by Nick Knight at No 6 to give England a lead of 53.

After losing their first two wickets for 34 on the last morning Pakistan were steadied by a stand of 98 between Ijaz and Inzamam-ul-Haq, whose running between the wickets (or lack of it) was often as entertaining as his strokeplay and they were 242-7 when stumps were drawn.

Thorpe's unbeaten 69 earned him the man-of-the-match award in England's six-wicket Texaco Trophy win over India that summer. Cork and Martin took three wickets apiece as India subsided to 158 all out in the 41st over and Stewart's unbroken alliance with his Surrey team-mate saw England home.

A century which began at Headingley with Jackson, Fry, Hirst, Trumper and Armstrong (and an umpire called Titchmarsh) ended with an unforgettable Test match and two epic contests in the 1999 World Cup.

Before that, however, England were again put through the mincer by the Australians, who in 1997 won by an innings and 61 runs in a game prolonged by the weather to lunch on the last day but was done and dusted in three playing days.

England brought in the diminutive Yorkshire-born left-armer Mike Smith for Andrew Caddick and were indeed made to look small. Put in by Mark Taylor, they were bowled out for 172 by the rampant Jason Gillespie, who bowled superbly but was aided by some rash, ill-executed shots. He took 7-37 and England lost their last six wickets for 18 runs in conditions that were not awkward enough to justify it.

Gough and Kent's Dean Headley made two early incisions each to reduce the Australians to 50-4 and England might have stayed in contention had

Thorpe not dropped the left-handed Matthew Elliott when he had made 29 of his eventual 199, the only such individual score in Test history at Leeds.

Batting became easier as the skies cleared and by the end of day two Elliott and Ricky Ponting had put on 208 in 49 overs. The humidity returned on the third day but not the spark to England's bowling as Ponting moved on to 127 and Ian Healy joined Elliott in another productive stand ended only by rain.

Mark Ealham, Kent's medium-paced all-rounder, hit back on the fourth morning but things continued to go wrong for Gough at Leeds and he was roughly treated by Elliott and Reiffel before getting a swinging yorker right to pluck out Elliott's off stump. Reiffel finished with 54 not out, Gough with 5-149.

Australia's declaration at 501-9 left them five sessions in which to bowl out England for a second time and it proved ample, though they were held up by a classy and courageous century by Hussain, who found stubborn support from John Crawley in a stand which revived England from 89-4 to 212-4 at the end of the fourth day.

Hussain's early, tame departure for 105 to a mistimed drive at Warne on the final morning signalled the end. Reiffel, with 5-49, was the main beneficiary as England lost their last five wickets for 16 runs in seven overs.

In May England had beaten the Aussies at Headingley on their way to a Texaco Trophy triumph. This was the year of the Hollioakes in one-day cricket and Adam took a couple of wickets as Australia were restricted to 170-8 in 50 overs before hitting an unbeaten 66 to take his side to a six-wicket win with an unbroken stand of 135 with his Surrey colleague Thorpe.

Early in 1998 it was another Surrey batsman, Alistair Brown, who shone with 59 against the South Africans. He and Knight put on 114 for the first wicket and England reached a target of 206 with 15 overs to spare after Shaun Pollock had revived the tourists with 60.

Headingley has never been a pretty cricket ground but was at its most evocative as 10,000 people took advantage of Yorkshiremen's favourite price (free) to watch the climax of the 1998 Test match against South Africa, played out in near-unbearable tension.

England had won the toss but thrown away their advantage by losing their last seven wickets for 49 runs in 19 overs. Yet another Surrey batsman, the left-handed Mark Butcher, drove well to compile 116, reaching his century with two edged fours through the slips before dragging a wide half-volley from Pollock into his wicket.

England included Andrew Flintoff and Ian Salisbury but little use was made of their bowling. Angus Fraser led the fightback on the second day with 5-42 in 25 overs, his victims including captain Hansie Cronje, who battled his way to 57 in three-and-a-half hours. England missed some chances but Ramprakash held a blinding catch at midwicket to get rid of the menacing Jacques Kallis for 40.

Atherton was out to the first ball of day three but Hussain took over his role to play an innings of supreme concentration, patience and skill on a worsening pitch. While he dug in, Stewart hammered Donald out of the attack with four searing boundaries and England, 22 runs behind on first innings, closed on 206-4 with Hussain still there on 83.

English optimism evaporated in 85 minutes of the fourth day as Donald and the admirable Pollock swept them aside with aggressive bowling. Hussain added 11 runs in a hour to his overnight score before being caught at mid-off and South Africa were left to make 219 for victory.

Gough at last delivered the goods at Headingley and with Fraser reduced the tourists to 27-5, England gaining the benefit of some debatable umpiring decisions, but there was another twist as Rhodes and McMillan took toll of some error-prone leg-spin from Salisbury. They added 117 before McMillan, having made 54, mis-hooked a bouncer from Dominic Cork and Rhodes moved on to a superb 85 before becoming Gough's 100th Test victim in his 25th game.

The possibility of an extra half-hour to conclude the gripping contest entered the equation but England dared not risk it with Gough and Cork on their knees. Gough spent much of the following night in the same position because of a stomach upset.

Pollock and Donald marched out on that final morning needing 34 runs to win; England needed two wickets. With nine runs added Donald edged Fraser to be caught behind the wicket and one run later, Pollock having exposed the inexperienced Ntini to Gough's inswing, umpire Javed Akhtar raised his finger for lbw and the crowd, in a collective release of tension, raised the roof to salute a 23-run win and an unexpected series victory.

South African opinion about the umpiring of Javed Akhtar is probably unprintable and Cronje declined

to go into print about it, taking the defeat with dignity. It turned out to be one of his last dignified acts before being disgraced in the match-fixing scandal which engulfed the game in 2000.

When the World Cup returned to England in 1999 Headingley staged three matches. In the group stages Pakistan overcame Australia by 10 runs, their innings of 275-8 containing six sixes, 23 fours and three run-outs. Abdur Razzaq made 60 and Inzamam 81 off 104 balls before being run out when he stumbled out of his ground after being hit on the foot by a yorker from Damien Fleming.

Moin Khan lashed three sixes – two off Glenn McGrath – in a rapid 31 not out at the end of the innings and Australia's reply faltered when Saqlain Mushtaq removed Ponting and Lehmann in the space of three balls. They recovered through Bevan, who hit Saqlain for six to reach a 66-ball half-century but fell for 61 when Wasim Akram returned for the 42nd over, ending a stand of 113 with Steve Waugh.

Waugh kept them going for a time but was out for 49, bowled by a fast, full-length ball from the thrilling Shoaib Akhtar, and the task of making 37 off the last five overs was beyond Australia, Wasim taking the last wicket to finish with 4-40.

Rain washed out the Super Six game between New Zealand and Zimbabwe, who had been dismissed for 175, but the match between Australia and South Africa turned out to be the most significant of the tournament.

On another fine one-day pitch Herschelle Gibbs hit a sparkling 101, adding 95 with Daryll Cullinan and a rapid 78 with Rhodes before Lance Klusener biffed a typically outrageous 36 off 21 balls to take them to 271-7.

Australia's win, gained with two balls to spare, was based on a scintillating stand of 126 in 23 overs between Ponting, who made 69, and Steve Waugh, whose majestic 110-ball innings of 120 not out contained the pivotal incident of the match and the entire World Cup.

On 56 he clipped Klusener to square leg where Gibbs appeared to take the catch but then let the ball squirm out of his grasp as he threw it up in celebration. When the teams tied in the semi-final at Edgbaston it was this win which took Australia through to Lord's and revenge over Pakistan in a one-sided final.

So to the year 2000 and a Test match against the West Indies which those prone to excessive blinking might have missed altogether. It was all over inside two days, giving rise to more grumblings about Headingley's pitch, though in reality it had as much to do with good swing bowling and incompetent West Indian batting. It was England's first two-day win since The Oval Test against South Africa in 1912.

The phrase "a strong Yorkshire means a strong England," so often trotted out without much substance, came gloriously true. White, who in a matter of months had turned himself from fringe candidate to key member of the England side, returned Test-best figures of 5-57 as the West Indies were shot out for 172 after winning the toss. Jimmy Adams, the captain, and Brian Lara were among the victims of his round-the-wicket attack on the left-handers from the rugby end.

England played an extra batsman and with Caddick coming in as nightwatchman Hick was down at No 8. It worked out well as he and Vaughan, who came of age as a Test batsman here, added 98 to rescue

England from a stuttering 124-6. Vaughan hit seven fours in his 76 in 196 minutes and Hick eight boundaries in 59.

Curtly Ambrose achieved personal glory by claiming Atherton as his 400th Test wicket but the West Indian support bowling was sub-standard and England gained a lead of exactly 100 runs.

Gough then produced a tremendous exhibition of inswing bowling with the new ball to leave the West Indies in turmoil at 21-4. His victims included Lara, who was lbw padding up for the second time in the match. Also from the rugby end, Caddick brought the match to a swift and financially costly conclusion with four wickets in the 23rd over and the West Indies, hapless and forlorn, were all out for 61, losing by an innings and 39 runs.

Fittingly, the 20th century had ended with some low opinions of the Headingley pitch but with high drama on it.

*West Stand, Headingley...third 15th june 2001*

*First time used at England v Pakistan game at Headingley*

# Chapter Thirteen

# Memories of Headingley

DOUGLAS VERITY,
son of Hedley

MY earliest memories of Headingley go back to 1938 when, as a five-year-old, I was taken with the rest of my family to watch my father play for England against Australia.

I remember clearly dad taking me into the dressing-room in the old pavilion, the distinct aroma of embrocation, and dad asking me to show the England players my forward defensive shot, which I had copied from watching his many rehearsals. This was greeted with great mirth as the bat was as big as me.

I remember being most impressed by the policeman guarding the dressing-room door, who performed some conjuring tricks for me.

During the game I must have lost interest, for I played with a toy under the seats. Suddenly there was a mighty roar and I asked my mother what it was and she said: "Your dad has taken a wicket." Looking this up in the records I find that it was Jack Fingleton, bowled for 30.

Another pre-War memory was of my father taking me to Headingley to see a rugby league match, Leeds v Bradford Northern. We sat in the main

stand on wooden tip-up seats, one with H Verity printed on it in black paint. Until recently on my annual visit to the Headingley Test I have made a point of sitting on the H Verity seat to eat my packed lunch.

Of course, Headingley was very different in those days. The western terrace and I think also the track round the boundary were covered in black cinders with simple wooden forms on the terraces. There were the trees on the grass bank at the Kirkstall Lane end and to any young cricketer called to the nets the unforgettable winter sheds, which were where the offices are now.

Under the main stand was the long bar which seemed endlessly long to me and behind the rows of red-faced drinkers my keen and permanently hungry eyes spotted the huge quantities of pork pies which I thought were just the thing for a growing lad.

After the war, with father gone with it, as a schoolboy cricketer and keen student of the game I used to pay at the turnstiles and sit on the western terrace, mostly on my own (my mother would never go to Headingley again). I used to hide in the crowd and never under any circumstances told anyone my name.

These were the days of sport-hungry, huge crowds with no shouting, except perhaps at the fall of an important wicket, just polite clapping. What a pleasant thought! Yorkshire and England were recovering slowly after a six-year lay-off. Some of the pre-War players were struggling on and some of the future greats were winning their spurs. Len Hutton was my great hero and to me is still the best all-round batsman I have ever seen. To think he was in pain, in every long innings after the War, with his injured left arm.

I saw all the tourist matches - Bradman's Aussies at Headingley, Hutton's ghastly duck in the first over to Lindwall on the next tour, Tayfield of South Africa making 'rabbit-holes' in the pitch with his toe, Peter May getting a century, Compton and Washbrook making successful comebacks and as the years rolled on Fred Trueman wrecking India and he with Mike Cowan on a dark evening devastating the mighty Surrey. What a glorious sight Fred was running in to bowl.

On again to Botham's match and what could be more dramatic than the year 2000 when England shattered the West Indies in two days?

I recall vividly, as a promising and reasonably successful Bradford League batsman, being called to the Headingley nets. I, like everyone else I ever met, faced batting with great trepidation in Arthur Mitchell's net. I found years later, as I spent many hours socially with him, that he was an old softy really.

The lovely Maurice Leyland once said to me as I batted in his net: "Don't lift your head lad until it's bounced off 't pavilion rails."

George Hirst, then a living legend, once came to see me play, which was a truly amazing experience. I was named George Douglas after Hirst and Jardine.

The most recent Headingley experience was when I took part in the opening of the Bowes-Verity suite above the offices. The lovely Bowes family were there in force and my wife Ann and I represented the surviving members of the Verity family. In my speech I spoke of how appropriate it was that Bill and my father should be linked together again, for after all they had hunted wickets together on cricket fields from Australia to Headingley, they plotted the downfall of batsmen almost to an art form and they signed on for the Army together.

I remembered how our families had shared the triumphs and subsequent tragedies of the 1930s and 1940s.

TED LESTER, batsman, Second XI captain and official scorer

THERE was a full house as usual for the first day of the 1948 Roses match at Whitsuntide and as we wet out to field Alec Coxon asked me if it was my first Roses match. When I told him it was he made me feel better by saying: "It's just like any other county match, so don't worry." I remembered his remark when I eventually went out to bat on the second day.

I had just got settled in when Peter Greenwood, a medium-paced off-spinner, came on to bowl at the Kirkstall Lane end. Thinking there might be easy runs available I tried unsuccessfully to hit him straight back over his head and was out for 25.

When I was in the dressing-room taking off my pads in strolled Herbert Sutcliffe. "What do you think you were doing?" he asked. Although I thought it was pretty obvious I said: "I was trying to hit him over the top."

"We don't play that way in Roses matches," was his final word as he walked out. He obviously disagreed with Alec.

During an England v Pakistan Test match I was going for a cup of tea when I was stopped on the stairs by a Pakistani gentleman (or so it appeared) asking for information. There was not a lot of time to get from the old pavilion, where we used to score, to the new pavilion for tea, so I was not best pleased to be confronted, but for the sake of diplomatic relations I reluctantly retraced my steps, got out all the scoring papers and provided him with the information he wanted. I was becoming more and more frustrated as I saw my cup of tea disappearing when I realised there was much hilarity in the adjoining Press box.

Looking down at the feet of my newly acquired 'friend' I realised that something didn't add up and I realised I had been taken for a ride. The 'Pakistani gentleman' was none other than Peter Laker, the cricket correspondent of I believe the Daily Mirror, who had acquired most of the correct attire and managed to cultivate a very good Pakistani accent.

I now understand that I was not the only one to suffer from his practical jokes over the years.

Friday July 1 1949 is a day I will always remember and not with affection. It was the last day of a game with Sussex and at the close of play on the Thursday we had taken three wickets and still had a lead of more than 300 runs.

As we travelled home that evening Vic Wilson and I thought the match would be over by lunch so we arranged to go racing at York. At 4.20pm the last day's play was called off with Sussex on 442-3. We had toiled all day while George Cox and Jim Langridge savaged our attack.

My father took me to my first Yorkshire practice at Headingley in 1939. I was shown into a room which I discovered years later was Yorkshire's dressing-room and sitting by the fire was George Hirst, the finest coach I ever met, together with half a dozen aspiring young cricketers. I sat down in a corner but he called me over to join the group. The great thing about him was that he always went out of his way to make the young players feel important and at ease and gave them the best advice possible..

The success of Yorkshire in the 1930s owed a great deal to this great coach. What a pity there is not a comparable Yorkshireman around today, so it would not be necessary to go abroad to find someone to improve the standard of our cricket.

Fourteen years went by before Johnny Wardle and I saw a photograph of some youngsters being coached by George Hirst and realised that we had made our first appearances at Headingley on the same day.

In 1951, because of the excellence of the batting pitches, we were finding it almost impossible to win matches at Headingley so an approach was made to the groundsman to prepare something on which the bowlers would have a chance.

Such a pitch was prepared for the Glamorgan game which we won by an innings at 2.20 on the second afternoon due to fine spin bowling by Bob Appleyard and Johnny Wardle.

After the match I said to the secretary, John Nash: "You won't want many matches like this one." His reply surprised me. "I wish they were all over in two days - we only lose money on the third." But I don't think his view was shared by the Leeds club and never again was such a pitch prepared.

In 1959 when a promising young batsman came into my Second XI I never dreamed that 18 years later I would be the England scorer at Headingley and be privileged to witness Geoffrey Boycott scoring his 100th first-class century.

I have to admit it was the most emotional moment

of my scoring career as I realised that here was one of my second team players creating cricketing history at his beloved Headingley - and in a Test against Australia.

DICKIE BIRD,
player and umpire

HEADINGLEY is the home of legends and is steeped in history. It has a unique atmosphere in the world of cricket. It's 50 years since I walked through the gates for my first practice and I can honestly say I was so proud I would have played for Yorkshire for nothing.

It was a privilege to have known and talked to some of the county's greats. There was none of this fitness work in those days - you were coached in the basics of cricket and learned the game by listening to the senior players.

My first Test match as an umpire was against New Zealand in 1973 and although it was an 11.30 start I was at the ground at 7.00, nervously preparing myself for the occasion. I sat in the football stand with not another soul in the ground and it seems like yesterday.

Graham Gooch's 154 not out against the West Indies in 1991 was the finest innings I witnessed as an umpire in a Leeds Test but of course the West Indies also provided me with one of my worst memories when, with Curtly Ambrose opening the bowling, water started to ooze up over his boots.

There had been a lot of rain, the water-hogs were everywhere and the groundstaff had done a great job in getting the ground fit enough for play to start at all. Curtly said to me: "Mr Dickie, we have a big problem man, come and look."

I suffered some fearful stick from the crowd, who tended to blame me for water whether it came out of the sky or out of the ground, but we had to come off. The story that went round later was that the drains had been blocked because they reckoned they needed to retain moisture in the square but what we really needed that day was some decent plumbers.

ASHLEY METCALFE,
opening batsman

FOR me Headingley will always mean green beans and uneven pitches. For 12 years the caterers served up green beans day after day for the players' lunch and I have grown to hate them.

People must wonder how a batsman ever fashioned a career on pitches where the ball seamed and swung and had uneven bounce and for the past 15 or 20 years the majority of Yorkshire's international players have been bowlers, which tells a story. Of the batsmen, only Martyn Moxon rose to England status in my time and I believe he would have played in dozens more Tests but for having to do most of his work at Headingley.

Mind you, the place was popular with many opposing players including Mike Gatting and Andy Lloyd because they knew the games would be short and it gave them more scope for socialising!

But to me it was not a poor pitch despite all the problems and I think much of the criticism has been unfair over the years. It has produced thrilling cricket at county and Test level - and results. Cricket is a public entertainment and to achieve that you need positive results.

Yorkshire players tended to learn how to play on it better than the opposition and that was particularly the case in our run to the Benson and Hedges Cup final in 1987 when we had a lot of cricket at Headingley.

Hampshire, for instance, arrived for the quarter-final and at 9.30 we saw them all out on hands and knees looking at the pitch with deep suspicion. Surrey in the semi were also a bit frightened of it and knowing that gave us a big psychological advantage before a ball had been bowled. In the championship we also did well for the first half of that season because we knew that by getting 240 to 270 we could dominate the game.

The highlights for me were a double-century against Middlesex in 1988 and that unbroken 242 opening stand with Martyn in the NatWest Trophy tie against Warwickshire two years later. That was especially satisfying for both of us because the pitch was by no means flat and we felt that Warwickshire's total would take some getting.

In between there was a four-day game against Notts that was over in a day-and-a-half, which showed that when the sun came out, which it did when they were batting, the ball did far less. I felt particularly sorry for young bowler Ian Priestley, who bowled his heart out but finished on the losing side.

To be honest the ground hasn't changed much since I watched Geoff Boycott make his 100th century in 1977. When you see how other grounds have developed you realise that Headingley has been left light-years behind. The Western Terrace had a great atmosphere of its own and it's a shame that they have cut back on its character because in big games those spectators could really lift the side.

In the changing-room, which was our inner sanctum, I was between David Bairstow and Boycott, the one all over the place and the other immaculate. I learned a lot from those two great figures. As for the committee room, we were only invited in if we had won. Players were not welcome and we found out what was going on in the club by reading about it in the Yorkshire Post.

The club is going forward with the players in mind now, and not before time. We practised indoors on two lanes with mats on concrete surfaces and no heating in the building. We looked forward to getting off to the Three Horse Shoes to thaw out.

GEOFF BOYCOTT,
on August 11, 1977.

I really did not want to bat that morning. When the cheers went up that England were batting - all the crowd wanted England to bat and see if I could do it - I was dreading it because I had not had any sleep and I was pretty up-tight about it. I thought I would not be able to keep my concentration and stamina going.

The pressure had been building from the moment I scored my 99th century. The very idea that I might pull a century of centuries out of the bag in a Test match was somehow preposterous, unreal, too fanciful to be true. And yet it was also a real possibility and the media weren't exactly unaware of it.

On the eve of the Test letters, cards and telegrams

arrived in huge numbers and I was still wading through them when we met for our traditional eve-of-Test dinner. We talked through tactics but when the conversation became more general I asked to be excused. I was uptight and Mike Brearley recognised as much without question.

But I couldn't sleep even after watching television. At 4am I sent for the night porter because I could not get the air conditioning to work. I took sleeping pills, which was most unusual for me, and woke up with a start to discover I was behind schedule. I rushed to the ground feeling tired and listless.

It was a beautiful, warm day for batting. The pitch was good and the crowd was on my side even if the bowlers most certainly were not. Mike Brearley got out in the first over but after 20 minutes, improbably enough, I felt relaxed and confident, purposeful at least. The ball was hitting the middle of the bat and the tiredness had disappeared, my concentration was good.

Len Pascoe bowled me a corker which brushed my left wrist band as I played forward. The Aussies did a war dance and I held my breath. Not out. Ray Bright bowled an arm ball and I went to glance it; it brushed my thigh pad on the way through and the Aussies went up again for a catch behind. Not out again and Bright was having apoplexy. Greg Chappell moved to cool him down and Bill Alley, who knew the language, told him where to get off.

My worst moment came when I was in the 70s and I helped a short delivery from Pascoe on its way towards fine leg. I knew as soon as I played it that it was in the air, a bit firmer than I intended, and as I set off for the single I dared not look. Max Walker was patrolling that area; if it carried the crowd would let me know. In the event it dropped short and bounced off his knee for four.

On 95 I pushed Pascoe into the covers for an easy single. Greg Chappell bowled the next over. Don't hook, even if he slips in the bouncer....my mind was working overtime before he bowled the delivery that mattered. I can see it now in slow motion. I saw it then with an amazing sort of clarity and something approaching elation. As soon as it left his hand I knew I was going to hit it and I knew where I was going to hit it. It was as though I was standing outside myself, watching myself play the shot. It was a fantastic feeling.

The stroke was outside to in, the ball hit the middle of the bat and went just past the far stumps on the on side as Graham Roope jumped out of the way. As soon as I struck it I lifted the bat high in the air. In the millisecond that followed I realised what it all meant and my arms folded over my head.

Somehow, I was destined to get a century that day. There is no other explanation for the memory and magic of it. Headingley and my 100th hundred was the greatest moment of my cricketing career. I may have played better and more importantly but this was the most magical moment of my life. I cannot remember who said what when the crowd flooded on to the field - it was just noise.

I was conscious that I was sharing something important with the people of Yorkshire. My people, right or wrong, good or bad, a source of immense inspiration.

DAVID WARNER,
cricket journalist

PITCH problems, real and imaginary, and a belief that the ball swings crazily under certain climatic conditions were part and parcel of the Headingley scene during my coverage of Test and county cricket in the final quarter of the 20th century.

But whatever devils may have lurked either on or above the surface they have been unable to prevent Headingley from consistently staging Test matches packed with memorable individual performances.

No other ground in the country can match it for the sheer richness of its contribution to cricket folklore in that period.

All of them have been well chronicled, starting with Geoff Boycott's 100th hundred in 1977. Then there was the epic England fightback against the Aussies four years later when Ian Botham and Bob Willis overturned the bookies' odds of 500-1 against a home win to make possible an almost unbelievable victory by 18 runs.

In 1991 Graham Gooch played the most disciplined and perfectly controlled innings on a difficult pitch that can be imagined to carry his bat for 154 and set up the win in the first Test against the West Indies.

Darren Gough was the national and local hero against South Africa in 1998 when his ninth wicket of the match was that of last man Makhaya Ntini and England had won by 23 runs.

The final day against the West Indies in 2000, of course, was not the fifth, the fourth or even the third, England storming home on the second evening at great financial cost to the ECB and Yorkshire.

All these are Test classics but for unrelenting drama packed into a first session of play none compares with the Roses clash at Headingley in May 1978.

There was disappointment before the game with the news that Geoff Boycott and Chris Old were injured but their absence was soon forgotten as one sensation after another left the large crowd dizzy with excitement.

Frank Hayes won the toss and decided to bat but by lunch the Red Rose side had been bowled out for 123 in 27.1 overs and Yorkshire were staggering on 10-2 in reply.

Contained in that frenzied passage of play were a career-best 8-65 by Graham Stevenson, five stunning catches by David Bairstow, seven ducks and a magnificent 58 in well under an hour from Clive Lloyd, who thrashed 50 of his runs (11 fours and a six) in boundaries.

Lloyd, shoulders drooped an wearing his best hang-dog expression, had come into the game carrying a strain and was not in the mood to run any singles if they could be avoided - which they generally were.

He came in after Stevenson had dismissed David Lloyd and Harry Pilling with consecutive balls and after denying him his hat-trick the West Indian smashed him for nine fours and a colossal hooked six before Stevenson ran him out off Geoff Cope's bowling.

With Lloyd out of the way Stevenson ripped through the rest of Lancashire's batting aided by the athletic Bairstow, who at that time was arguably the best wicketkeeper in the world when standing back to fast bowlers.

During this carnage I was filing 'running copy' and 'running' was the word because in those days the Press phones were down a flight of steps at the back of the Press Box and out of sight of the action, which meant that I missed quite a bit of what was going on.

The pace slackened but the game continued to produce remarkable cricket, not the least being Phil Carrick's maiden century which rescued Yorkshire from 49-5 and took them to 260.

With the fearsome Colin Croft bowling like lightning, Carrick survived and indeed profited by slicing many a ball high over the slips but when Croft was rested the tension eased.

Howard Cooper, the best bowler never to be capped by Yorkshire, destroyed Lancashire second time round with 6-26 and he was helped by Steve Oldham, who claimed the other four wickets. Lancashire were routed for 105 by 5pm on the second day to bring Yorkshire victory by an innings and 32 runs.

Being Headingley, of course, the pitch was reported to Lord's at lunch on the first day by umpires Eddie Phillipson and David Evans and the TCCB pitches' inspector Bernard Flack made one of his regular visits to the ground a few hours later but on this occasion nothing came of it.

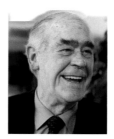

BRIAN CLOSE

I RECALL my first game at Headingley, when I made 88 not out against Essex and hit one ball on to the roof of the Main Stand in 1949. In that same year we had a game against Sussex where we didn't take a wicket at all on the last day, which just shows how good the pitches were for batting in those days.

I then went to Catterick for National Service and after doing my square-bashing I could get a pass to play for Leeds in the Yorkshire Council and on Sundays for Jack Appleyard's XI in Roundhay Park. When I was batting for Leeds I remember hitting Tommy Mitchell, a leg-spinner who had played for Derbyshire and had been on the Bodyline tour to Australia, all over the park. He was annoyed about that.

People always thought I was at my best against the fast bowlers but I loved playing the spinners, though I sometimes got out to them because I was always playing for fun.

In 1952 Len Hutton showed his artistry with a big hundred against Kent. People often ask me to compare him with Bradman, which is impossible because I didn't see Bradman. But Len was the best I ever saw, his artistry was out of this world, and remember this was after the war when he had one arm shorter than the other.

In 1952 Surrey began their run of championship wins but we beat them by nine wickets thanks mainly to Johnny Wardle and Eric Burgin, who took 6-43 with his inswingers.

My first Headingley Test was in 1959 when I took some wickets against India with off-spin but I didn't play for England again until 1961 and my first full series was in 1963.

In 1959 Colin Cowdrey got a century against us for Kent and that was the first time he had succeeded against Yorkshire, mainly because Ronnie Burnet would not let us crowd him early in his innings.

We declared about 140 behind to try to set up a finish and we had a bowler at that time called David Pickles, who had been so quick the previous year that batsmen were actually trying to get to Fred Trueman's end for a bit of respite.

But David completely lost it in 1959 and when he opened the bowling in Kent's second innings he was all over the shop. I told Ronnie that it could not go on and he might as well let me have a go and I got 8-41 in 19 overs. Even so we had to get 240-odd at a brisk rate and I made 52 as we won by two wickets in a great finish.

I was England captain when Boycott was dropped after making a double-century against India at Headingley in 1967. To be fair, he was not in great nick coming into that game and he made matters worse by making a habit of taking a single of the last ball of the over.

We won the game but at the time the Press were campaigning for more entertaining cricket and although I argued for Geoff I lost out to the selectors, Doug Insole, Don Kenyon, Alec Bedser and Peter May. The same sort of situation cropped up later that summer against Pakistan when Kenny Barrington played a slow innings and there were calls for his head but I saved him because that time it was a wet wicket and it was a real scrap for runs.

When I was captain I brought Ray Illingworth back into Test cricket. I argued that he had been badly handled by previous captains but I felt I knew what made him tick and what he was capable of. They said he had no variation but I knew he was a fine bowler and I think I got the best out of him.

My worst memory of Headingley is being summoned to the ground after the committee had

decided to get rid of me. I thought the meeting was to discuss plans for the following season but I was presented with two statements, one of which was my resignation and the other my sacking.

Brian Sellers had turned against me for what I had said about one-day cricket and how it would kill English cricket but everything I said at that time has turned out to be true.

I knew there would be a stink about it anyway, so I opted to resign. I felt sick on the way home and all the colour had drained out of me. I was then advised that I should not have resigned and I rang John Nash, the club secretary, to tell him I had changed my mind and they would have to sack me. It took me half an hour to get through because the lines were jammed.

Reg Hayter, a reporter I knew well, rang me to tell me to get out of the house as all hell would break loose. He told me to get down to London and I saw a England international at Wembley that night and also went on David Coleman's sports programme.

Unfortunately it left my wife to deal with the mayhem. There were reporters all over the place and two of them even got into the house to check that I was not hiding in a wardrobe. They even tried to check if my toothbrush was still there.

For me, Yorkshire's planned move to to Wakefield was always a mistake and I argued against it, though for a couple of years it looked as if it would come off. I couldn't see where we were going to get the money from and it seemed daft to me to be losing cricket in Yorkshire's major city and from a ground with so much heritage. I had been a spectator when Bradman led the Aussies to victory in 1948.

The problem was that Yorkshire had not taken advantage of their position at the ground just after the war, in the 1940s when they had plenty of money but didn't buy it from the rugby league club. They could have had it then for about £10,000 and they would have been in control of the place, but they didn't want the responsibility of running the place and paying people to do the various jobs. They have been paying for that lack of vision ever since.

BOB APPLEYARD

ONE of the most memorable days of my life was in July 1934 when, as a 10-year-old member of the school cricket team, I was taken to Headingley to watch the fourth Test against Australia as a treat.

After a journey from Bradford by tram and train and a long queue down Kirkstall Lane we did not get into the ground until half an hour after play started and were ushered down to sit on the grass behind the boundary, as was the custom for children in those days.

The days began with Australia on 39-3 but by the lose they had reached 494-4. Bradman and Ponsford were batting when we left 10 minutes early to avoid the crowds but as soon as we got out of the gates a great roar was heard. Ponsford had stepped back on to his wicket having made 184. Bradman was 271 not out and they had scored 455 runs in 387 minutes. We hadn't seen a single wicket fall.

During the 1955 Adelaide Test match the Don invited Colin Cowdrey and I to dinner and the two of us listened enthralled at his cricket stories, for he had a wonderful memory but was an extremely modest man. I was pleased to relate my first impression as a 10-year-old schoolboy and how I hated him for his treatment of my heroes Bill Bowes and Hedley Verity.

Headingley was never my favourites pitch to bowl on. In the 1950s, compared with other grounds the bounce was low and the ball did not come on to the bat. Batsmen had to graft and when bowlers found the edge the ball did not carry to the catchers. The turn was slow and these were not the best ingredients for attacking cricket.

Years later when I was on the club's committee we were having problems and were in danger of losing Test status. The Sports Turf Research Institute at Bingley St Ives was consulted and new drains were installed at the Kirkstall Lane end of the square and down either side in order to control the moisture level.

During a dry spell, because of the build-up of various types of top dressings from Humber silt to Surrey loam used over a long period, the surface was breaking up into a crazy paving pattern, producing uneven bounce and variation of movement of the pitch.

In a dry spell before the England-West Indies Test match of 1988 we decided that the drains were taking away too much moisture, so we blocked them up so that the square could retain enough moisture to prevent cracking.

Keith Boyce had prepared one of the best Test pitches I had seen at Headingley but the weather turned against us on the eve of the match when a thunderstorm flooded the ground. In the morning the rain stopped and the groundstaff did a superb job to get the game going after only a short delay.

This game coincided with Sir Leonard Hutton's 50th anniversary of his 364 in the Oval Test of 1938 and a dinner had been arranged to mark the occasion at the Queen's Hotel, Leeds. We invited surviving members of that 1938 Australian side but Don Bradman, Bill Ponsford and Bill Brown could not make the trip and instead Neil Harvey and Ray Lindwall came over with their wives.

The game started with Curtly Ambrose bowling from the Rugby end and suddenly a water spout shot up in front. No one had seen anything like it before and when I asked Ray Lindwall what he would have done in those circumstances he replied 'I would have run round it,' which I thought summed up the Australian attitude quite well.

The problem was that the water from the mopping-up operation had been poured down the manhole drain on the edge of the square but at least we avoided the problem of crazy paving pitches on that occasion.

I wonder if the Headingley square will ever have the pace and bounce needed for good cricket. Keith Boyce made a lot of improvements in his time but with more and more artificial covering pitches throughout the country have changed.

It would be intriguing to do a comparison between the scoring rates during the 67 years since I made my first visit to Headingley to the 2000 Test match, which lasted only two days.

# Index

*Illustrations are in italics*

152

153

# Subscribers

Paul Abraham
J P Adams
Philip Akroyd
Norman Alderman
Paul Allam
J C David Allan
Stephen Allinson
Stephen Allison
Rodney Annison
Edgar Appleby
Mike Appleton
R Appleyard
David U Armitage
Robert J Ashall
Barry Ashdown
Terry Ashford
Dr Winifred Ashton
Michael Aspinall
George A Astle
Robert Atkinson
Douglas Ayre
Paul Andrew Bagnall
Andrew J Bailey
Malc Ball
Alan Barker
Barbara Barker
Geoffrey Barker
John Barker
N H C Barker
James W Barr
D B G Barraclough
Margaret Barraclough
W Barrett
Harry Barron
Edna Bashford
Robert Battey
David Beachell
Ken Beanland
John Beckett
Angus Bell
David Bell
Keith M Bellwood
Dennis Bennett
Keith Bennett
Ben Bennett Jr
Bob Bentley
Dudley M Berry
John R Binks
Leslie Binns
Michael Binns
Paul Birch
Donald Birchall
H D Bird
David Birks
Nigel Blackburn
F Blades
Mike Blanchard
Mary Elizabeth Bland
Edward Bloxham
Steve Boddy
Jim Boddy O.B.E.
Paul Bolton
Thomas P Booth
Paul Boothroyd
Alan G Bowker
Stephen R Bowman
G Boycott
Allan Bradbury
M N Bradley
J D Bramley
John Bramman
Nigel David Bratton
John E Brereton
Charles V Brewster
Clare Brewster
Bill Bridge
Robert Trevor Brook
Laurence Brookes
Peter Brookes
Raymond Brown
Rupert D E Brown
Kenneth Browning
Peter C Brumwell
Peter S Bryson
Brian Buckley
Ian Buckley
Gerald Burkin
Alan Burstwistle
Howard Burton
Martin Henry Burtt
Philip G Calvert
Alastair Campbell
Frederick Canty
Athel Carr
David Carroll
Steve Cashmore
Dereck Cattaneo
Paul A Cattermole
Paul Challenor

Jonathan Chalton
Paul V Chapman
Brian Childs
John Clamp
John C Clapham
Donald Clark
Michael J Clark
Reverend Trevor Clark
Ian Clarkson
Paul Clegg
Duncan Cliffe
D B Close
Ian & Matthew Clough
Nigel Clough
Aubrey Clover
Brian Coates
Peter Coates
Andrew Coldrick
David Ian Coldwell
J Collett
J Cook
Donald Cooke
Philip Cousins
Geoff Cowgill
Lawrence Craggs
Norman Crampton
Frances Craven
Ian Creighton
George Crompton
Derek Cromwell
John Crosland
Damian Crosse
Roger Crossley
Matthew Crowther
T J Crowther
Charlie Crummey
Alan Cruse
Tony Cumiskey
Allan Daffern
Brian Dalby
Nick Davis
John Dawson
Carl Frederic Denison
Richard Dermott
John Dickens
John Dickins
Raymond & June Dixon
Steven J Dobson
J A Dollive
Val Dooks
R Martin Downs
Richard Downs
Arthur Drew
Isobel Dring
John Duncalf
Stephen Dunning
John Durham
Cyril Earnshaw
Martin Eastwood
John F Edwards
Royce Elliott
Richard H Emsley
James B Entwistle
Michael J Entwistle
Vernon Escolme
John Eyre
Roy Eyre
John Falshaw
Robert J Fawthrop
John Filer
P J Finan
John Edgar Finney
Peter Flower
Brian Foster
Philip Foster
Richard Fountain
Thomas Frank
Pete Frankland
David Fraser
Nicholas G Fraser
Michael L Freeman
Chris Furniss
James H Gaimster
Keith Galliford
Keith Gamble
Sheila Gaythorpe
Brian Gibson
Colin Gilks
Neil Girling
Tony Glew
Ian M Goddard
John Edwin Goodyear
Gordon Gravil
Donald C Grayson
Ernest A Green
Geoffrey Green
Ian Greenhalgh
Richard K Gudgeon

Peter L Haigh
David S Hall
P M Hall
William Hall
Peter Halsall
Keith Handley
Arthur Hanley
Colin Hanley
Donald C Hanson
Kenneth E Hanson
Paul Harburn
M Hardcastle
Brian Hardgrave
Gordon Harker
Haydn Harker
Janet Harker
Bob Harrison
George Harrison
Mike Harrison
Richard Harrison
Sean Anthony Harrison
James Carl Hart
Ken Harvey
Chris Hassell
Bob Hayhow
Malcolm L Hayton
Brian Heald
John B Heath
Derek Heaton
Fred Heaton
Brian Hebblethwaite
Ian Hebblethwaite
Tony Hector
Dr Edward Heeley
Philip Hellawell
Trevor Heylings
Hedley Higgins
Donald Hill
Jack Hill
John P Hill
John Hills
Alan D Himsworth
George Hird
David Hirst
D Hodgson
Gerald Hodgson
M G Holden
Graham Holmes
T John Holmes
Peel H Holroyd
Ronnie Holroyd
Tony M Hopper
Carlton Houseman
J R Howard
Matthew Howson
Bill Hudson
David Ellis Hudson
Michael W Hudson
Steve Hudson
Alan Hufton
John Hunter
Ron Hutchinson
Stephen Hutchison
John Idell
Anthony Ireland
Jonathan J Isles
James Winship Jackson
Martin Paul Jackson
Matthew Jackson
Peter James Jackson
Chris Jameson
Michael W Jeffels
Andrew Alan Johnson
Timothy L Johnson
Winston M Johnson
David Jones
Eric Michael Jones
Malcolm Jones
Malcolm Jowett
Wally Jude
Brian Kennedy
Jeremy Kettlestring
Sam W Kilburn
Michael C Kirby
James A Kirby-Welch
Steven Kirk
Ken Kitching
Raymond Kitching
Harold Calvert Knight
Michael Knight
Dr Bernard Knowles
David Laidler
Ronald Lawrence
Kenneth Lawson
Mark Lawson
Andrew R Leach
Brian Leach
Raymond Leach
Edric Leadbeater

Michael Leak
Bruce Lee
John Lees
Peter Lees
Jeff Leetham
Chris Lennox
Ian Lennox
John Lennox
E I Lester
David J Lewis
Granville M Lidgett
Logan Dean Lindley
John Lister
Roger Lloyd
John Loades
Alan Lofthouse
Tony Lofthouse
Edward C Longshaw
Simon Mark Lonsdale
Gary C Loran
Fred Lovell
Gary Lowe
Tim Mallinson
Andrew Manby
Stephen Mann
Steve Marginson
John Philip Marsden
Glyn R Marsh
Denis A Marshall
Gerald A Martin
Ron Martinson
Derek Roy Mason
Peter Mason
Brian C Maw
Geoff Mawson
Colin A McAnna
Richard McDonald
Dorothy McEvoy
John G McNamara
Michael J Mead
Frank Melling
A A Metcalfe
Tony Metcalfe
John Middleton
Keith Middleton
Rowland Midgley
Robert Mills
Peter Millward
Brendan Mitchell
Maxine Mitchell
David Moore
Jim Moore
Robert Moorhouse
Jonathan Moreland
Jon Morley
Daniel Morris
Michael T Morris
Alan Morton
John Richard Morton
John Morton
Andrew Mould
John Moulson
Andrew C Muckle
D Mulholland
Ruth Musgrave NEE Gaunt
Geoff Myers
Roger C Myers
Patrick J A Neal
Phil Neale
Mel Neary
Nudger Needham
Michael Newbould
M S Newboult
Geoff Newton
Anthony Nicholson
Richard Nicholson
Don Nixon
Michael G North
Stuart W North
John W Nurden
Barrie Oakes
Pat Ogden
Tony Ogley
David I Oliver
Geoffrey Ounsley
John Oxley
Alan Pagdin
Keith Parkin
J Michael Parkinson
Brian Charles Parks
David Parry
Simon Parsons
Ralph B Patterson
Ian F Pattison
Mark G Pawson
Geoff Pearson
Nigel Pearson
Richard Pearson

Bob Pegg
Simon Penniston
Michael Penson
Roy Peters
John Pickering
David Malcolm Pickles
Graham Pickles
John Pickles
Michael Pitchforth
Doug Pointon
Eric Poppleton
Malcolm Potts
Jeff Powell
William A Powell
Dave Priestley
Damien Jon Quirk
Philip H Rack
Andrew Rammell
Dr S R Ramnani
Margaret Ratcliffe
James Douglas Raw
Richard Rawson
J H Reed
Archibald Reid
John Rhodes
Susan M Rhodes
Daryl M M Richardson
Brian Ridsdale
Brian Rimmer
William H Roberts
Mike Robertson
Neal Robinson
Peter Robinson
Peter Robinson
Michael Rodgers
Dave Roebuck
Peter Room
Chris Ross
Paul Rowbotham
Don Rowland
Michael Rowntree
John W Ruddock
Peter Ruder
Alan Rumford
Ian Ryder
Stephen Ryder
Andrew Sadler
Melvyn Sadofsky
Michael Sanderson
Martin Schofield
Mick Scott
Richard Scruton
Martin P Sedgwick
John Selway
Geoffrey Selwyn
Bob Shackleton
Donald Shearing
Peter Shepherd
Eddie Short
Frank Simpson
J Alex Simpson
John Simpson
Malcolm Simpson
Peter Simpson
John A Skelton
Colin Skippins
Kenneth G Skirrow
Charles Smailes
J Smales
Alan Smith
Barrie Smith
Bob Smith
Clifford Smith
Geoffrey Smith
Geoffrey Smith
John B Smith
Mark David Smith
Peter Smith
Robert E Smith
Robert Smith
M W Stanley
P J Stanley
Wilfred Stenton
John Stephenson
T L Sterriker
Dennis Stockton
William Stoker
Timothy C Sugden
Joe Sutcliffe
John Sutcliffe
Edward David Sutton
Norman H Swinney
Alan Sykes
Ken Sykes
P A Tandy
Major Robin Tarr
Paul Tatterton
Darren Taylor
Dave Taylor

Keith Taylor
Tony Taylor
Allen Teale
Craig Tennant
Henry Thompson
Nick Thompson
Peter Thompson
Matthew J Thornton
P Anthony Thornton
Phillip M Thornton
Ronald Thornton
Jack Timewell
Andrew J Tomlinson
Harry Tordoff
Ian E Torr
Brian Townend
Dave Townend
Robert Trafford
David Tunbridge
Michael Turner
Keith A Umpleby
D Verity
William Fred Vickers
Bill Wakefield
John Chambers Waldron
Enid Walker
Gordon R Walker
Ruth Walker
Glenn Wallace
William J Walsh
Andrew Walton
Hugh Walton
John Lawson Walton
Graham Ward
D Warner
Andrew Warren
Bob Watson
Chris Watson
David M Watson
Ian Watson
Tony Watson
David Weatherburn
Chris Webster
Tony Webster
Philip Welch
Ken Wellburn
Christopher Wells
Philip Wells
Richard Wetherell
Stephen Whalley
P B Wharmby
Pat Wharmby
Brian & Barbara White
Cecil White
John Alfred White
J E Whitehead
Robert Whitehead
Ruth M Whitehouse
David Whiteley
Barrie Whitham
Robin A F Wight
Stephen Wilkiinson
Brian Wilkinson
Roy D Wilkinson
H Willett
Jack Willey
Andew Williams
Claire E Williams
Brian R Wilson
Carl F Wilson
Joanne Wilson
John R Wilson
Robert Wilson
Tony Wilson
William Wilson
David M Wood
Dennis Wood
Donald Wood
Michael Wood
Mick Wood
Paul Daniel Wood
Sir John Wood
Trevor Wood
Howard Woodall
John F Woodcock
Marc Woodcock
John Gordon Woodhead
Derick Tom Wray
Ron Wray
Andrew L M Wright
Gerry Wright
Andrew George Wyles
David C Young
Shane Yoxall